The Integrity of God

The Integrity of God

R. B. THIEME, JR.

R. B. Thieme, Jr. Bible Ministries
Houston, Texas

This book is edited from the lectures and unpublished notes of R. B. Thieme, Jr.

A catalog of available tapes and publications will be provided upon request

R. B. Thieme, Jr., Bible Ministries
5139 West Alabama, Houston, Texas 77056

Printed in the United States of America

ISBN 1-55764-039-4

Contents

Chapter 2 Integrity in Action

Chapter 3 Integrity and Hope

Chapter 4 Conclusion

Preface

Before you begin your Bible study, be sure that, as a believer in the Lord Jesus Christ, you have named your known sins privately to God (1 John 1:9). You will then be in fellowship with God, under the control of the indwelling Holy Spirit, and ready to learn doctrine from the Word of God.

If you are an unbeliever, the issue is not naming your sins. The issue is faith in Christ:

> He that believeth on the Son hath everlasting life: and he that believeth not the Son shall not see life; but the wrath of God abideth on him. (John 3:36)

1
Integrity and Love

LANGUAGE OF ACCOMMODATION

EARLY IN LIFE you became aware that God exists. When you wondered about the source, the cause, the nature, or the purpose of things, your natural curiosity pointed you toward a Supreme Being. But imagining that God exists is much easier than understanding Him.

Everyone reaches God-consciousness—at least everyone above minimum intelligence and age (Rom. 1:19, 20). But the herculean task of understanding God requires more than native curiosity. It demands positive volition—an active desire to learn about Him, the willingness and self-discipline to submit to learning the truth. Positive volition is a matter of individual choice, and most people turn aside long before reaching the goal of understanding. Even those who do want to know God are caught in the dark labyrinth of ignorance and human limitations. All kinds of religious and philosophical theories promise to lead us into the light only to deadend in falsehood and evil (Rom. 1:21-23). How do we find our way out of ignorance? How can we come to understand the integrity of God?

For as the heavens are higher than the earth, so are my

> ways higher than your ways and my thoughts higher than
> your thoughts. (Isa. 55:9, AV)[1]

> But as it is written, Eye hath not seen, nor ear heard,
> neither have entered into the heart of man, the things
> which God hath prepared for them that love him. (1 Cor.
> 2:9, AV)

We are spiritually blind. We cannot discover God's character or personality. But into our darkness shone the grace of God; He has revealed Himself.

When we respond positively to God-consciousness, God is responsible to provide Gospel information whereby we can believe in Christ and thus enter into an eternal relationship with God.[2] God has revealed Himself in the Bible, the Mind of Christ (1 Cor. 2:16): the Gospel is one category of Bible doctrine. Toward us, God has "magnified His Word above His own reputation" (Ps. 138:2b). The doctrines of the Word of God, resident in our souls, are the only means by which we can know who and what God is and thus come to respect and love Him. Only through learning Bible doctrine can we accord Him the recognition, honor, and glory that He deserves.

But how does God enable us to understand what is normally beyond our comprehension? How does He accomplish the seemingly impossible task of communicating His spiritual, infinite, perfect attributes to our temporal, finite, imperfect minds? How does He give us the capacity to receive "the things which God hath prepared for them that love Him"?

Our blindness is perhaps darker than you realize. The unbeliever, called the "natural man," lacks a human spirit (1 Cor. 2:13-16). Spiritually dead, he is simply not equipped to understand spiritual phenomena. Even the simple truth of the Gospel would elude him were it not for the convincing (or convicting) ministry of God the Holy Spirit: the Third Person of the Trinity must stand in as a Substitute for the missing human spirit in order to make the Gospel clear and understandable (Gen. 6:3; John 6:44; 16:7-11; 2 Pet. 2:21). Only then can the unbeliever make his decision to accept or reject Jesus Christ as Savior.

At the moment of faith in Christ, the new believer acquires a human spirit (1 Thess. 5:23) as part of the grace apparatus for perception (GAP). GAP is the nonmeritorious system by which every believer can learn the

---

1. Bible verses marked "AV" are quoted from the Authorized Version (King James). Unmarked verses are corrected translations that more faithfully represent the original text.

2. See R. B. Thieme, Jr., *Heathenism*.

whole realm of doctrine and grow spiritually regardless of his educational background or human IQ.

In GAP, God provides every step, from doctrine resident in His own mind to doctrine resident in the believer's soul. He furnishes the Bible itself, the spiritual gift of pastor-teacher, the local church as the classroom where doctrine is taught, the privacy of each believer's priesthood that allows him to be objective as he learns. The human spirit, in conjunction with the soul, completes the "inner equipment" of GAP which is needed to convert doctrine from something merely comprehended into something thoroughly understood and useable for both spiritual advance and application to life.[3]

But even acquiring a human spirit does not enable us to understand God. God the Holy Spirit, who takes an active role leading up to our salvation and who provides certain blessings connected with salvation itself, must continue *after* salvation in His imperceptible, behind-the-scenes work of glorifying the Lord Jesus Christ (John 16:12-15). At salvation the Third Person of the Trinity personally takes up residence in our bodies (1 Cor. 6:19, 20). From His permanent headquarters in the body, the indwelling Spirit seeks to control the soul. The Bible describes the believer under the Spirit's silent, energizing control as being "spiritual" (1 Cor. 3:1), "filled with the Spirit" (Eph. 5:18), "walking in the Spirit" (Gal. 5:16).[4] GAP can function only under the filling of the Holy Spirit. The filling of the Spirit is therefore the link between salvation and the eventual understanding of Bible doctrine that constitutes spiritual maturity. The filling of the Holy Spirit is mandatory for both the intake and the application of the Word of God.

God has provided remarkable assets so that we might learn the truth about Him. But even with all of these, we are not yet out of the dark. God had to design in the Scriptures themselves a very simple approach to complex and advanced doctrines. For the sake of clarity, therefore, when describing the character and function of infinite God, the Bible often resorts to language of accommodation. In other words, to make certain that His thoughts, policies, decisions, and actions are lucidly explained, God takes into account our inherent limitations and basic ignorance. He graciously describes Himself as having human feelings, human passions, human thoughts, human anatomy—even human sins—in order to communicate things to us for which otherwise we would have no frame of reference. Of course, God possesses none of these characteristics; He uses them as teaching aids, known as anthropopathisms and anthropomorphisms.

Derived from the Greek *anthropos,* "man," plus *pathos,* "a function of the soul with an outward manifestation," an anthropopathism credits to

---

3. For a complete description of GAP see Thieme, *Grace Apparatus for Perception.*

4. See Thieme, *Old Sin Nature vs. Holy Spirit.*

God some human emotion, thought, or mental attitude sin. From *morphos,* "body," an anthropomorphism depicts God as having some physical characteristic of man. Both categories are figures of speech, not descriptions of God's true nature or essence.

God does not hate, even though the Bible declares that "thou hatest all workers of iniquity" (Ps. 5:5). Nor is He jealous, in spite of the sobering idiom that His "jealousy shall smoke against that man" who turns away from the Lord (Deut. 29:20). When the "eyes of the Lord are over the righteous . . . but the face of the Lord is against them that do evil" (1 Pet. 3:12), true functions of God are described—He indeed blesses the mature believer and disciplines the reversionist.[5] But God is an immaterial, spiritual Being; He has no eyes or face.

God's purpose in using these teaching aids is certainly not to keep us in the dark as to His true character, nor even to cater to our ignorance, but to enable us to learn. He comes down to our frame of reference when presenting what otherwise would go as far over our heads "as the heavens are higher than the earth."

The Word of God employs such imagery primarily to dramatize the Gospel to unbelievers and to make basic doctrines vividly clear to immature believers. As we become aware of anthropopathisms and anthropomorphisms and of how they are used, our ability to understand the Scriptures greatly increases.

Let us note several familiar anthropopathisms and see how they relate to the attributes that God actually possesses. Of the many examples, one that often confounds believers is the description of God in the days of Noah.

GOD'S REPENTANCE

> And it repented the Lord that he had made man on the
> earth. . . . (Gen. 6:6*a,* AV)

Over three hundred years ago, the translator evidently thought that the Hebrew word, which he rendered "repent," meant to feel sorry for sins, to renounce some obnoxious habit, or to feel remorse over some wrongdoing. Many believers today define repentance in such terms. But how can God repent? He does not sin. He does not have bad habits or make mistakes. He has nothing to feel sorry for! The translator knew something was wrong; he had a "problem passage" on his hands. What was he to do?

He might have recognized that God knows what He is doing and that the exact wording of the Scriptures was inspired with a deliberate purpose in

---

5. See Thieme, *Reversionism.*

mind.[6] But no, he tried to hide the problem by reversing the word order. "It repented the Lord" is a timid translation, even by seventeenth-century standards. The Hebrew comes right out with it: "And the Lord repented. . . ."

When we stop juggling English syntax and look to the original language, we find no reference to sin or failure. The Hebrew verb *nacham* is equivalent to the Greek *metanoeo* in the New Testament; both are translated "repent," but they mean simply "to change one's mind." Neither word has anything whatever to do with emotions or with feeling sorry for sins. The translator's problem is laid to rest.

But another problem rears up in its place. God *cannot* change His mind! He is omniscient and immutable (Isa. 46:10; Ps. 102:25–27; Mal. 3:6; Matt. 10:30; Heb. 4:13).[7] There is no variation or instability in Him, not even a "shadow of turning" (James 1:17). He knows perfectly and eternally all that is knowable; there is never a circumstance—personal, historical, or of any other kind—that comes as a surprise to Him or that could possibly require Him to change His mind.

God may appear to change, but He does not. When He seems to change, He is actually preserving His changeless integrity! He is simply expressing His character differently as called for by differences and changes in man or in history. He treats each person as an individual and every historical situation according to the facts of the case (Ps. 33:13–15; 139:1–18, 23, 24; 147:4, 5).

I do not want to leave any doubt in your mind. God's "repentance" is an anthropopathism and nothing more. We will see that it is by noting a few details about how God actually thinks.

Divine thinking can be categorized under three headings: Self-knowledge, omniscience, foreknowledge.[8] A note of caution about these terms: they do not mean what, at first glance, you might assume them to mean; they have technical definitions. First, God's Self-knowledge is His cognizance of His own Person, essence, and attributes. Infinite and never changing, God knew all about Himself — and each Member of the Trinity knew the other two Members — when nothing had yet been created. God has that same information at this very moment, and He will always have it throughout eternity future. Second, omniscience is defined as God's eternal knowledge of everything outside of Himself. Omniscience is related to creation and includes both actual reality — past, present, and future — and all the other possibilities — which will never occur. Finally, the term "foreknowledge" applies to a very specialized subcategory of God's knowledge. Based

---

6. See Thieme, *Canonicity*.

7. See below, Appendix A, The Doctrine of Divine Essence.

8. See below, Appendix B, The Doctrine of Divine Decrees.

on knowing (omniscience) how each believer would use his free will, God decreed in eternity past that certain things would occur in that believer's life. God's awareness of those events, which He Himself decreed, before they come to pass in human history, is called foreknowledge. Only believers (and Christ Himself) are said to be "foreknown." Let us concentrate primarily on the second category—God's omniscience—in illustrating how He thinks.

In His omniscience, He at all times perceives all events with all their causes, conditions, and relations—from the most vast to the most minute —as one indivisible system of things, every part of which is essential to the integrity of the whole.

Not only does God know in complete detail what *will* happen, but He also knows what *would* have happened had He decided to adopt some course of action other than the one He chose. Try to visualize how awesome the mentality of God really is. If the "one indivisible system of things" were different in even one detail—if Alexander the Great had not cut the Gordian Knot, if the Apostle Paul had drowned in the shipwreck at Malta, if you had been born one day earlier, if ever the course of one single atomic particle were different—the entire system would be changed. One variation would lead to another and another and another in a vast, intertwining system of cause and effect.

Now, God's intelligence is such that He could take any event in all of creation at any moment in the history of the universe, change it in one of an infinite number of ways, and then tell you exactly what would happen differently because of the change. Without any strain He could carry out all the intricate ramifications of that one change throughout history to the end of time—and beyond time into eternity! But what is more, at the *same* time He could also trace out *all* the implications of *all* possible changes to *all* events!

That is exactly what He does. He has all the possibilities and the one actuality clearly focused in His mind at all times. His genius is endlessly vast; "His understanding is infinite" (Ps. 147:56).

In reading about the past, we often indulge in "iffy history." We wonder "what if" a certain person had done something other than what he did. "What if" this or that event had occurred instead of what actually did? What if Adam and Eve had never sinned? What if the Confederacy had won the War Between the States? What if Franklin D. Roosevelt had never been elected President? Things would certainly be different. We would not be in such a mess today. (Or at least we would be in a different mess.) We speculate from time to time, but speculation is mere wishful thinking. To God, however, iffy history is not speculation; it is perfectly clear and exact. He knows precisely what would have happened (Matt. 11:23), and I imagine that He will have some fascinating stories to tell us in heaven about what might have taken place but did not.

God knows the future as clearly as the past. His knowledge is not subject to development; He never needs to learn anything because He already knows everything. Furthermore, He always acts rationally, but He never needs to reason things out: He knows the conclusions and the premises at the same time, the end from the beginning. He knows both the good and the bad. He knows every terrible thing that we know, and many more besides, but His knowledge never causes Him to regret the past or dread the future. You can see that His thinking is quite a bit different from ours!

If you think you are keeping any secrets from God, relax and forget it. He knows your soul, your every thought, and He has known them for billions of years. His genius comprehends infinite, endless things, but He always finds the time to concentrate His full attention on you. In fact, He is always totally concentrating on you.

He foresaw your life from beginning to end and stockpiled everything you will ever need. Even if you cut off your intake of doctrine and take a spiritual nosedive into reversionism, He has just the right type and right amount of divine discipline ready to meet the need. He knows the best way to bless you; and in discipline, He knows exactly where it hurts most. In spite of everything that He knows about you, in spite of your yet future failures (which would shock you if you knew about them), God is perfectly relaxed about you. He faithfully supplies all the logistical grace necessary for you to advance day by day in learning the Word of God.

The Word of God reveals the absolute truth of the mind of God, but His perspicacity extends infinitely beyond what He has chosen to reveal to mankind (Rom. 11:33). Whether in the Scriptures or in the undisclosed realms of divine cognizance, the smallest mistake, miscalculation, or oversight would mean that God was not God. By His very nature, He cannot be complicated with ignorance or with absurdity.

It *is* absurd to suggest that omniscient God might run into a situation in which He would have to change His mind. That is impossible and contrary to His infinite nature. But man—limited, imperfect, and often stupid—can change his mind every minute on the minute. The female of the species is renowned for her legendary accomplishments in this field. We can change our minds out of instability and indecisiveness or as part of flexibility and even moral courage. We revise our opinions as a routine, legitimate, and necessary human activity; we are all familiar with this human function. Thus, when Genesis 6:6 states that *God* changed His mind, we are looking at a strictly human function ascribed to God to make His functions clear to human beings!

God had promised mankind a Savior, the "Seed of the woman" (Gen. 3:16). God always knew that such a promise required Him to preserve the human race so Christ could be born as true humanity. But Satan, constantly on the offensive, conspired in the days of Noah to infiltrate fallen angels into the human race in an attempt to destroy the lineage of Christ (Gen. 6:1–13; 2 Pet. 2:4, 5; Jude 6).[9] Satan enjoyed fantastic success! The antediluvian population fell right into step with his plan. After a few generations of this intermarriage, true humanity began to disappear, and evil became rampant on the earth. God's character was on the line. Would He welsh on an obligation? Would He fail to complete something He had begun? No. God always keeps His promises. After giving man every opportunity to change his own mind (Gen. 6:3), God judged all but Noah and his family, the only remaining believers of pure human descent.

God did not change; God had not made a mistake; God did not learn something new. *Man* had changed, as God always knew he would, under a satanic conspiracy that God always knew would occur. The Flood came as an act of divine justice designed to prevent the compromise of God's character and to protect and perpetuate His matchless plan of grace. In communicating it to man, God translated this policy of His justice into an anthropopathism: repentance. What more emphatic way to express His unswerving and just attitude toward evil men than to declare that He had just plain changed His mind about creating the human race? If anything could catch the attention of Noah's calloused, unbelieving contemporaries, that would.

This language of accommodation in which God "repents" is not unique to Genesis 6; it is common throughout the Old Testament (Ex. 32:14; Num. 23:19; Judges 2:18; 1 Sam. 15:35; Ps. 90:13; Jer. 15:6; 42:6; Amos 7:3, 6). Each time we find it, a different facet of God's character has come to bear on a new situation in the human race, but God has not changed.

GOD'S ANGER

The anger of the Lord is another anthropopathism, and again God recruits a familiar human attitude into the service of expressing divine policy. God is said to be angry toward reversionism.

> . . . Because they have cast away the law of the Lord of hosts,and despised the word of the Holy One of Israel. Therefore is the anger of the Lord kindled against his people. . . . (Isa. 5:24*b*, 25*a*, AV)

---

9. See Thieme, *Victorious Proclamation.*

> . . . I shall execute judgments in thee in anger and in fury
> and in furious rebukes. I the Lord have spoken it. (Ezek.
> 5:15b, AV)

God's "anger" expresses the terrible harshness of the stages of divine discipline against the reversionist or the reversionistic nation. Reversionism is the believer's recession from any stage of spiritual growth. It is a process characterized by indifference toward or rejection of Bible doctrine, an attitude which leads to various malfunctions of the soul. Reversionism is first brought on by a reaction to one of the many reactor factors that will periodically arise in any normal life. For example, there is no excuse for reacting to disillusionment, loneliness, boredom, self-pity, or a guilt complex by embarking on a frantic search for happiness which carries you away from doctrine and leads to even worse disillusionment.

Divine cursing toward the reversionistic believer begins with warning discipline (Rev. 3:20), continues through more and more intensive discipline, and culminates, if the believer does not recover, in maximum discipline—the "sin unto death" (1 Cor. 11:30; 1 John 5:16). When a nation is saturated with reversionists, it is cursed and warned through five cycles of discipline (Lev. 26:14–46; Hosea 4:1–6). The fifth cycle ends in military defeat—the destruction of the nation and the enslavement of its survivors (Jer. 7:24–34).

But does God do this out of anger? Emphatically not! Again, let us briefly describe His true attitude and thus underscore the fact that God's "anger" is only an anthropopathism.

God possesses only the ultimate in happiness. He is perfect; His happiness is perfect. He is eternal; His happiness is eternal. He is immutable; His happiness cannot be diminished or increased. He is justice; He is happy about always being entirely fair. He is perfect righteousness—this is His glory. He recognizes His own perfection and takes pleasure in His own glory. God *enjoys* claiming all glory for Himself simply in the interest of absolute truth.

Happiness is part of God's character. It is impossible for Him to be unhappy or angry since He thoroughly enjoys every facet of His own existence. For example, God is satisfied and delighted with His plan of grace. In grace, He shares His own happiness with believers through Bible doctrine resident in their souls—and He does so right under the devil's nose.

God's pleasure depends on *His* character, never on yours. In other words, regardless of any overblown opinion that you might entertain about your own importance, you are incapable of either adding to or detracting from His happiness. God cannot be more happy than He already is, and nothing you can think, say, or do can make God unhappy. This does not mean that He is overjoyed by your negative volition or by your failure to fulfill His will and desire for your life. Nor does it mean that He is indifferent toward you. It means that His plan calls for *you* to share *His* happiness, not for Him to depend on yours. In fact, God is the only Source of the spectrum of happiness—from orientation and tranquillity to stimulation and ecstatics—which characterizes the mature believer through all the varied circumstances of life (Deut. 28:63; Ps. 43:4; Rom. 1:25; Phil. 4:4). God has provided for your soul everything necessary to develop capacity for happiness. This provision is Bible doctrine. You might as well come aboard through GAP and enjoy the ride.

The only hindrance is your own free volition. If you utilize the divine operating assets and grow up spiritually, you will come into blessing. But if you reject doctrine and go off on your own—as if you were the designer of happiness and knew more about it than God does—you will inevitably come under divine cursing. But even discipline from the Lord is designed to alert you to your need for doctrine and to motivate you to return to the daily intake of your spiritual food.

Whether He blesses or curses, God is absolutely fair, and being fair, He is totally content. But the reversionist has no doctrinal frame of reference; he does not understand God's attitude; and he lacks inner happiness or true satisfaction of any kind. If God described His own fantastic happiness to such a person, would it make much of an impression? Would it slow down his subjective reactions? Would it instill a sense of urgency regarding the importance of Bible doctrine? Can the reversionist associate his own lack of happiness with the infinite pleasure of God? Not likely. Therefore, God communicates through an anthropopathism. The message comes in loud and clear when God hits him with discipline and explains in no uncertain terms what is known in Latin as *ira deum,* "the wrath of God."

There are many other anthropopathisms in the Bible, such as jealousy (Ps. 79:5; Ezek. 39:25; Zech. 8:2; 2 Cor. 11:2), scorn (Ps. 2:4; 37:13; 59:8; Prov. 1:26), grief (Eph. 4:30), nausea (Rev. 3:16), and longsuffering (Ex. 34:6; Rom. 2:4; 1 Pet. 3:20; 2 Pet. 3:15). Anthropomorphisms abound as well. For example, God is given hands (Ex. 15:6; John 10:28, 29), arms (Ex. 15:16; Deut. 5:15; 33:27; Isa. 52:10; 53:1), or "many breasts" (Gen. 17:1) to depict divine guidance, protection, and provision. Each use of human attitudes or anatomy communicates an aspect of God's Person or plan.

Among all of these figurative expressions, there is one anthropopathism which is almost always misunderstood. So routinely is it taken to be a literal characteristic of God that many Christians have come to believe something that is not true. The results have been devastating. By clinging tenaciously to an erroneous idea of what God is like, many believers who sincerely and even sacrificially strive to honor Him simply do not. They do not understand His true character; they are therefore ignorant of how He deals with us and of how we conform to Him. To their own disadvantage and unnecessary discomfort they force themselves into false molds of legalism and emotionalism, which they mistakenly call spiritual maturity. Truly expecting to please God, they incur only His wrath. Hoping all the while to be happy, they always seem to come up short. The seriousness of this situation cannot be overemphasized.

The crux of the problem is that many believers have an inaccurate understanding of the love of God. This discolors their entire viewpoint on life. It automatically distorts their motivations, decisions, and actions. When reality is obscured, orientation is lost.

GOD'S LOVE

Perhaps the best known verse in the Bible is John 3:16.

> For God so loved the world that he gave his only begotten
> son that whosoever believeth in him should not perish but
> have everlasting life. (John 3:16, AV)

This familiar sentence encompasses God's entire plan of grace. The verse begins with eternity past when the destiny of the Second Person of the Trinity was established—to be born a true man (literally, "His uniquely born Son") that He might go to the Cross to be judged for the sins of mankind. It specifies the mechanics of our entering God's plan—faith in Christ. And it concludes with one of the advantages gained from believing in Him—eternal life.

A great deal of basic doctrine is covered in John 3:16 because in it our Lord was presenting the plan of salvation to Nicodemus, a religious unbeliever.[10] Jesus was explaining the Gospel to him in extremely simple terms, drawing such analogies as being born again or hearing the wind blow. But even with a picturesque, nontechnical explanation from the greatest Teacher of all time, this intellectual Pharisee was still slow to catch on. If he was struggling with these basic doctrines, certainly he could not understand the inner functions of God's nature! Jesus could not speak to Nicodemus as He might have spoken to a mature believer. No wonder then that Christ used

---

10. Religion is man's presumptuous attempt to gain God's approbation. Only Jesus Christ is worthy of divine approbation, and He earned it for all who will accept by faith His work on their behalf. Religion rejects such grace and always builds on the quicksand of human arrogance; religion always fails to impress God. Satan sponsors it as his best method of blinding the thinking of unbelievers and believers alike. The Christian's relationship with Christ is not a religion.

an anthropopathism to describe the Father's motives in sending His Son into the world.

In Jesus' day, as today, few people understood the essence of God, but nearly anyone could comprehend love in some sort of human relationship. Therefore, just as human anger, human jealousy, human patience, and human changes of mind are ascribed to God, so also is *human love.* There is a vast difference, as we shall see, between divine love and human love. But how do we know that divine love is not in view in this famous verse?

Do you know what would be entailed if God loved the world? The world is Satan's kingdom (John 12:31; 14:30; 16:11; 2 Cor. 4:4; Eph. 2:2). This fallen supercreature rules his domain according to a plan and policy called "good and evil" (Gen. 3:5), or more simply, "evil" (Gal. 1:4).[11] Evil is the sum total of Satan's genius; it is the thinking of Satan as opposed to the Mind of Christ, Bible doctrine. Satan sponsors many different—even antithetical—ideas and false systems of thought by which he seeks to gain control of the human soul (Matt. 6:3; 15:19) and hence of the entire human race.

When we understand Satan's reason for revolting against his own Creator and recognize his current objectives, we have a frame of reference for understanding evil. Satan revolted because of arrogance. And his objective both then and now is to be like God and to usurp the throne of heaven (Isa. 14:14). He wants to prove that he is as good as God. In order to do so, the devil is determined to solve all the problems of life independent of God's design and Bible doctrine. Thus, he promotes human good—any good deeds accomplished apart from the filling of the Spirit and doctrine or any solutions contrary to the laws of divine establishment.[12] Evil thinking leads to evil function, and such satanic doctrines as altruism, philanthropy, legalism, socialism, and communism lead people to sincerely pursue "noble" ends at the expense of human freedom, privacy, property, prosperity, and spiritual growth. Satan operates under the proposition that the end justifies the means; therefore, he resorts to violence whenever necessary to accomplish his "good" ends (John 8:44).

Satan intends to prove God a liar, to supplant God's perfect design, to win the angelic conflict, to expose God as unfair for sentencing so wonderful a creature as himself to eternal judgment in the Lake of Fire (Matt. 25:41).

In short, the devil's world, *cosmos diabolicus,* is totally, violently hostile to the essence of God, to the plan of God, to the freedom of man, to the salvation of man, to the spiritual advance of believers—to everything

---

11. See Thieme, *Reversionism,* Appendix A, The Doctrine of Evil, 2d ed., 1978, p. 135.

12. See Thieme, *Divine Good vs. Human Good* and *Divine Establishment.* Incumbent upon believer and unbeliever alike, the laws of divine establishment are God's design for the protection, orderly function, survival, and blessing of the human race.

related to God. There is absolutely no basis for compatibility between God and Satan's world (Job 34:10; James 1:13).

> For you are not a God who takes pleasure in wickedness;
> no evil dwells in you. (Ps. 5:4, AV)

Indeed, God judges evil and the primary characteristic of evil, arrogance.

> Thus I will punish the world for its evil and the wicked for
> their iniquity. I will also put an end to the arrogance of the
> proud and abase the pride of the dictator. (Isa. 13:11,
> AV)

Not only is the world enemy territory, but since the Fall of man when Satan usurped the earthly throne from Adam, every person born into the human race (except virgin-born Jesus Christ) is a natural citizen of the devil's realm. We are all born under divine condemnation, physically alive but spiritually dead (Rom. 5:12-21). Adam rejected God's provisions in the Garden, decided instead to eat from the tree of the knowledge of Satan's plan—good and evil—and plunged the entire human race into spiritual death under Satan's new regime. We shall study this in depth when we examine the doctrine of imputation; for now, we need to see only that we are totally incompatible with God.

As fallen Adam's progeny, we have his original sin imputed to us at birth (Rom. 5:18). Furthermore, we inherit the trend (called the old sin nature) which Adam acquired as a result of that first sin (Rom. 6:6). Further still, we exhibit our fallen condition by committing all categories of personal sins—mental, verbal, and overt. To say the least, we are not very attractive to God. We are spiritual corpses infested with Adam's sin, the old sin nature, and personal sins. We are repulsive to God.

> For all have sinned and come short of the glory of God.
> (Rom. 3:23, AV)

The glory of God is His perfect essence with emphasis on His righteousness. There is absolutely no way that God could love the world or any member of the human race without first laying aside His own essence. If He loved us, He would not be God; it is as simple as that.

God does not love Satan. God does not love the world. God does not love fallen man. All we can offer Him are sin and human good, but both are equally objectionable to His absolute righteousness (Isa. 64:6; Titus 3:5). What the righteousness of God rejects, the justice of God condemns.

Therefore, God can no more love us than He can be angry, jealous, impatient, or changeable. "Love" in John 3:16 is simply an anthropopathism.

Now before you go into shock, let me assure you that divine love *is* directed toward the believer, but *how* it is and *why* it is make all the difference in the world as far as our lives are concerned. It is simple for us, but it is no simple matter for God.

Recall that in John 3:16 Christ was explaining divine motivation to someone who had no frame of reference to understand anything about God's essence, let alone about God's true and magnificent attribute of love. Nicodemus, for all his intelligence, religious education, and respectability, was an ignorant man regarding the attributes of God. We know that he was on the wrong track because as a legalistic Pharisee he had been striving all his life to impress God with human morality. Morality is necessary and commendable; indeed, it is ordained by God between members of the human race. But only a person who was misinformed about God's character—who was too proud of his own accomplishments to recognize man's depravity—would be so brash as to expect *divine* approbation for *human* morality![13] To give such an ignorant person an opportunity to remedy his ignorance, Christ ascribed a human characteristic to God. Our Lord was giving Nicodemus a chance to learn! But don't look down your nose at the ancient Pharisee—we all start out at zero, and we all have our blind spots. Yet God is always fair to each of us in that He accommodates our stupidity long enough for us to learn basic doctrine as a foundation for more advanced doctrine.

This explains the existence of many passages throughout the Scriptures in which God is the subject, and we, fallen man, are said to be the objects of His love. In such statements, made to those who are doctrinally unenlightened but who do know something about human love, He makes His policies and motives clear.

Actually, God's motivation is the sum of His entire essence. But what does that mean to someone ignorant of divine essence? Not a thing! On the other hand, "God so loved the world that He gave" is perfectly clear. Love, as a motive for giving, registers in nearly everyone's mind and permits people to comprehend the basic principles of salvation.

If you are having difficulty in understanding how God's love could possibly be an anthropopathism, let's look at a passage that ascribes the opposite attitude to God.

> As it is written, I loved that Jacob, but I hated that Esau.
> (Rom. 9:13)

---

13. See below, pages 93, 204.

In these contrasting statements, God evaluates a pair of twin brothers. Jacob had believed in Christ, the promised Messiah, for eternal salvation; but Esau had remained an unbeliever all his life. Therefore, God has a different attitude toward each, consistent with His own perfect character. But the moment we bring God's character into the picture, we see that God could not possibly hate Esau. Hatred is a mental attitude sin. God is not a sinner; He does not sponsor sin, tempt to sin, nor condone sin in anyone else. God cannot compromise His own nature; to suggest that He does is blasphemous. Hatred, then, is obviously a human characteristic which is ascribed to God to express His judgment against unregenerate Esau.

Now look at the other half of the comparison, the description of divine thinking toward Jacob. Through faith in Christ, Jacob's relationship with God is one of eternal blessing. But the opposite of *human* hatred toward Esau is not *divine* love toward Jacob—it is *human* love! God neither hates nor loves the way humans do. Thus we have two anthropopathisms; the contrast between love and hate creates an image anyone can understand. In Romans 9:13, therefore, God has handed down a judicial opinion regarding unbelievers and believers. His position is represented on one hand by a human sin—personal hatred—and on the other by a legitimate human attitude—love.

LOVE₁ VERSUS LOVE₂

Christianity today has failed to recognize that human love is sometimes ascribed to God. As a result, the anthropopathism is not properly differentiated from God's actual attribute of love. This confused mixture of the human and the divine is at the root of a widespread misinterpretation of Scripture which produces a superficial, distorted, blasphemous concept of God. In the Bible, God is credited with two kinds of love. To avoid confusion, let us call the attribute he actually possesses "love₁," and the human love ascribed to Him, which He does not possess, "love₂." Thus, "for God so loved the world" and "I loved that Jacob" are examples of love₂. Immediately the question arises, What is love₁ like?

Love₁ is perhaps the most difficult of all divine attributes for us to understand, and, unlike love₂, it is mentioned only rarely in the Word of God.

> . . . For God is love. (1 John 4:8*b*)

Notice that John uses love in an intransitive sense; that is, it does not take an object. Never is such a phrase used of man. We might love someone or something, but we are never said to *be* love. God's actual characteristic of love, however, is related directly to His Being; He possesses love₁ as an absolute attribute of His divine essence.[14] By "absolute attribute" I mean simply that God's love is not a "relative" attribute; it is not *related* to an object of love; it is independent of anything that God has created. Love₁ functions today exactly as it did before the creation of man, angel, or universe; before anything existed apart from God Himself.

God is absolutely independent. He is more than independent; He exists eternally, not created or sustained by any source outside Himself. In fact, He does not even sustain Himself! He is the Source of all sustenance, but another of His absolute attributes, the attribute of spirituality, includes the fact that He exists as an infinite Person who needs no sustenance, no maintenance, no help, no support, no fulfillment from anyone or anything. He always existed, complete and perfect, long before He brought you or me on the scene; and His love, like all of His absolute attributes, is totally independent of what He has made (Prov. 8:22–36). Love₁ is so constant and so superior to our love that it does not require an object.

Before we discover anything else about love₁, therefore, we know from its eternal existence that in whatever way it functions, it does so equally with or without an object, with or without a particular occasion for love. In spite of all the changeability within God's creation, nothing can change the love₁ in God's essence. This is perfect love, so far above ours that were it not for Bible doctrine, we would not know it existed.

We understand human love as an attitude directed toward an object. For us, "to love" is a transitive verb: it has a subject, the one who loves, and an object, the recipient of love. Now, you might have an abundance of capacity yet lack an object, but in the human race even the greatest capacity for love is not love unless it has somewhere to go. Obviously you could not love your friends or a member of the opposite sex were there no such people! You could not love to watch an Arizona sunset were there no such thing as an Arizona desert! It simply does not make sense to think you could. There must be something that inspires love in you.

Some people love good automobiles. Others love superb firearms; yet others, beautiful music or rare antiques or fine wines. We all love different things. Whatever it is, however, an object is mandatory in human love. But human love is exactly what God does *not* possess—except in language of accommodation. God's love₁ remains the same, object or no object.

Love₁ is different from love₂ in yet another way. Not only does our love require an object, but it always involves emotion as well. If you love the grandeur of the high desert at sundown, a sweeping emotion in your soul will

---

14. See below, Appendix A.

reflect all that darkening beauty when it stretches out around you. For us, a properly functioning emotion means stimulation and enjoyment, but God does not have or need emotion. His happiness is part of His character. He is not up one minute and down the next. He always focuses His infinite mentality on everything at once so that He is not subject to the variations we experience as our lives unfold in time. Since we do not possess the infinite, perfect attributes of our Creator, He has equipped us with emotion as part of the essence of our souls. And we can be glad He did! Through emotion we express our appreciation for the objects of our love.

In other words, our emotions are designed to support and to respond to the contents of what I call the "right lobe"—the dominant, thinking portion of the mentality of the soul. When you see breathtaking scenery, for example, the sight fulfills the norm or standard in your right lobe that identifies beauty. Your vocabulary and categorical storage areas come into play, also through the memory center of your frame of reference, enabling you to recognize the scene for what it is. This is how an emotional response is elicited, along with whatever application might lift off from the launching pad—whether a comment, some type of artistic expression, or simply silence.

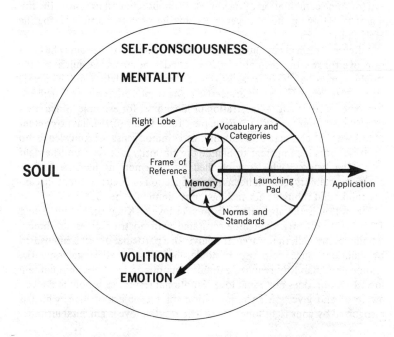

Emotion is part of human capacity for love. If your right lobe is saturated with Bible doctrine, you as a mature believer have capacity for love, for life, for happiness, for prosperity, for all the blessings that God has waited to pour out upon you. Because of the doctrine in your soul, your emotions respond when you recognize certain Biblical truths or apply them in your daily life. For instance, you will be stirred emotionally when you hear so powerful an expression of grace and divine establishment as the fourth verse of The Star Spangled Banner.

But emotion is a two-edged sword. When capacity for life does not pervade the soul, human emotion becomes the instrument, not of a spectrum of happiness, but of a spectrum of misery—unhappiness to match any occasion. If your right lobe is saturated with evil, your emotions will respond to and encourage evil, making you a misfit, completely out of touch with reality. Likewise, if you respond to your old sin nature and thereby overthrow the inner authority of the Holy Spirit, then instead of *responding* to the doctrine in your right lobe, your emotion will *dictate* to the right lobe. The Holy Spirit works through the doctrine you know; but when you quench the Spirit, by turning over control of your soul to the old sin nature, the doctrine in your soul ceases to have its influence. Instead, you produce sins, human good, or evil (or some combination of the three). Without rebound to restore the filling of the Holy Spirit, you eventually sink into reversionism, grieving the Holy Spirit.

Reversionism always involves an emotional revolt of the soul. The emotion overthrows the mentality; the responder becomes the initiator; the "right woman" of the soul starts to give orders to the "right man." The early stages of reversionism are characterized by a frantic attempt to compensate for some reactor factor—frustration or loneliness, for example. Since emotion, like an "empty sack" (*koilia* in the Greek, Rom. 16:18), has no content of its own—no character, no stability, no common sense, no knowledge, no doctrine—it is incompetent to handle the authority it seizes from the right lobe. The believer who is controlled by his emotions likewise has no character, stability, common sense, or application of doctrine. Emotion cannot think; and thought, not feelings, must dominate the soul.

Emotion is the appreciator in human love (1 Kings 3:26; Phil. 1:8; 1 John 3:17). When a right lobe saturated with doctrine or establishment dominates the soul, the awareness of love for a particular object is intensified by emotion. Such response is noble, beautiful, gratifying, romantic. Although human love requires emotion, emotion in itself does not contain love. Emotion does not equal love. Emotional responses simply make you aware of and give you an appreciation for the object of love, which is recognized by your right lobe. There love resides; love is a mental attitude.

HOW LOVE₂ IS MISUNDERSTOOD

Not only do many believers think that love₂ is love₁ but they even have a misconception of human love. How are we to understand an anthropopathism if we do not understand its basis in the human realm? Much could be said about human love—it has kept the poets (and lawyers) busy for thousands of years. But for our purposes, at risk of being far too brief, it has at least four characteristics: 1) thought, 2) emotion, 3) sex, and 4) respect.

Thought is the part of love that is so often missing. Now, if you are always preoccupied with sex, you probably do not do much thinking. When you truly love someone, that person becomes the topic of your thoughts. This first characteristic of love, then, occurs in the soul.

The second factor also pertains to the soul. Emotion sustains love, and we call that being romantic. If a woman says she loves a man, she means that she has thoughts about him and likes what she thinks. But when she says she is *in love* with him, she carries it a step further. Her emotion is involved; he has her soul's full attention! The emotion does not add to the value or depth of the love; it simply stimulates the love, carries it along, and makes it romantic.

Point three brings in the physical aspect of love between a man and a woman. Here is where love so often gets fouled up. Some people give sex top priority and lose track of the other aspects of love, while others cling to the ascetic trends of religious legalism and insist that sex be endured only for procreation. Neither view is correct. God designed sex not merely to perpetuate the human race; sex is primarily for the recreation of husband and wife. Even so, sex is not love; sex is one expression of love.

Since the first three points address the soul and the body, for lack of a better term I call the fourth characteristic of human love the spiritual factor. True love, especially a woman's love for a man, actually begins with this point. The spiritual factor of awe—even fear—lays a foundation that eventually supports a wonderful structure of respect and admiration. Whether in Hebrew or Greek, the word for respect also means fear.

If you take our list of characteristics and cross out points one and four, what remains is the idea of love held by most people today. Thought is the root and foundation of love, but few bother to do much thinking at all. You cannot be a good lover unless you think and concentrate. And when thought goes out the window, respect or awe goes out right behind it. What is left? Emotion and sex.

1. ~~THOUGHT~~

2. EMOTION

3. SEX

4. ~~RESPECT~~

Anyone can emote; it takes no character or effort. Emotion that is not based on the doctrinal or establishment content of the right lobe is superficial and meaningless at best; at worst, it is self-destructive. When you hook up an emotional revolt with sex, sex also becomes meaningless and self-destructive. Young people who are emotionally and sexually frustrated often assume that marriage (or nowadays "living together") is the solution to all their problems. But as soon as they get married under such false premises, everything blows apart. Emotion and sex are not love. Emotion will not sustain a relationship any more than people can have sex every minute on the minute! Thought and respect are the driving forces of human love; emotion and sex go along for the ride and make for some very pleasant moments in life.

Now let's take a believer who has a superficial idea of human love and show him "for God so loved the world." He has understood the point of the verse well enough to be eternally saved, but when he goes back to take a closer look at God's attitude, he misses the point. The only way he can relate to this anthropopathism is through his own limited frame of reference. Even though he may have a high IQ, he never considered thought to be *the* essential element of love. He therefore does not consider the issue of what God thinks. Furthermore, awe and respect are certainly not his idea of what constitutes love; thus, he fails to consider that the perfect standards of God's absolute righteousness must be met before God can respect anyone. This believer does not realize that God cannot possibly think well of the devil's world or respect and love its sinful human citizens. All that exist in his hazy concept of love are emotion and sex. Of course, sex related to God is no issue; that went out with Greek mythology. The ignorant believer therefore jumps to the only conclusion he has left: emotion.

This believer, then, ignorant of Bible doctrine, looks at John 3:16 and sees sentimental, emotional love; human love at its superficial worst. He distorts the anthropopathism when he lowers God to the level of empty-headed man. He has the temerity to suppose that God loves everyone! Even a human being knows better than to love just anyone, let alone everyone![15]

This ignorant believer has the colossal gall to imagine that God somehow ignores sin and evil, somehow throws away His perfect standards, and somehow falls in love with mankind. He assumes that God cannot quite get along without us and that we will be welcomed into heaven with open arms if only we do our best and behave ourselves. He imagines, with a devotional look on his face, that down deep God is really a sweet, soft-hearted guy. Certainly He would not send His creatures to hell! (How Satan loves to hear that!) Whether they realize it or not, believers who stumble to such con-

---

15. Regarding commands to love your neighbor or your enemy, see below, page 207.

clusions are tied up in their own emotional shoelaces, and they assume that God shares their blasphemous confusion.

God does not love in the same emotional, unthinking, unstable way that man loves; in fact, the Members of the Trinity do not love as man does even at his human best. Divine love is far superior to our love; it is more demanding and, hence, far more exclusive.

People who take John 3:16 or any other example of love[2] to mean that God is somehow attracted by fallen man have completely missed the point of this often-quoted verse. Those who expound such all-loving, all-forgiving, all-sweetness "theology" do not realistically portray the truth of the Word of God.

On the false assumption that a distorted anthropopathism is an actual divine attribute, believers leap to the conclusion that God's plan of grace is built on love, that God's love is the driving principle of the universe. Consequently, they try to base their lives, their relationships with others, and their relationship with God on this hazy, nebulous, ambiguous feeling called love. Such people speak in terms of brotherhood, of loving everyone, with never a reference to honor, integrity, or justice—only to sweetness and light. Tragically, they try to orient to life with little or no reference to reality.

When this erroneous interpretation of God's love, this penchant for emotionalism, gets tied up with religion, the evil result is no surprise. A person who thinks God operates on feelings toward him will naturally try to operate on feelings and emotion toward God. What is the result? Holy rollers. The tongues crowd. Emotional "drunkards." Even those Christians who stop short of talking gibberish and rolling in the aisles want to *feel* spiritual or *feel* close to God. Everyone seeks an emotional experience. He wants to feel good from doing good deeds; he wants to feel the approbation of a pastor patting him on the back; he wants to hear preaching, devoid of content, that inspires him to say, "It was thrilling to have been here!"

This notion of Christianity is divorced from the truth. The believer's true relationship with God is based on thought and respect—the content of Bible doctrine in his soul. Doctrine enables the mature believer to know God and to stand in genuine awe of the Members of the Trinity. Emotion happily and contentedly tags along as a response to the saturation of doctrine in his right lobe.

This is true human love for God, occupation with Christ. Our love works the same way toward right man or right woman, toward friends and family. From among all the mental attitudes familiar to us, Jesus selected genuine human love to help explain to Nicodemus certain things about God. Examples of this anthropopathism can be found throughout the pages of Scripture. Just as our "repentance" is used to portray the action of God's immutable fairness, and just as our anger helps communicate the calm deliberation of His justice, so also love$_2$ stands for some true function of divine essence. So far in seeking to discover what that function is, we have merely eliminated one possibility. We have found that human love and divine love are so radically different that love$_1$ is the one divine attribute which love$_2$ does *not* represent.

What *is* God's attitude toward His fallen creatures? What divine characteristic provides, guarantees, and undergirds the magnificent relationship which He offers through simple faith in Christ? For the rest of our study, we shall answer two questions: What divine attribute does love$_2$ represent? and, Since love$_1$ does not function like love$_2$, how does love$_1$ function? The answers to both of these questions are found in the same doctrine—the doctrine of the integrity of God.

PAUL EXPLAINS THE GOSPEL

By now we have developed sufficient frame of reference to proceed. We are about to examine a passage from Romans that will explain how the statement "for God so loved the world" works. Paul will give us the key to understanding how God can love rationally, without an object, without emotional variations, and without compromise to His divine perfection. The principle is so obvious that it is almost surprising! Paul will explain that perfect God loves a perfect Object. With love$_1$, God loves Himself!

Anyone can memorize "God is love" and quote it to justify all manner of imbecilic activity, but its true meaning lies in discovering what is worthy of God's love.

> For I am not ashamed of the gospel of Christ: for it is the
> power of God unto salvation to everyone that believeth;
> to the Jew first, and also to the Greek. For therein is the
> righteousness of God revealed. . . . (Rom. 1:16, 17a, AV)

Paul was the greatest Jew who ever lived (with the possible exception of Moses, and of course not considering the God-Man, Jesus Christ). Without a doubt Paul was the greatest Roman. Both during his lifetime and century upon century thereafter, down to the present moment, his influence far exceeds that of any other citizen of SPQR.[16] Some secular scholars consider him to be the last great intellect in history. Through his intake of the Word of God, he exploited grace to the maximum, and God blessed him with the most

---

16. *Senatus Populusque Romanus,* "The Senate and People of Rome," was the title of what we call the Roman Empire. The official name was commonly shortened to SPQR just as our nation's title is often reduced to US or USA.

complete knowledge of doctrine that any believer has ever possessed. His incisive mentality, his occupation with Christ, his vigorous capacity for life as a mature believer made him objective, enthusiastic, and eminently prepared to tackle any situation life could offer.

When a genius of Paul's stature begins to explain why he is so strongly motivated, we are compelled to sit up and take note. An aspect of his motivation is brought to light as he, the foremost apostle, reveals the mental attitude of a communicator of doctrine. His attitude should be shared today by every pastor-teacher and, likewise, by every believer regardless of spiritual gift.

The Greek compound verb *epaischunomai* combines the preposition *epi,* "over and above," with the verb *aischuno,* "to be ashamed." With the negative, the compound literally means "to not be ashamed, to be above being ashamed." In other words, Paul never hung his head regarding anyone or anything with whom or with which he was associated. Lack of such embarrassment means freedom from subjectivity and can indicate that reversionism is absent as well. When a person is so subjective, weak, or cowardly that he worries about the opinions of others—afraid they might ridicule him or think him a little strange—he does not know enough doctrine to come in out of the rain! Children who are ashamed of their parents, and parents ashamed of their children, fall into this category; as does the person who is ashamed of his background, occupation, or lack of education.

We all have something of which we could be ashamed, yet our lives are to be free from shame and guilt. The grace of God cures these cancers of the soul through rebound and the consistent function of GAP. Paul, therefore, is not describing the immature believer. Anyone with a guilt complex can work himself up emotionally to overcome his natural reticence and "do great things for God." But only the mature believer knows what it means to be supremely blessed of God; only he has the poise from spiritual growth to be truly relaxed, confident, and unashamed of the doctrine in his right lobe. He knows that the opinions of people are insignificant and inconsequential compared to God's thinking expressed in the Word of God. He knows, furthermore, that he does not have to prove anything to anyone but that he is designed to live his life as unto the Lord.

The noun *euaggelion,* "gospel," is often misunderstood. We think of the Gospel as being the salvation message of Jesus Christ and His work on the Cross. That is the technical meaning of the word, but that is only part of its overall connotation. *Euaggelion* means "good news, news of victory or good fortune," referring to something of intrinsic value. The "good news" includes the entire Word of God, only a small part of which applies to the unbeliever. Which aspect of Bible doctrine is in view will be indicated by the context. Paul is not ashamed of *any* doctrine, but in Romans 1:16 he narrows down the field to that information necessary to bring an unbeliever to the point of faith in Christ. We know this from the explanatory clause that follows. (The phrase "of Christ" in the King James Version is not in the original text.)

Paul explains why he is not merely unashamed of the Good News but is *proud* of it and even boastful (1 Cor. 1:31; 2 Cor. 12:5; Gal. 6:14): "for it is the power of God unto salvation to everyone that believeth." Paul asserts the dogmatic and unqualified fact that there is a certain portion of Bible doctrine that results in eternal salvation for those who believe it. The Gospel is therefore called "the power of God."

The Greek word for "power" is *dunamis.* Derived from the earliest Indo-European language and having a counterpart in ancient Sanskrit, this word's oldest meaning was "ability" or "capacity." As the noun passed through Homeric into Attic Greek, the idea developed that an individual's spiritual and intellectual life could be traced back to his *dunamis* or IQ. Therefore, in the classical Greek of the fifth century B.C., *dunamis* meant "ability, IQ, perspicacity, the capacity to learn, the ability to concentrate in learning." Developing further into the Koine Greek of the New Testament, the word denotes power in the sense of competence or capacity. When linked with the possessive genitive of *theos,* "belonging to God," the phrase should be translated, "for it [the Gospel] is the ability of God."

When you communicate the Good News to an unbeliever, you explain the simple message of salvation. But without going into detail that would confuse the issue and confuse the unbeliever, you are actually declaring *God's ability* to save, *God's ability* to bless, *God's ability* to provide. The meaning of *dunamis* throws salvation back on the actual capacity and character of God Himself.

This is exactly what Jesus was doing as He spoke John 3:16 to Nicodemus! Our Lord was explaining the Gospel. But in reality He was talking about "the ability of God"—God's capacity, God's essence. Could He come right out with an enthralling discourse on His own divine attributes, which were the same as those of the Father and the Holy Spirit? Could He go into detail with this uninformed unbeliever about motivation within the Godhead? That might have been a feast for a mature believer, but it would have left poor Nicodemus starving! If the Pharisee was to be saved, simple language was needed; thus, Christ used the anthropopathism of love₂. He compared God's thinking to human love and left it at that.

Both John 3:16 and Romans 1:16 teach the same subject, the Good News of salvation. The Gospel is the "power of God"—the ability and capacity of divine essence—to guarantee that believers "should not perish but have everlasting life." Paul comes out and identifies which attribute of divine essence is involved, whereas Christ merely represented this divine attribute in language of accommodation when evangelizing a religious unbeliever. And what does Jesus' statement "for God so loved the world" point to in the actual essence of God? Which divine attribute produces the action in saving us? After assuring both Jews and Gentiles of divine impartiality—"to the Jew first, and also to the Greek"—Paul gives us the answer.

THE THINKING OF A JUDGE

The Apostle begins Romans 1:17 with the particle *gar* used as an inferential conjunction to introduce an explanation, a profound explanation as far as our understanding of God is concerned. "For," he writes, "by this same [Gospel] the righteousness of God is revealed."

The word for "righteousness," *dikaiosune,* is one of the most significant words in the New Testament; it means much more than simply "righteousness." It is a second-stage development in the Greek language in that it comes from two older words, the noun *dike* and the adjective *dikaios.* The difference between *dikaiosune* and its two predecessors is the suffix *-sune,* and that suffix makes all the difference in the world.

The Greeks developed a system of abstract thought that reached its peak in Athens in the fifth century B.C. Concurrent with this brilliant advance in thinking, they refined their language over several generations until the Attic Greek of classical times was rich enough to reflect all the literary sophistication and nuance of meaning conceived of by such men as Plato, Sophocles, Aeschulus, Euripides, and many others. The suffix *-sune* changed the meaning of a noun or adjective from the simple to the complex, from the concrete to the abstract.

The Greek word for beauty does not take the *-sune* suffix, but we can use the concept of beauty to illustrate the change in Greek thought. In Homer's day, in the ninth century B.C., a young warrior might exclaim, "That woman is beautiful! She's a beauty!" Perhaps you remember from the *Iliad* that a Trojan prince named Paris caused a great deal of trouble by saying essentially that. He snubbed Hera and Athena, handing the golden apple of discord to Aphrodite because she promised him the hand of Helen, the most beautiful woman on earth. Unfortunately, Helen was already married to the king of Sparta. Enter, Trojan War. In the words of Aeschulus:

> What hast thou done, O Helen, blind of brain?
> O face that slew the souls on Ilion's plain.
> One face, one face, and many thousands slain.

In more ways than one, Paris' thinking went no farther than external appearances. But among the philosophers of Athens four hundred years after

Homer, the conversation turned away from mere feminine pulchritude. Beauty itself became the topic. To these thinkers beauty was an abstract concept of balance and symmetry, the "golden mean" of inner beauty of the soul and outer perfection of the physical form.

The concept of justice underwent a change, too; and the development from the specific to the abstract is reflected in the change from *dike* and *dikaios* into *dikaiosune*. *Dikaiosune* was first used in the fifth century B.C.; the historian Herodotus used it in telling the story of Solon, the farseeing statesman whose laws had saved Athens over a hundred years before.

In Soion's day, the government leaders had woven a web of decrees that tyrannized and exploited the citizens of Attica, the city-state of which Athens was capital. These rulers tried to play God. They coveted power; they poked their noses into the business of law-abiding citizens; they continually passed new laws. Without regard for freedom or free enterprise, which is the true source of national prosperity, they attempted to remove the problems of mankind through legislation, especially through laws designed to solve the problems of one percent of the population with "solutions" imposed on all.

Solon witnessed this abuse of authority, which was all too similar to what we see in the United States today. As an aristocratic member of the ruling assembly, he eventually became the archon, and while serving his term, he persuaded the Athenians to adopt a new code. The old tyranny was set aside. Solon's new system guaranteed freedom for every citizen. Privacy and property were protected; free enterprise became the order of the day.

Solon was confident. He knew he had the right answers, and he did a very clever thing. He convinced the Athenians to pass one final statute decreeing that no one could add to or subtract from the law—except Solon himself.

Did he then wait around, wringing his hands, wondering which new law he would have to enact in the face of the first crisis? No! Remember that Solon was a brilliant man. He immediately set out on a ten-year sabbatical and simply left the Athenians to live by the excellent laws already in force! Even today his code is considered to be one of the best legal systems of all time. It helped the city-state to eventually become one of the powerful empires of antiquity.

The legislation of Solon greatly influenced the development of the meaning of *dikaiosune*. With Solon absent, his laws could not be expanded or rescinded; the people of Athens had to adjust to what he had left them. Under this system of law, Herodotus first coined *dikaiosune* as a legal term, meaning "the thinking of a judge in alloting to each one what is due him"; in other words, good, clear, objective thinking that gives everyone a fair shake before the law.

The abstract concept of fairness indirectly included those under the law so that the citizens who adjusted to the justice of Solon were said also to possess *dikaiosune* or "civil virtue." The connotation of the word, however, is not the justice of a people but the justice of the person in authority, the judge in a court of law. Many classical writers, including Plato, used the term in this sense. *Dikaiosune,* therefore, means "adjustment to the law," and that is the sense in which "righteousness" is a correct translation; but "justice" is an equally accurate rendition.

In 280 B.C., over a century after the Golden Age of Greece, the Old Testament Scriptures were translated from Hebrew into Greek by seventy-two scholars in Alexandria, Egypt. In their amazingly accurate version called the Septuagint, *dikaiosune* stood for the Hebrew words *tsedeq* and *tsedeqah,* which can mean either righteousness or justice. The concepts are so inter-related that sometimes they cannot be distinguished, and the Hebrew does not attempt to separate them. Whenever God's justice or righteousness is mentioned in the Old Testament, *dikaiosune* appears in the Septuagint. God, instead of Solon, becomes the norm; and believers, instead of the citizens of Attica, are called *dikaiosune* when they observe the will of God, that is, when they have adjusted to the justice of God.

Both Philo and Josephus employ this ancient word in extrabiblical literature contemporary with Christ and Paul. Philo, a Jewish philosopher living in Alexandria, makes *dikaiosune* a divine attribute in terms of the ethics of stoicism. Josephus, the Jewish historian, follows his many predecessors in using *dikaiosune* as adjustment to the law, hence, "legal righteousness" or righteousness in judicial thinking. It emphasizes the judge's sense of justice, his ability to pronounce a fair verdict by scrutinizing all the evidence in the light of his expert knowledge of the law. It does not refer to the judge's own personal morality or immorality because the issue is not his private conduct but whether or not he can think in court! Josephus also notes that failure to adjust to the law brings legal retribution or judgment; therefore, he recognizes *dikaiosune* as the source of both blessing and cursing.

By the time it entered the Koine Greek of the New Testament, *dikaiosune* carried a wealth of meaning. It is therefore frequently mistranslated. It means "justice" as a characteristic of a judge, as the legal thinking of a judge, as the professional integrity of a judge. It means "righteousness," not merely in the sense of being good, but as a principle leading to correct thought and action. It means "to be fair and equitable in dealing with others"; it means "virtue, justice, integrity."

Both Philo and Josephus applied this word to God, using the same phrase we find in Romans 1:17, *dikaiosune theou.* But these writers possessed a limited or erroneous concept of God's character, whereas the human authors of the New Testament, under the inspiration of the Holy Spirit, gave the term its full, doctrinal meaning. In Scripture, "the *dikaiosune* of God" means one of three things: 1) the overall "integrity" of God, 2) His "righteousness" as the *principle* of His integrity, or 3) His "justice" as the *function* of His integrity.

The genitive case of *theos* makes the difference between these definitions: it is both a subjective and possessive genitive. A noun in the subjective genitive is the subject of the action; that is, it produces the action of the word it modifies: God's integrity in *action* is His justice. On the other hand, *theos* in the possessive genitive indicates something that God possesses as a principle: God's integrity in *principle* is His righteousness. Whatever its specific translation, however, *dikaiosune theou* is an abstract term; it always in some way connotes God's integrity set against the background of all His attributes. Divine integrity is, therefore, infinite, perfect, eternal, unchangeable—and incomprehensible apart from its revelation in doctrine.

As a principle, *dikaiosune theou* involves God alone, apart from man; but as divine action, it can include man. In this sense, *dikaiosune* is sometimes used as a synonym for *eusebeia,* "godliness" and becomes a technical term for spiritual maturity. Maturity is the believer's maximum adjustment to the justice of God or total relationship with the integrity of God.

Yet another technical usage encompasses not just the spiritually mature but all believers; even the reversionist is included. In this legal or forensic sense, *dikaiosune* means "justification." God is the expert Judge; He has all the evidence and can pronounce only a fair, objective verdict. When a person believes in Christ, God is free because of the Cross to credit to that person His own righteousness, the very principle of divine integrity. Immediately, from the bench of the supreme court of heaven, God recognizes this new piece of evidence in the case. Since the believer now possesses God's perfect righteousness, God pronounces him *"dikaiosune!"*—justified, righteous. This is the essence of salvation.

In due course, we shall study both forensic justification and maturity adjustment to the justice of God. Both of these applications of *dikaiosune theou* to the human race include the concept of vindication by grace. Grace means that God does all the work and receives all the glory. At salvation we are justified as possessing *His* righteousness; at maturity we are vindicated as having in our souls Bible doctrine, the thinking and verbalization of *His* integrity. Our human righteousness and personal achievements have nothing whatever to do with our justification before God.

Dikaiosune theou was the unmentioned subject of the conversation when Christ used love₂ to help Nicodemus understand the Gospel. The power, ability, or capacity of God to save mankind is not a matter of love; love₁ can have nothing to do with fallen man. Instead, as Romans 1:16, 17 tells us, the Gospel reveals the function of His *integrity*. Love₂ truly represents an attribute of divine essence, and that attribute is the justice of God.

This opens the door. We can now begin to see how God can bless the totally depraved, spiritually dead citizens of the enemy's kingdom without destroying His own perfection. Love$_1$ does not have to descend to our depraved level and thus cease to be love$_1$. Salvation does not mean that God must love the unlovely; that would be a fatal contradiction of His character.

Salvation means that God treats us in justice. He does not condescend to save us. He never condescends to do anything! The unbending strength of *every* facet of His absolute essence is fully behind *everything* He thinks or does toward us. *That* is divine integrity. He never makes exceptions. He does not act on emotion. He never feels sorry for the "poor, lost sheep" so as to be overcome by sentimentality. Nor is anything He accomplishes done on impulse. His works are never tentative or short-sighted, and therefore His plan never needs to be revised, undone, or corrected. Nothing He does *can* be undone—not even by God Himself. No loophole will ever have to be closed because no loopholes exist! Therein lies our security, our comfort, our blessing.

GOD LOVES HIS OWN INTEGRITY

Dikaiosune theou becomes the focus of our study. We find that it brings together both types of love that the Bible credits to God: love$_2$ represents His justice; love$_1$ is directed toward His justice and His righteousness. In other words, with love$_1$ God loves His own integrity. God loves Himself. Love$_1$ is internal! God needs no object to love because *He* is the Object!

> He is the Rock, his work is perfect: for all his ways are
> judgment [justice]: a God of truth and without iniquity,
> just and right is he. (Deut. 32:4, AV)
>
> He loves righteousness and justice. . . . (Ps. 33:5a)
>
> For the Lord loves justice. . . . (Ps. 37:28a)
>
> For I the Lord love justice. . . . (Isa. 61:8a)

God's Self-love should not surprise you. In His infinite knowledge, He knows Himself to be totally beyond comparison, to be totally worthy of admiration to an infinite degree in every possible sense. He claims all glory for Himself simply in the interest of absolute truth. If He did not recognize His own incomparable greatness and demand all glory, something would be wrong: He would have to be either ignorant of His own attributes or unimpressed with the most tremendous of all truths, the fact of His infinite glory. If He did not love Himself, there would be no reason for us to love Him. But He does love Himself, and through the accumulation of Bible doctrine in our souls, we must follow suit. In fact, He commands us to learn what He already knows and has always known about His own essence.

> For who has come to know the Lord's mind, who shall instruct Him? We keep on having the mind of Christ [the Word of God, Bible doctrine]. (1 Cor. 2:16)

In God, subjectivity is not the hotbed of arrogance and evil it is in mankind. God's subjective love for Himself is not narcissism but a recognition of the facts. He is truly worthy of love; His integrity is the one thing most important to Him. He respects His own integrity, honors it, loves it. In particular, He devotedly loves the principle of His integrity, His perfect righteousness. God is righteous, and He expresses His righteousness in every act of His will. This is clear revelation of how much He loves His integrity. To use the concise language of theology proper: "in righteousness is divine love for holiness [integrity] revealed."[17]

Perhaps you are beginning to see that what truly impresses God and what you may have assumed impresses Him are two different things. Imperfect, sinful man has nothing to offer God that is worthy of His love. Even after salvation, we cannot earn divine approbation or blessing. The only things we have that please God are what God Himself has given us, first at the moment of salvation and subsequently through the filling of the Spirit and the intake of doctrine.

Sooner or later you must learn two things, so you might as well be prepared for the shock. You have to learn, first of all, that God is not impressed with you. He is not pleased with your self-righteousness, with your personality, with your talent, with all the human good deeds you perform. He is not excited even a little about what you were, are, or plan to become. And that is the second thing: not only is He unimpressed with you now, but He never will be impressed with you. It is an absolute impossibility for you to make any kind of positive impression on God. You and I have no ability to attract His love. We lack the talent, the brains, the personality, the righteousness; not even our very best can make the grade.

But when most Christians today read "God is love," do they ever latch on to that! Do they ever foul that up! They immediately assume that *they*

---

17. See below, Appendix A.

must be the objects of God's love. Without a moment's thought or hesitation they rush to the conclusion that somehow God deeply appreciates them, that He is charmed by their little ways, that He sees all the "good" in them, that He could not quite get along without their "Christian service," that He truly respects the "dignity of man," that He cannot contain Himself from showering them with fatherly approbation.

"God is love," they say, with deep conviction. "Surely He'll bless me!" But in the next breath, after reversionism and divine discipline have knocked them flat, they whine and complain, "How could a loving God let this happen to me?"

What is wrong? Why the disillusionment? Answer: these people are ignorant of doctrine. They are maladjusted to the justice of God. They have no idea that *justice,* not love, is their point of contact with God. They have been rationalizing human sentimentality into divine love. They do not understand that God demands that we do things *His* way, not ours, and that His way is doctrine resident in the soul—doctrine taken in today, tomorrow, the next day, and every day. They are totally in the dark regarding the absolute, infinite, perfect character of God.

All the good deeds you perform do not inspire God to love you. His righteousness rejects your human good and His justice will judge it (1 Cor. 3:11–15; Rev. 20:12). Nor does He put any stock in your great personality. Your personality is how you relate to people, not to God. Others see you as a face, a body, a personality, a person of some accomplishment and with a certain amount of intelligence and human integrity. That is fine. You certainly should not renounce these wonderful assets simply because they do not relate you to God. Value them in their proper human place, but never attempt to superimpose the way *people* form an opinion of you over the way *God* evaluates you. The Latin proverb, notwithstanding, the voice of the people is *not* the voice of God.

There is no point in playing games with God or in trying to make deals with Him. He knows better than to fall for that, so between you and God, who are you kidding? No one but yourself (and perhaps a few impressionable friends). God does not suddenly like you because you stop doing this or that and stop going with the girls who do. God does not reward you for being good. He set up the laws of divine establishment, including the principles of morality, to protect human freedom and to provide prosperity within the nation where establishment is observed, but *God* is not bribed by your good deeds. Nor does He revel in your emotions, not even in those experiences that you associate with being "near to God." You are not even in the ballpark! God is in another league! He is not swept off His feet by your wonderful self, but He is mightily impressed with His own integrity!

We simply do not have anything of ourselves that pleases God. On the other hand, this does not mean that we are to grovel in the dust. We would be just as arrogant to think that self-abnegation satisfied God as we would be to assume that He was impressed with our human good works. We need to understand the truth and to see ourselves in our true relationship to God's immutable, impartial, unimpeachable perfection. No human gimmicks apply; we must learn how justice operates.

THE NATURE OF DIVINE INTEGRITY

GOD'S ESSENCE, THE ULTIMATE SOURCE

Several basic principles give us a running start at understanding God's integrity. We must realize, first of all, that everything God does or sponsors comes from His essence, from who and what He is. Whether the law of gravity, the principle of limited government and free enterprise, or the work of the Cross—every law of nature, every principle of divine establishment, every jot and tittle of Bible doctrine is based on the attributes or character of God.

Let us take one example. The grace of God is often defined as "unmerited favor"—not an inaccurate definition but an oversimple one, and one which permits believers to easily confuse grace with sentimentality. Far from being sentimental, God's grace toward mankind is rooted in His essence. Since His attributes are perfect, nothing He does for us in grace is ever less than perfect, nor does it ever compromise His divine nature. Let us point out this characteristic in every category of grace.

Saving grace removes the condemnation of spiritual death under which we are born and places us into a permanent blessing relationship with God. The doctrine of propitiation explains how the work of Christ on the Cross satisfied the uncompromising justice of God on our behalf and shows how God provides salvation without compromising His essence.[18]

Logistical grace keeps us alive and enables us to grow spiritually even though we live in the devil's world. Based on who and what He is, God has established certain objectives for us in the angelic conflict. In general, He keeps us on earth after salvation to learn Bible doctrine, which gives us the capacity to possess and enjoy fantastic divine prosperity. Blessing is the objective. If we are to seize this objective, this tactical victory in the spiritual combat of life, we require a great deal of provision and support—Bible teaching, air to breathe, food, shelter, clothing, transportation, friends. Logistical grace is indispensable in fulfilling the plan of God; thus, it is totally consistent with the essence of God.

---

18. See Thieme, *The Barrier.*

Supergrace includes the basic stages of spiritual maturity, supergrace$_A$ and supergrace$_B$. Supergrace$_A$ is that wonderful, tranquil period upon reaching maturity—the Christian soldier on "rest and recuperation." Supergrace$_B$ is the testing of adversity, opposition, and distraction—like crossing "no man's land"—as the mature believer continues to advance in doctrine. In either stage, supergrace is the tactical victory in the angelic conflict: upon the supergrace believer God pours out spiritual blessings, temporal blessings, blessings by association, historical impact, and blessings related to undeserved suffering. Because God is glorified when He blesses us, His essence is not only uncompromised in providing supergrace, it is emphasized!

Ultra-supergrace is the advanced stage of spiritual maturity, attained by the believer who continues and even intensifies his intake of doctrine after reaching supergrace. God does more than derive glory from blessing the ultra-supergrace believer; God is pleased by him and accepts him into friendship. Abraham and Moses, for example, were called the friends of God (2 Chron. 20:7; James 2:23; Ex. 33:11; cf. Rom. 14:3). Maximum doctrine in the soul gives the ultramature believer the capacity for blessings even under concentrated satanic opposition (2 Tim. 3:8a; cf. Ex. 7:11, 12, 22; 8:7; 9:11). Thus God demonstrates His perfect character in a special, concentrated way, proving again that "greater is He that is in you than he [Satan] that is in the world" (1 John 4:4b). The ultra-supergrace believer's capacity frees the essence of God to pour out intensified blessings without compromising any divine attribute.

Like all other categories of grace, *dying grace* is also furnished by the perfect essence of God. God transfers the mature believer from time to eternity in such a way that dying becomes the most relaxed and wonderful blessing of his entire life. God expresses His changeless nature even in how He calls the mature believer home.

Finally, *surpassing grace* blessings are awarded in heaven to the believer who learned enough doctrine on earth to develop capacity for supergrace or ultra-supergrace blessings in the devil's world. What God gives is permanent, and the blessings of time are parlayed into greater blessings in eternity. Such blessings and rewards bring unending glory to the Lord Jesus Christ as well as happiness and vast prosperity to the one so rewarded. The fact that some believers will be rewarded more richly than others is further proof of the uncompromising nature of God's perfect character (Mark 4:3–21).

From sustaining the universe to blessing believers, everything God does is based on the attributes of His essence. Therefore, before you can appreciate what God gives you (or what God is tapping His foot *waiting* to give you [Isa. 30:18]), you must first come to appreciate God Himself. Thus the importance of understanding the doctrine of divine essence, and thus the importance of distinguishing attributes from anthropopathisms.

GOD'S PERSON, NEVER DIVIDED

Not only do all God's actions reflect His attributes, but since He is a Person (Ex. 3:14), all His actions always involve His *entire* Person. Certain things He does exhibit only this or that attribute, but actually all His characteristics always function together in perfect coordination and harmony. An analogy to light will help you see what I mean.

When sunlight falls on a blue dress, blue is the only color seen; when on a bright red shirt, only red. A yellow object shows only yellow while, say, a Highlander's tartan would boast many colors, each in its own order in the sett. How can one beam of light suddenly be a different color every time it strikes a different spot?

The differences occur because a ray of white light contains all the colors of the spectrum, and whenever it strikes an opaque object some colors are absorbed while others are reflected. The blue dress is blue because it absorbs the reds and yellows; it reflects only the blue we see. The red shirt absorbs yellows, blue-greens, and blues, reflecting its specific shade of red. If a dress absorbed no color, it would reflect the entire contents of the white light and would obviously be white. The opposite, a black dress, would absorb all colors and reflect none. Even though each object shows its own color, the entire visible spectrum is still present in the white light shining upon it. The difference is not in the light but in the selective absorption of the object.

Likewise, God's essence might manifest certain characteristics in one situation but others in a different situation. The Lord Jesus Christ displays His awesome omnipotence as the Creator and Sustainer of the universe (John 1:3; Col. 1:16; Heb. 1:2, 10). Omniscience and sovereignty come into prominence when we study the doctrine of divine decrees (Rom. 8:28-30; Eph. 1;4-6).[19] The existence of the canon of Scripture emphasizes yet other attributes, especially His veracity (Ps. 138:2). And when He sustains us through all the uncertainties and instabilities of life, His immutability stands out (Deut. 31:6; Heb. 13:5*b*, 8). In every case, no matter which attribute is reflected, God's total, indivisible Person is completely involved.

In other words, no divine attribute can be bypassed, overlooked, or violated in anything God does; His right hand always knows what His left hand is doing. God does not put aside His sovereignty when He manifests His veracity. He does not switch back and forth between omnipotence and omniscience. He does not ignore His righteousness and justice in order to deal with us strictly out of love.

---

19. See below, Appendix B.

JUSTICE GUARDS DIVINE ESSENCE

God never has the slightest trouble keeping His attributes straight. One never compromises another. Even when He deals with imperfect, sinful, fallen man—and especially when He *blesses* us—He is not lowering Himself to our imperfect level thus destroying His own perfection. The reason He can bless us is that one of His attributes stands guard, as it were, over all the rest. The justice of God, the function of His integrity, is the guardian of God's essence in all that He does toward imperfect creatures.

When one Member of the Trinity is concerned with Himself or with the other Members of the Godhead, there is no need for a guardian. There is never a possibility of compromise because all three Persons are perfect, co-equal, and coeternal; all Three possess the same integrity. Thus, in Himself, God is free to regard His personality—the fact that He is a Person—as most important.[20]

Related to man, however, there is almost unlimited opportunity for compromise. Man violates God's character at almost every turn. Here God must keep His integrity first and foremost. Thus, God's point of contact with us can be only His justice. Let me emphasize this: our point of contact with God is His justice.

> But the Lord of hosts shall be exalted in judgment, and
> God that is holy shall be sanctified in righteousness. (Isa.
> 5:16, AV)

> He is the Lord our God: his judgments are in all the earth.
> (1 Chron. 16:14; Ps. 105:7, AV)

The justice of God is the origin of everything we receive from Him, both blessing and cursing. This is true of unbeliever and believer alike; God functions toward all mankind from His justice, both now and forever. The reversionistic believer's *discipline* comes from divine justice, but then, so does the mature believer's *blessing*. Both the unbeliever's eternal agony in the Lake of Fire and the believer's ultimate sanctification and reward in heaven come from the same Source! Everything God does toward us from any of His attributes goes through His justice. Justice is the half of God's integrity which functions or acts; justice is the final source of all divine action related to mankind.

---

20. God's personality is an aspect of His absolute attribute of spirituality. See Appendix A.

How can I make this clear? Think of the essence of God as a box with an opening in the bottom. Inside the essence box are all of God's attributes, and right over the hatch is His justice. Whatever comes from God to man can come only through that opening. God's justice is also our point of contact with Him; therefore, when we come to God, His absolute fairness is the attribute to which we must adjust. This explains why Romans 1:16 and 17 dogmatically state that God's ability to save man is not His love, not His sovereignty, not His omnipotence, not any divine attribute but justice.

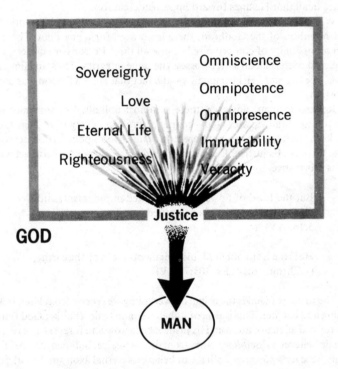

If God's point of contact with us were His sovereignty, *He* would choose who would go to heaven; *He* would program us to mechanically enact every detail of our lives on earth. We would be automatons; human freedom would not exist; the angelic conflict could not be won. This is the position of Hypercalvinism which distorts the sovereignty of God.[21] If, on the other hand, God's point of contact with us were His omnipotence, He would be a tyrant.

---

21. See below, Appendix B.

It would be impossible for us to fulfill the will of God because He would do everything Himself by direct fiat. He would force people to believe in Christ. Again, there would be no freedom, no volition, no divine establishment; human history would not be permitted to run its course as part of the angelic conflict. As perfect as these attributes are, they are not the basic frame of reference in God's relationship with us. We have already diagnosed the plethora of human sentimentality, instability, compromise, and emotionalism that develops from the false assumption that love is God's point of contact with us. Of all the attributes in the essence box, justice is the only one that protects His entire essence. For this reason, and for other reasons that we shall see, God's justice is our point of reference with Him.

RIGHTEOUSNESS GUARDS DIVINE JUSTICE

In the exercise of His justice, however, God is never arbitrary or capricious. His justice has a "guardian" of its own. Divine justice can never be corrupted because it always functions according to the standard of fairness found in God's perfect righteousness.

> And he shall judge the world in righteousness, he shall minister judgment to the people in uprightness. (Ps. 9:8, AV)

In the same way that justice is the watchdog over God's entire essence, righteousness is the watchdog over His justice. Whereas justice is the function of divine integrity, righteousness is the principle of divine integrity. What righteousness demands, justice executes.

Absolute righteousness is the key to the character of God; all else depends on it. If he did not have absolute righteousness, God would not be God. But He does have it. He has always existed as God, and there never was a time when He did not exist as God. Inviolable righteousness is at the very core of His Being (Isa. 6:4); God cannot tolerate less than His own perfection. Again, what the righteousness of God demands, the justice of God must perform: if righteousness rejects something, justice condemns it; if righteousness approves, justice blesses.

Righteousness rejects sin; therefore, justice condemns sin. Righteousness also rejects our human good because, being relative, it falls short of the absolute standard of divine good; therefore, justice condemns all our legalism, religiosity, human works, and self-righteousness. Righteousness likewise rejects evil; justice totally condemns it.

On the positive side, God's righteousness approves of the perfect God-Man, the Lord Jesus Christ. Righteousness also approves of His perfect work on the Cross in payment for our sins. Therefore, justice *blesses* anyone who believes in Christ. Justice, not love₁, accomplishes this. It is the fairness of God that bestows upon every believer the thirty-six amazing blessings that we call eternal salvation.[22] Here is a definition to note and remember: *grace* is the policy of the *justice* of God for *blessing* mankind.

> Therefore, the Lord waits to be gracious to you [God constantly desires to bless believers], and He is on high to have compassion on you. For the Lord is a God of blessing and justice [all the blessings He waits to give come through His justice]. How blessed are those who wait for Him [the daily function of GAP]. (Isa. 30:18)

Perhaps you are wondering why you have never before heard of the "integrity" of God. "Where is that found in the Bible?" you ask. The Authorized or King James Version of the Bible calls the combination of righteousness and justice the "holiness" of God. But the word "holiness" fails to communicate; it is anachronistic, antiquated, about as useful as a Model T. The meanings of words in any language change over a period of time, and in the past 350 years, the English language certainly has been no exception.

If someone today were described as being "holy," people might picture asceticism, straightlacedness, self-righteousness, or some other form of pseudo-spirituality. When the Bible says, "Holy, holy, holy" (Isa. 6:3), it certainly does not mean self-righteousness or self-denial! What does it mean? Well, we might observe the repetition and say that it speaks of the Trinity, which it does. We might sing it with great vigor, but responding emotionally does not add to our understanding. I'll tell you what Isaiah 6:3 means to most believers. Not a thing! And it never will until explained in other terms. Today, if the word "holy" is not ambiguous, it is vague; if not vague, evanescent. We need not tie ourselves to an obscure, emotion-tinged word, especially when an excellent, meaningful, twentieth-century term is available. "Integrity, integrity, integrity." *That* begins to communicate!

God has always possessed integrity as part of His eternal, infinite, perfect essence. It is a quality of His unchangeable Self so basic to His character that He does not have to sustain it by His will or sovereignty. God does not have to continually decide to perpetuate His integrity; He simply has it. His integrity is totally superior to ours.

We are not perfect. Nor are we immutable; we are likely to change at any moment (in fact, we continually change). You can see that whatever integrity

---

22. See Thieme, *The Plan of God,* Appendix.

we can achieve comes only through a continuous series of decisions, through the proper and honorable use of volition. And in the same way that we gain human integrity, we can also lose it.

We must constantly decide to do the right things and not to do the wrong things. For example, we must daily decide to expose ourselves to the teaching of doctrine and not to be distracted from concentrating on it. In that way, we develop correct norms and standards. As we saturate our souls with the Word of God to the point of spiritual maturity, we must also make decisions to apply doctrine to the circumstances of life. We have integrity if we make enough decisions in favor of what we know to be right. But if we make too many decisions in violation of what we know to be right, we have no integrity.

Human integrity is not natural to us, but perfect integrity *is* natural to God. It is the sum total of His perfection. The integrity of God is not merely the absence of evil; it is the very quintessence of His nature.

Thus, everything God does toward mankind is a reflection of His perfect integrity.

> The Lord is righteous in all his ways and Holy [He has integrity] in all His works. (Ps. 145:17, AV)

His sovereignty decrees only what is consistent with divine integrity. His omnipotence accomplishes only what integrity has endorsed. His perfect attribute of love$_1$ is directed only toward what meets the standards of integrity. And what meets that perfect standard? What qualifies as an object worthy of God's love? Does fallen man? Does Satan? Does the devil's world? Certainly not! These are proper objects for condemnation and judgment. God can love only what is perfect: divine integrity itself.

Because God loves His own integrity He does not require an object in order for His love to function. Love$_1$ is internal. But God's love is not merely internal. There are three Members of the Trinity, each with the same integrity; therefore, love$_1$ is external as well. Divine integrity in each Member of the Godhead is the object of God's love, so that God the Father loves God the Son and God the Holy Spirit with the same infinite love which He has for Himself. Likewise, the Lord Jesus Christ loves the Father and the Holy Spirit, and the Spirit loves the Father and the Son. Subjectively, God's love is rational, perfect, and *internal;* but objectively, it is rational, perfect, and *external* from one Person of the Trinity to another.

God's love, we might say, is rather exclusive. We cannot intrude on it. We are not worthy. A person who thinks he can elbow his way into the love of God is a crass, ignorant boor. We are *left out* as far as God's love is concerned. But God has not abandoned us.

INTEGRITY TAKES PRECEDENCE OVER LOVE

The doctrine of divine integrity fires a powerful broadside against our pride, but it does not leave us shipwrecked and alone. We may feel like clinging to the flotsam of the false ideas we have served for many years—ideas built on the assumption that God cannot quite do without us or that He is somehow obliged to show us undying affection. But no, when Bible doctrine clarifies God's love and sinks our arrogance in the process, we are not cast adrift.

Although you and I do not merit God's love, He has something for us that is *greater* than love. Now, that's a shock! You never thought that anything could be greater than God's love! But something is, and God has it toward you. Integrity.

The tremendous value of our relationship with divine justice will become clear once we see that, when dealing with mankind, God's integrity takes precedence over His love. This precedence is proven at the Cross.

God the Father loves God the Son with an eternal, infinite love. The rapport between the Members of the Trinity has never been less than total. They have enjoyed the most magnificent relationship since eternity past, and nothing changed in that relationship when Christ became a man through the virgin birth. In both His impeccable humanity and His perfect deity, the Lord Jesus Christ was acceptable to the righteousness of God; the Father deeply loved Him.

Yet in spite of this great love, of the Father for His Son, God over-ruled love, at the Cross. When Christ hung between heaven and earth, the justice of God the Father poured out upon Him all the personal sins of the human race. Justice came before love. The Father judged the Son. No punches were pulled. Jesus Christ suffered the unmitigated full measure of spiritual death as the penalty for sin (Gen. 2:17; Rom. 3:23).

Our Lord was insulted, abused, and virtually skinned alive. His back was a mass of lacerations and exposed nerve endings; His face was barely recognizable. His great physical strength was so debilitated that He stumbled in the road. Nailed to the cross, He had to force His feet and wrists against the spikes to relieve the weight on His lungs so He could breathe. From the time of His arrest, through long hours of mental abuse and physical torture, never once did He cry out (Isa. 53:7; Acts 8:32-35). But when the Father imputed our sins to Him and executed divine judgment upon Him, He screamed in pain. From the *justice* of the Father, who kept on loving Him, our Lord suffered an excruciating agony that will never be felt by any other human being. For three hours He repeated, "My God [the Father], my God [the Holy Spirit], why have you forsaken me?" His mind was perfectly clear, and from the doctrine in His soul He knew perfectly well why He was being forsaken. He was quoting Psalm 22:1 to express the agony of spiritual death. He knew He was being "made . . . sin for us . . . that we might be made the righteousness of God in Him" (2 Cor. 5:21).

Christ died twice on the Cross: first spiritually, then physically.[23] His spiritual death paid the penalty for sin. His physical death indicated that His work in the First Advent was complete. Furthermore, His physical death set the stage for His resurrection, ascension and session, which complete both our salvation and His strategic victory in the angelic conflict. But during the entire three hours in which He suffered spiritual death, Christ was still physically alive. We know this because as the darkness covered the hill, He kept screaming under the unspeakable pain of the judgment that should have come to us. Only a living person can scream. During those hours He paid for our freedom from the slave market of sin (redemption), broke down the barrier between God and us (reconciliation), and freed God to take us in and bless us without compromising His essence (propitiation). When our Lord's work was complete, He shouted, "It is finished!" Salvation was accomplished, and He was free to die physically. Nothing remains to be done in salvation but for us to accept it.

At the Cross the Father faced a choice between love, and justice: His love for Jesus Christ versus an act of judgment against Him. The Father's attribute of love never dimmed or went out—it never even flickered. With His love still infinitely bright, He decided to overrule His love and judge Christ for our sins. Christ was sent to the Cross because when God deals with sinful mankind, divine integrity always takes precedence over divine love.

When that first sin struck our Lord and His body was shot through with the pain of divine judgment, when the Father heard that first cry from the One He loved, admired, and esteemed so dearly, did He call off the judgment? Did He revert from justice back to love? He did not! He was totally impartial in the function of His integrity, and the judgment continued until the final sin of all human history had been judged. God's love never interferes with His justice.

We generally think that Christ alone provided salvation, but actually the entire Trinity was involved. Both the Father and the Holy Spirit had to forsake Him while He was identified with our sins (Ps. 22:1). But the Father had, as it were, the most nightmarish job of all. He had to deliberately pour out the full wrath of His justice upon the One He loved so perfectly. For infinite eons before man was formed out of the dust—long before even the dust existed—the Father had loved Christ, and He continued to love Him while judicially imputing our sins to Him and executing

---

23. See Thieme, *The Blood of Christ.*

judgment upon Him. The closest the Father could come to expressing His love was to blanket the hill in a darkness so total that neither man nor angel could watch our Lord's ordeal.

The way in which God treated His Son on the Cross demonstrates conclusively that when God deals with us, divine integrity has higher priority than divine love. When He deals with Himself or with the other Members of the Godhead, His integrity is not challenged. But our imperfection sounds an alarm in the essence of God. If God had to design a coat of arms to represent Himself before fallen man, the motto would read, "Integrity Before Love."

THE IMPARTIALITY OF GOD

God's integrity is perfect; He is never better or worse. He is immutable; never has He varied in the least since eternity past, and never will He throughout all eternity future.

> Jesus Christ, the same yesterday, today and forever.
> (Heb. 13:8, AV)

The Being of God is unalterable, absolute, totally consistent. If God is fair in anything He does, He is necessarily fair in all His dealings with us. This is a principle: God is impartial and unprejudiced.

In Romans 1:16, Paul interjected a theme which he pursues throughout the book of Romans (especially in chapters 9 through 11): "to the Jew first and also to the Greek." The Jew is mentioned first because Israel is God's chosen people, having been given special responsibilities and accompanying privileges related to the custodianship and dissemination of the Word of God. The principle, however, is that both Jews and non-Jews— that is, all people—have access to the same opportunities and blessings in this dispensation. No race or culture has greater privilege than another in the royal family of God,[24] nor is any race or culture excluded. No individual is treated with special favor, and no one is ignored. Race, culture, personal traits—none of these is an issue in the plan of God. The issue is: either you adjust to the justice of God, resulting in blessing, or the justice of God will adjust to you, resulting in cursing and discipline. The impartiality of divine justice is a concept you must understand before you can get even a good start in the Christian life.

---

24. See below, page 199.

For there is never partiality before the God. (Rom. 2:11)

Since we deal with the justice of God we must get away from certain misconceptions. Because of culture, background, or some practice advocated by legalistic religion, many people think they have a special "in" with God. Perhaps they grew up in a Christian home where certain taboos were observed; perhaps they faithfully worked around the church or witnessed or prayed every day or read the Bible from cover to cover. At some time in life they followed some procedure that they *know* impressed God. Arrogantly, they reject the truth that we can do nothing to impress infinite God, that God is impressed only with what *God* does, that divine righteousness and divine justice demand no less than divine righteousness and divine justice!

From their blind arrogance comes self-righteousness, and from self-righteousness the erroneous assumption that God is partial to them. After all, they insist, we have been good, clean, respectable people; we have sweet, pleasing personalities; we smile; we do a good turn now and again; we contribute to charitable organizations; we have spoken in tongues; we have been baptized or circumcised; we have kept the Law (at least the Ten Commandments).[25]

All these "letters of recommendation" are destroyed by the impartiality of God's justice. He never gives special consideration to anyone. He has set up His own system, consistent with His own essence, to which everyone must adjust; and no other system can compete—not yours, not Satan's, not anyone's. Blessing from God is a matter of divine integrity, and the plan of God states that all direct blessing to you depends entirely upon your consistent, daily adjustment to the justice of God.

The verb in Romans 2:11 is the present active indicative of *eimi,* translated "there is." The customary present tense, with the negative *ou,* means that there will *never* be a time when God makes exceptions for anyone. God is totally wise, totally fair, totally unchanging. He wrote the rules for His own creation, and His rules are always in force in every case. There is no slack anywhere. He treats us in grace, but grace is the policy of His justice. Grace is not a sloppy program of sentimentality. God is not some huge mass of love. He is a Person of incorruptible, awe-inspiring integrity, and His grace is an efficient, well-run plan.

The word for "partiality" is the noun *prosopolempsia,* from *prosopos,* "face," and *lambano,* "to receive." Being partial or "receiving face" connotes bias, an inclination to favor one person over another, a

---

25. See Thieme, *The Ten Commandments.*

predilection or fondness toward a certain person. Divine justice is completely free of it; human relationships abound in it.

A man who loves a woman and thinks she is entirely wonderful is partial to her. A woman in love who thinks her man is the most noble person on the face of the earth is definitely biased. Parents are partial to their children; friends are partial to friends. People in any category of love are partial, and something would be wrong were they not. Sometimes bias goes too far, and people are left with no ability to judge objectively. But God is not that way. He deals with us in justice, and in every instance without exception, justice demands justice.

For example, God does not look down on shining white faces and say they are best; nor does He say that black, yellow, or red faces are best. No race is best; no individual is best. There is no preferential treatment. God is unbending and impartial. Your special "in" with Him fades like a mist; the light of divine justice illuminates reality.

That ought to startle you and, at the same time, please you above all else. Startle you because you have been on the wrong track! You have been nice to people you couldn't stand just to get God's attention; you have tithed so that God might bless your business; you have toed the line so God might drop your right man or right woman in your lap. The light of divine justice should sober you because here you are trying to bribe God, and suddenly you see that He cannot be bribed! Just think of all the time and energy you have wasted trying to stay in God's good graces! But life is not designed to be a strain; you cannot work your way into God's favor, nor can you work to stay there. Grace is extended through His justice. You simply adjust to the justice of God. If you entertain any other idea, don't worry, the justice of God will adjust to you—with punishment and discipline.

On the other hand, the light of divine justice ought to delight you—you are assured that God always treats you fairly, that when He demands something of you He has already provided the means of execution, that whenever God does something for you or promises you something, it is absolutely guaranteed forever.

There are two approaches to understanding God's freedom from prejudice. First, from the viewpoint of salvation, we *all* start out at zero. As of the moment of physical birth we are all spiritually dead, and God simply does not care to pass the time with a bunch of rotten corpses. God is obviously impartial because in His estimation we all start at the same level—the absolute bottom, divine condemnation. Furthermore, He provides identical salvation for each of us "zeros" who believes in Christ.

The second approach to a realization of God's impartiality begins on the other side, not with man but with God Himself. Go back to the essence of God; perfect righteousness stands guard over divine justice while justice guards God's entire essence. If justice played favorites it could not properly protect God's character; God would not be God. The very definition of absolute justice precludes any possibility that God ever makes exceptions for anyone.

Every great believer understood God's incorruptibility. Many of them —Abraham, Moses, David, Paul—discovered it the hard way. You can repeat their mistakes by assuming that God somehow treats you as a privileged character; or you can learn it the easier way by submitting to God's system: the consistent intake of the Word of God. If you choose to learn the hard way, you will discover that no believer anywhere—you included —is exempt from being destroyed, disgraced, instantly recalled to heaven! Any punitive action that God can take against any believer He can take against you! On the other hand, if you choose the easy way, you will not only come to understand and appreciate His perfect justice but in that justice you will also discover His system for blessing you. The same rules apply to all. If you take in doctrine and crack the maturity barrier, you will be blessed by God in such a phenomenal way that it can be described only as "exceeding abundantly above all that we ask or think" (Eph. 3:20).

To the extent you think you are a privileged person, you are divorced from reality. If you consider yourself to be great in God's eyes because of something you have done or refrained from doing, if you think that keeping the Ten Commandments makes you a special case before God, if you imagine that your sweet personality means you are close to Him, you have lost contact with reality. This basic disorientation is what makes the study of divine integrity difficult for so many believers. A steady diet of devotional sermons, sentimentalism, and human good has dulled their taste for the truth.

Only by learning doctrine can we orient to the truth and in doing so advance to spiritual maturity. As mature believers, we have resident in our souls what God has revealed of Himself; we are read in on His plan of grace; we are occupied with the Person of Christ; we are fully adjusted to the justice of God. Orienting to the justice of God *is* orienting to reality.

That might be a completely new thought: reality *is* the justice of God. Reality is more than the overt events of history or of our own daily lives. We might be enjoying prosperity; we might be under intense pressure. We might be happy or unhappy, in supergrace or reversionism; but no matter what our attitude or situation today, that is only the surface. To orient to life we must understand what lies beneath the surface. We must understand the principle that gives meaning to the things we see: reality is God's righteousness put into action by His justice.

Here our study turns from defining and describing the integrity of God to delineating the plan of God based on that integrity. God is continuously working in our behalf; we must see His integrity in action. To discover the link between God's justice and God's plan, let us brush the dust from a basic category of doctrine.

2
Integrity in Action

IMPUTATIONS: THE FRAMEWORK FOR UNDERSTANDING DOCTRINE

THE DOCTRINE OF IMPUTATION is an undeveloped area of Biblical teaching. It is almost completely ignored. Rarely is it lifted down from dusty seminary shelves, and then only to fill in a gap here or there in the doctrines of sin or salvation. As a separate category, the full scope of the doctrine of imputation is not understood, let alone communicated from pulpits.

Yet imputations are the outline of our lives. Imputations erect the framework upon which is built all other doctrine pertaining to our relationship with God; they are the bones of the skeleton; they give structure and strength to every principle and concept related to the Christian way of life. The delineation of imputations is the story of grace, the story of how divine justice accomplishes the purpose for which God created mankind.

We are alive to be blessed. And all blessing from God to man revolves around the fact that the justice of God imputed human life to our souls at birth, Adam's original sin to our old sin natures, our personal sins to Christ on the Cross, divine righteousness to us at salvation, and eternal life to the human spirit at the new birth. A study of these five basic imputations will permit us to see the phenomenal implications of divine justice as our point of contact with God.

Did you ever wish that a single doctrine might pull together your understanding of the Word of God? Have you ever wanted a categorical peg on which to hang all the diverse details of God's plan for your life? Here it is!

The doctrine of imputation provides a relatively simple series of pegs which will bring order out of chaos in your doctrinal closet.

The doctrine of imputation presents the integrity of God in action throughout the full history of man. Let us therefore begin at the beginning, in the Garden of Eden with the original man and woman. From the first couple we can trace the policies and actions of God's justice down to our own lives today and on into eternity future.

LOVE₁ AS ADAM'S POINT OF CONTACT

THE AGE OF PERFECTION

Adam was perfect as he came from the hand of God; so was the woman, who was constructed from Adam's rib.[26] Not only were the first two people perfect, but so was their environment. Perfect persons plus perfect environment equals a perfect age.

Once and for all we should throw out an old, lingering misnomer. The epoch of man in the Garden is often called the Age of Innocence, but no one was "innocent" in the Garden. How can you have wonderful sex every day and be innocent (Gen. 2:24, 25)? How can you attend Bible class every day taught by the Lord Jesus Christ Himself and be innocent (Gen. 3:8)? You cannot. And they were not! Theirs was an age of perfection, not of innocence.

Here a principle comes into play: love₁ can be directed only toward perfection. In its internal sense, love₁ does not take an object; God loves His own integrity. But in its external sense, the love of God goes toward the other two Members of the Godhead—and toward the perfect products of divine creation. Nothing imperfect can come from perfect God; therefore, the man and the woman came under the divine attribute of love₁. In the Age of Perfection, man's point of contact with God was love, not justice. Their situation was very different from ours.

Everything we have from God comes via justice; everything they had came via love. In love, God provided the trees "good to the sight" as stimulation for their souls, and the trees "good for food" as delicious sustenance for their bodies (Gen. 2:9). Since Adam and the woman were created as adults who did not have to grow up, love₁ even supplied them with instantaneous

---

26. Adam's wife was originally called *Ishah,* "the woman." Not until after the Fall, and after she had believed in Christ as her Savior, did Adam rename her *Howah,* transliterated "Eve" and meaning "the mother of all living." Her new name recognized that Christ would be the "Seed of the woman" (Gen. 3:15, 20).

capacity to appreciate their lives in the Garden. They acquired this capacity of soul simply by eating the fruit from the tree of lives. Not from the "tree of *life,*" in the singular, as translated in the King James Version, but from the tree of *lives,* plural. This tree represented positive volition toward God's plan for them in the Garden and gave them capacity in many categories. They had a perfect right man-right woman relationship. They had leisure. They did not have to work for a living. They thoroughly enjoyed their surroundings. They dominated all the rest of creation. And every evening, Christ came in the cool of the day to teach them Bible doctrine. Love₁ blessed them in every way—body, soul, and spirit—and supplied the capacity to enjoy all these things.

> And God saw everything that he had made, and behold, it
> was very good. (Gen. 1:31*a*)

NO JUSTICE, NO GRACE

All the blessings of the Garden came from the love of God, but there were several things Adam and the woman did not have. Two things were missing because they were not necessary. First, there was no justice in the Garden in the sense of being man's point of contact with God. As perfect individuals, still sinless, the first two human beings offered no compromise to the character of God. As the guardian of divine essence, justice was not challenged and, as it were, had nothing to do. God was free to provide for them strictly out of love. Second, therefore, there was no grace.

Grace is the plan and policy of the justice of God for blessing fallen man. But Adam and Ishah were not fallen nor was justice their point of reference. Grace is for the undeserving, but they were neither undeserving nor deserving. They were simply the perfect work of perfect God, and they would stay that way as long as they did not reject God's authority. Now remember, their situation was different from ours. Since the Fall, God has dealt with us through His justice so that grace rules both now and forever (Rom. 5:21). But grace did not reign in the Garden. There, everything was *perfect* provision but not *grace* provision.

Only one reference to the justice of God existed in the Garden. This was a warning that justice would become their point of contact if they ate from the forbidden tree of the knowledge of good and evil. The nature of this tree, like that of the tree of lives, has been long misunderstood. Some, with a cynical and superficial knowledge of the Scriptures, have gone so far as to say that God opposes knowledge! That is ludicrous. We know that the greatest virtue in the Christian life is maximum understanding and application of the

Word of God (Prov. 1; Hos. 4:6; Rom. 10:2). What, then, does this tree represent?

In contrast to the tree of lives, which gave man and woman an opportunity to express their positive volition toward God's plan, the tree of the knowledge of good and evil embodied Satan's plan. The connective "and" is not a contrast; it is a *link* between similar concepts. "Good *and* evil" was, and still is, the sum total of Satan's policy for ruling the world and for proving himself to be as good as God; to eat from this tree was to acquiesce to the Prince of Darkness.

Satan did not rule the world during the Age of Perfection. His usurpation of the throne and his tyranny of good and evil were merely potential. Adam was the sovereign of the earth and of all that was in it, including his wife. He and she were placed on earth to resolve the angelic conflict, but originally they were not subordinate to the arrogant, good-and-evil ambitions of Satan. They were created perfect. They were therefore insulated from the spiritual warfare which already had been raging for an unrevealed length of time, and which in fact was being waged unseen all around them. They would continue to be protected from Satan's influence as long as they stayed on positive volition toward God and Bible doctrine. The two trees in the middle of the Garden represented the opposing sides in the angelic conflict.

Today, Satan is the sovereign of the world, and he rules through the policy which he naturally calls "good" but which God calls "evil." As we study past history or look about us at contemporary history, we see that the satanic system pervades every aspect of life. The United States is being destroyed in the name of "the greatest good for the greatest number"! We face many temptations to "get involved" in doing "good," but in the Garden, only one good-and-evil issue was at stake: God's prohibition of that one tree. This was a test of perfect man's volition; he could become imperfect only through disobedience to the divine command. As long as he accepted God's authority, he would remain in perfect status quo and would enjoy all the blessings that divine love could lavish upon him.

NO ETERNAL LIFE, NO STABILITY

Here again, the implications of a principle come out: as always, integrity is greater than love. Man lived under the love of God in the Garden, but there are some things that even perfect love cannot do. It cannot provide grace, but neither can it provide eternal life. There is no permanence in a relationship based solely upon love.

God's love, like all His attributes, is immutable, eternal, perfect; but man with his free will could change at any moment and become imperfect.

All he had to do was eat the forbidden fruit. God's love could not guarantee that man would never sin, and therefore God's love could not guarantee that man would be qualified to live with Him forever. Today, as believers in the Lord Jesus Christ, under the justice of God, we have the tremendous blessing of eternal security. We are members of the royal family of God forever, and nothing—not even God Himself—can remove us from our position in Christ (Rom. 8:32). In fact, we have more than eternal security; when we reach spiritual maturity, we also have complete temporal security for the blessings we receive from God in time.[27] Not so for Adam.

Every day when the Lord came to the Garden at sundown, He provided all the doctrine that Adam and the woman needed; He repeated the prohibition each day and warned them of the results of disobedience. And if our original parents had gone through that particular day without violating His command, He renewed the contract with them for another twenty-four hours, never more, never less. In perfection, man was given one day at a time (Gen. 2:17).

Perhaps Adam and the woman went on for thousands of years with the contract renewed every day; or they might have lived in the Garden for a month or a year. The length of time is not revealed, but no matter how long they lived in the Age of Perfection, they enjoyed a wonderful mental, spiritual, and physical relationship.

Love₁ was unable to provide Adam and the woman with eternal security, but moreover it was unable to stabilize them even a day at a time. Divine love provided doctrine, and doctrine does sustain. But divine love itself cannot sustain even perfect man in the face of temptation. Human volition is the spoiler.

When the woman was tempted, she failed to resist the subtleties of Satan because sometime between her creation and her fall she had lost respect for authority. She had rejected all authority but her own; instead of responding, she had begun to react. And having turned her back on Adam's leadership and protection, she demonstrated a complete lack of common sense: she started talking to a stranger, Satan, as though he were an old friend. She should have recognized Satan's cynical innuendoes as being anti-doctrinal and immediately told Adam. But no, she had rejected her husband's authority.

Adam was not the only authority over her, however. The other Authority designed to protect her was the Lord Jesus Christ and the Bible doctrine that He communicated. Even though she had been attending Bible class every evening, she had stopped concentrating. She apparently resented the Lord's teaching, especially His prohibition of the tree.

---

27. See below, page 117.

> But of the tree of the knowledge of good and evil, thou
> shalt not eat of it; for in the day that thou eatest thereof
> thou shalt surely die. (Gen. 2:17, AV)

The Hebrew verb *muth,* "to die," is doubled so that a literal translation would read, "dying, you will die"; as an idiom it actually indicates the intensity of the death. Spiritual death is in view—the "wages [subsistence pay] of sin" (Rom. 6:23)—which includes total condemnation from the justice of God.

The woman's rejection of the Lord's authority was clearly demonstrated in her conversation with Satan; she leapt at the prospect of becoming as smart as God. Furthermore, given an opportunity to comment on a point of doctrine (Satan was flattering her by asking), she gave the wrong interpretation. Christ had taught her, "thou shalt not eat of it," but in her vanity she added to the Word of God.

> But of the fruit of the tree which is in the midst of the
> garden, God hath said, ye shall not eat of it, neither shall
> ye touch it, lest ye die. (Gen. 3:3, AV)

She distorted the Lord's words when she said, "I cannot eat *or touch* the forbidden fruit." She added to the truth by suggesting that the tree was somehow poisonous, which it was not. She evidently believed that it was, however, for after eating she carried around the fruit as if to mock the Lord. If her soul had been saturated with doctrine, she would have been impervious to flattery. But instead, her soul was filled with vanity which actually drew in Satan's false compliments! She was deceived by being flattered. Her vanity was not sinful because the only sin possible in the Garden was disobedience to the divine prohibition. But she set herself up for the Fall by rejecting every authority designed to protect her. She cast aside the awe and respect which hold together true love. Wanting to be a "free spirit," she ended up spiritually dead.

DIVINE LOVE CAN ONLY BLESS

Throughout her temptation by the serpent, the woman's point of contact with God was His attribute of love. Why could not love₁ sustain her in the crisis? The answer to this question will emphasize the superiority of justice as our point of contact.

Love₁ can do only one thing: it can only bless. It has no dynamics in a negative situation. It provided doctrine in the Garden, but where negative volition rejected the authority of the Word of God, love was helpless. But justice is a different story. The justice of God is free to bless *or* punish. Justice is a much stronger motivator to resist temptation than is the love of God. Love, required Adam's and the woman's positive volition; justice can function equally well toward positive or negative volition, toward believer or unbeliever, for blessing or cursing.

The Bible frequently communicates this dual function of divine justice by ascribing to God human love.

> For whom the Lord loveth he chasteneth, and scourgeth
> every son whom he receiveth. (Heb. 12:6, AV)

Love₂ is in view here. The parent-child relationship attributed to God is an anthropopathism which illustrates the two functions of the justice of God, both the discipline and the security involved in belonging to the royal family of God. The human parent's integrity overrules his natural love so that he does not spare his child the pain of discipline and proper training. Divine integrity also takes precedence over divine love. Indeed, we shall see that because of what justice has done for us, in both cursing and blessing, we are much better off, even though we live in the devil's world, than were our original parents under love, in the Garden!

THE FALL OF MAN AND THE GRACE OF GOD

The woman rejected love, as her point of reference with God; she disregarded every system of authority that God had designed to protect her from her own vanity; she succumbed to flattery; she was deceived by Satan; she ate from the forbidden tree. Immediately she became spiritually dead. The warning, "dying, you will die," came true; her personal sin had two instantaneous results. "Dying" meant that she acquired a sin nature; "you will die" signified her spiritual death—her condemnation from the justice of God.

As the first spiritually dead person in the human race, she naturally wanted to share her new-found situation with her husband. So she took the fruit to Adam. There he stood, the ruler of the world, the original perfect man, the man of genius intellect, the man whose soul was saturated with Bible doctrine. He faced the choice of perfection with God in the Garden versus spiritual death with the woman outside the Garden. In full knowledge of what he was doing, he took the fruit from her hand and deliberately sinned. His wife may have been deceived by Satan into disobeying God, but not so Adam. Just like her, however, when he ate of the fruit he too immediately acquired a depraved nature, which we call the old sin nature, and became spiritually dead.

At the Fall, Adam and the woman came under a new system. No longer perfect, they ceased to be objects of the love of God. Their new, depraved condition demanded something greater than love. Justice was called for, and justice immediately went into action.

Remember that justice is one half of the integrity of God: righteousness is the principle of His integrity while justice is its function. Justice is always taking action in one of two ways: it is either blessing or cursing. And the policy of divine integrity is quite simple: righteousness demands righteousness; justice demands justice; what the righteousness of God demands, justice executes. Under this policy, righteousness demanded something at the Fall of man.

Let us stop and think this over for a moment. The Garden was characterized by perfection; the period after the Garden is characterized by grace. Under perfection, grace was impossible, but under imperfection, grace becomes imperative. Now, what was it that carried man over the line from perfection to grace? You might quickly answer that *sin* brings us to the point of needing grace. That is absolutely false. Sin never advances the plan of God in any way.

> What shall we say then, shall we continue in slavery to the
> old sin nature that grace may increase? Definitely not! . . .
> (Rom. 6:1, 2*a*)

Sin brings man to the point where he needs condemnation and judgment, not grace! God's immovable righteousness sees sin and demands that man be condemned. Justice immediately condemns us. This is the action that qualifies us for grace, an action performed not by us at all but by the justice of God.

Grace is designed for the undeserving, and once condemned by the justice of God, we are *totally* undeserving! *That* is how we come into line for grace. This becomes a principle of God's justice: cursing always precedes blessing. Condemnation precedes justification. God offers saving grace only to those who *need* saving. He would never waste grace on those who were not condemned. He would never send His Son to the Cross unnecessarily! Therefore, at the Fall, God immediately condemned Adam. He did so by imputing Adam's original sin to his newly acquired sin nature, resulting in his spiritual death. This is what we call a real imputation.

REAL AND JUDICIAL IMPUTATIONS

Imputation is the function of the justice of God in ascribing, reckoning, or crediting something to someone for cursing or for blessing.

Imputations fall into two categories: real and judicial. A real imputation credits to a person something which belongs to him, something antecedently his own. There is thus an affinity between what is received and the one who receives it. A real imputation must have a place to go, a target ready and waiting. What is given in a real imputation goes where it rightfully belongs. Stated even more simply, a real imputation must always have a home.

On the other hand, what is judicially imputed does not have a home in the person to whom it is given; it is *not* antecedently his own. When something is credited where it does not rightfully belong, where there is no affinity, where there is no target or direction, God must immediately take some form of judicial action to rectify the situation. In other words, to complete a judicial imputation divine justice must immediately pronounce a verdict, whether of cursing or of blessing. A judicial imputation emphasizes the Source, the justice of God, rather than any affinity between the giving point and the receiving point.

There are five great imputations related to salvation; three are real, two judicial. We must examine these divine operations if we are to understand how the justice of God functions toward us and if we are to see the tremendous advantage of having justice as our point of contact with God. Each believer, whether he knows it or not, has already been involved in all five.

IMPUTATION OF HUMAN LIFE

The first two imputations from the justice of God—both real—occur at the moment of physical birth. Human life (which we also call *soul life*) and Adam's original sin are imputed to every member of the human race. A distinction must be made between biological life and soul life. Biological life begins at conception and is the means of transmitting the old sin nature. Soul life is created by God and imputed at physical birth as the means of transmitting the human soul. The combination of biological life and soul life becomes a physically alive human being.

In the fetus, the sensory, intermediate, and motor nerves stimulate muscular action, called reflex motility. Because the fetus is mother-dependent, its movement is often in sympathy with the mother's metabolism or emotional state (Luke 1:41). But the developing body within her is not a human being with life of its own until God sovereignly imputes human life, or soul life. Only God has the power to create a human being. You are not a biological accident; God personally created you.

This first imputation occurs when the viable fetus emerges from the womb. Human life begins when God imputes the breath or spark of life. This *neshamah,* in the Hebrew, is the same "breath" that God breathed into the nostrils of Adam, whose body He "formed from the dust of the ground" (Gen. 2:7). Human life always comes in the same way, directly from God, whether to Adam as an adult or to Adam's progeny as infants.

> For I will not contend forever, nor will I always be angry,
> for the spirit should fail [would faint] before me, and the
> souls which I have made. (Isa. 57:16, AV)

God is describing here the policy of His justice toward the Jews of Isaiah's generation. But we are specifically interested in how this passage describes human beings. The word "souls" is the same Hebrew word used in Genesis 2:7, *neshamah,* "breath" or "soul life." Used in the plural, it shows that God gave the spark of life not to Adam only but individually to each human being (cf. Job 33:4). As with Adam, so in Isaiah's day, and so today, God always provides physical life in the same way–by a real imputation–and always for the same purpose–for our happiness and blessing.

But where does the spark of life go? What is the home for this real imputation?

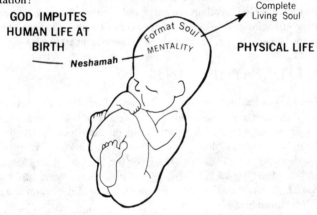

GOD IMPUTES HUMAN LIFE AT BIRTH

— Neshamah

Format Soul
MENTALITY

Complete Living Soul

PHYSICAL LIFE

As the body develops within the mother's womb, there also develops within its cranial area the form of a soul which we call a format soul. It consists of the genetic format for the mentality, inherited from the mentality genes of both parents. The word *nephesh,* often translated "spirit" or "life," refers to this format soul prior to birth. Following birth, it refers to the soul's fully formed, immaterial essence which is provided at the moment the spark of life is given. The breath of life turns the format soul into "a living soul" (cf. Gen 2:7). Developed in this way, the human soul is the home for the imputation of human life. The spark of life is the soul's ignition, and only upon ignition at the moment of birth does the fetus become a living human being.

Life can be imputed only where it has a home; whether human life to the soul at birth or eternal life to the human spirit at salvation, the giving of life is always a real imputation. Furthermore, this first imputation at physical birth —like all imputations from God—is a permanent arrangement. The breath of life resides in the soul forever.

Even when your soul leaves your body in physical death, your life is still in your soul; your life is never separated from your soul. Do not confuse the immaterial with the material. If your body were destroyed as part of your death—even if you, as a soldier, took a direct hit square in the middle of your forehead from an enemy shell so that your brain was vaporized and sprayed all over the battlefield—your soul would still be uninjured, and your life would remain intact in your soul. There is no such thing as soul death or soul sleep.

You have no choice as to whether or not you remain alive forever. You will! We might call this "human security." Your choice lies in *where* you will spend eternity. If you refuse to believe in Christ, your soul will depart from your body into the fire of Torments when you die (Luke 16:23-25). You will be resurrected with a body of damnation (John 5:28, 29; Rev. 20:3). You will stand trial before the great white throne of the Last Judgment, and you will be cast into the Lake of Fire where you will live forever in terrible, indescribable, hopeless suffering (Matt. 25:41; Rev. 20:10-15).

If, on the other hand, you believe in Christ, the moment your soul departs from your body you will be "absent from the body, face to face with the Lord" forever (2 Cor. 5:8). We call this "eternal security." What you do with the human life which God permanently imputed to your soul is strictly up to you.

> The Lord is . . . not willing that any should perish, but that all should come to repentance [a change of mind about Christ]. (2 Pet. 3:9, AV)

> . . . Believe on the Lord Jesus Christ, and thou shalt be saved. . . . (Acts 16:31, AV)

IMPUTATION OF ADAM'S SIN

THE GENIUS OF DIVINE JUSTICE

In the same moment that human life is imputed to the soul, the second real imputation occurs as a result of Adam's deliberate sin in the Garden. Adam's original sin is imputed to its home, the old sin nature. This is a real imputation because there is an affinity between Adam's sin and Adam's trend (or sin nature), between his act of disobedience and the corruption that it caused in him. The result of this imputation is that we are born physically alive but spiritually dead.

"But," you ask, "what does Adam's sin have to do with *me?* I've hardly even heard of it! I'm certainly not responsible for what he did! How is it fair that *I* am *born* condemned? I'm not even given a chance! You say justice is God's point of contact with me. What kind of justice is *that?*"

I'll tell you what kind of justice that is. That is the most brilliant stroke of justice possible! While fulfilling to the letter the total condemnation demanded by the righteousness of God, the imputation of Adam's sin lays the foundation for every advantage you will ever enjoy in time or eternity. It makes the Cross possible; it makes your salvation possible! Were the justice of God to treat you in any other way, you would go straight to hell.

SPIRITUAL DEATH

Adam's original sin plus Adam's sinful trend equals spiritual death. But these two factors come to us in different ways. Adam's sin is directly imputed by the justice of God at the moment of physical birth; Adam's trend is passed down genetically through the male in copulation. The *genetically formed* old sin nature is the home for the *imputation* of Adam's sin, and the result of this affinity is spiritual death.

Spiritual death has been defined in the past as separation from God or a total lack of relationship with God, but that is an oversimplification. Spiritual death is not separation from God. God is *present.* Indeed, God is thoroughly involved, but He is involved in *condemning* us. The first function of the justice of God toward fallen man is condemnation. Therefore, our initial relationship with the justice of God is spiritual death because justice must condemn before it can bless.

God condemns sin. Hence God is not the author of sin; Adam is. To implicate God with sin is blasphemous. God is neither the source of sin nor does He sponsor sin, tempt to sin, or ever fail to judge sin. A perfect God could create only perfect creatures; therefore, no sin and no old sin nature existed in the human race prior to the Fall. Moreover, He gave the original man and woman everything they ever could have needed to remain in a sinless status like the original status of angelic creatures. If Adam and his wife had not decided of their own free wills to eat from the forbidden tree, God would have continued to perpetuate the Age of Perfection day by day indefinitely. Although Satan was the first sinner among all of God's creatures, Adam was totally responsible for the Fall of man. We must be absolutely clear on this point: God is not the source of sin.

The immaterial soul that God prepares as the home for human life is perfect. Whether in the original couple or in us, the soul and its human life are flawless and sinless as they come from the hand of God. The soul is tainted only because it comes under the corrupting influence of the old sin nature. In Adam, this contamination occurred at the moment he sinned; in us, at the moment of birth.

Thus, at birth, we become facsimiles of Adam at the Fall: we become slaves of the old sin nature. During the Age of Perfection, Adam was the ruler of the world and the authority over the woman. He was the head of the human race as it existed in the Garden and consequently was the federal head of all mankind. We were seminally in him when, through his own choice, he fell under the sovereignty of the old sin nature (1 Cor. 15:21, 22).

Even though the woman was the first to disobey, it is Adam's sin, not hers, that plummets mankind into condemnation. There was a difference between the sins of the first two human beings.

> For Adam was first formed, then Eve. And Adam was
> not deceived, but the woman being deceived was in the
> transgression. (1 Tim. 2:13, 14)

These verses come from a context describing authority. The statement that Adam was created first refers to his position of responsibility as the federal head of the human race. But he is further responsible for our condemnation because when he sinned, he knew exactly what he was doing. The woman, completely taken in by the smooth line that Satan handed her, did not know what she was doing. Of course, ignorance is no excuse before God; she was just as guilty and just as spiritually dead as Adam. But the only sin that can be imputed to mankind for condemnation is a sin of cognizance; therefore, even though Adam was not the first sinner in the human race, his sin, not the woman's, is imputed to us for condemnation.

These principles related to what is imputed—Adam's sin—also hold true of the target—the old sin nature. *Adam's* old sin nature, not the woman's, becomes our old sin nature because he was the head of the human race and because he sinned in cognizance. The sin nature, however, is not transmitted to us by imputation; it is transmitted genetically.

THE GENETIC PERPETUATION OF THE SIN NATURE

We must recognize that the old sin nature is not part of the soul but that it resides instead in the cell structure of the human body. That is why this inherent distorter of life is called the "flesh" (Rom. 7:7-18; 8:3-5), the "body of sin" (Rom. 6:6), and the "sin" that "reigns in your mortal body" (Rom. 6:12). Reflecting its ancient origin, it is also known as the "old man" (Eph.

4:22; Col. 3:9) or, as we call it, the "old sin nature." While not part of the soul, Adam's sinful trend, from its command post in the body, influences the soul. It sponsors mental attitude sins and causes the "heart" or right lobe of the mentality of the soul to become the area of motivation for evil (Jer. 17:9; Matt. 12:34, 35).

The old sin nature or Adam's sinful trend is both material and immaterial. The material part is its residence in the cell structure of the body. The immaterial part is the function of its specific trends toward sin, toward human good, and toward evil. We refer to these three specific trends collectively as "Adam's trend" or, in keeping with the Biblical nomenclature that emphasizes sin, as "Adam's sinful trend." Everyone's sin nature includes all three of these specialized trends which function in different combinations at different times.

The specific trend toward sin tempts you to produce all categories of personal sins: mental, verbal, and overt. The trend toward good tempts you to produce human good, which includes all attempts to earn salvation or the approbation of God, all production not from the filling of the Holy Spirit, and all misguided efforts to improve the world through the betterment of man. The trend toward evil is the intensification of the other two trends—sin and human good—with emphasis on the trend toward good. "Good and evil" is not only the policy of Satan as the ruler of the world, it is also the function of the old sin nature as the sovereign of human life.

On the material side, the old sin nature resides in the human body, contaminating every cell. Regardless of a cell's structure or function—whether muscle, fat, skin, blood—each contains forty-six chromosomes. The chromosomes in every cell carry the same pattern of genes which, like a blueprint, determine all of that person's physical traits—eye color, height, bone structure, IQ. These chromosomes also carry the old sin nature. Each chromosome in every cell is contaminated with Adam's sinful trend.

For growth, repair, or replenishment, the body's cells divide by a process called *mitosis* in which one cell becomes two. The two new cells are exactly alike, and both are exactly like the single cell from which they came.

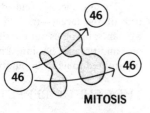

MITOSIS

The reproductive cells, however—the male sperm and the female ovum —are produced by a specialized process of cell division, a double process called *meiosis*. After meiosis, each new cell has only half the original number of chromosomes, or twenty-three instead of forty-six. In this way the male and female reproductive cells prepare for fertilization in which their chromosomes combine in the offspring. In other words, the child derives his characteristics from both father and mother yet ends up with no more than the normal forty-six chromosomes.

In the male parent, one immature reproductive cell with forty-six chromosomes divides once into two cells, each with twenty-three; then each of these divides again into two mature sperm, again each with twenty-three chromosomes. Thus, from one cell come four sperm.

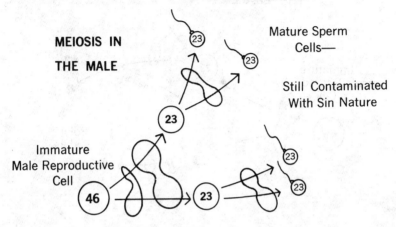

MEIOSIS IN THE MALE

Mature Sperm Cells—

Still Contaminated With Sin Nature

Immature Male Reproductive Cell

In the female, a unique additional process occurs. Again, meiosis is a two-step operation, but instead of producing four egg cells, the original cell yields only one. Approximately once a month, this single egg is produced by a process called oögenesis. In both stages of meiosis, this process throws off unneeded cell matter—and the contamination of the old sin nature—into small, non-functional polar bodies that soon disintegrate. All contamination crosses over into the polar bodies, leaving one large, uncontaminated ovum ready for fertilization.

That one cell in the female, which is produced every month and (if not fertilized) discharged in menstruation, is the only pure cell in the human body—indeed, the only pure cell since the Fall of man. In this normal biological process God made provision to fulfill the promise that Christ, "the Seed of the woman" (Gen. 3:15), would become the Savior. In female meiosis, God paved the way for the virgin birth by which the Second Person of the Trinity entered the world as perfect, uncontaminated Man, qualified to go to the Cross as our Substitute.

The twenty-three chromosomes in the mature ovum are totally free from the old sin nature, but each sperm is contaminated in all of its twenty-three chromosomes. When the ovum is fertilized by the sperm, it is also contaminated by the sin nature carried in the sperm. Thus, through genetic

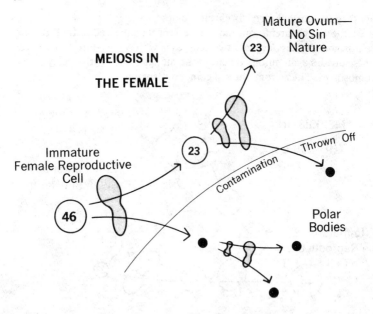

MEIOSIS IN THE FEMALE

Mature Ovum— No Sin Nature

Immature Female Reproductive Cell

Thrown Off

Contamination

Polar Bodies

transmission, the blastocyst, embryo, fetus, then eventually the person, possesses an old sin nature. If the child is a girl, she has a sin nature; if a boy, he too possesses the sin nature. Both male and female are carriers of Adam's trend, but because Adam, not the woman, sinned in cognizance, only the male transmits it.

> For this reason, just as through one man [Adam] the sin [of Adam] entered the world and so the [spiritual] death through the sin [of Adam], consequently the [spiritual] death spread to all mankind because all sinned [when Adam sinned]. (Rom. 5:12)

The entire passage from Romans 5:12 to the end of the chapter is elliptical. Paul is excited, stimulated; his genius is running full throttle. He wastes no words. When something is already understood in context, he leaves it out; when already comprehended, he brushes it aside. He breaks off sentences; he shortens them to their barest, most dramatic structures to focus on some of the most vital principles in the entire Bible. Driving straight to the point, he leaves as much as possible to implication.

This does not mean that the implied words and phrases are unimportant, just that they are already understood or are reserved for later explanation. In other words, I am not adding to the Word of God when I say "the sin [of Adam]" or "the [spiritual] death," or "all sinned [when Adam sinned]." I would never dream of adding to the Word of God. I am merely filling in an ellipsis in translation as well as in interpretation. This elucidation is perfectly legitimate; in fact, essential.

The reason you do not find such an expanded translation in your King James Bible is not that I am adding it but that King James' translators left it out. They overlooked the significance of the definite article, translated "the," which is the key to understanding the Greek in this passage. Here the definite article identifies a technical point as being already familiar in the context. The translators forgot that Paul was a genius, and for the most part they ignored such principles of ellipsis as brachylogy (leaving out words) and aposiopesis (breaking off sentences) which he uses throughout this passage and which must be accounted for if we are to understand the doctrines at hand.

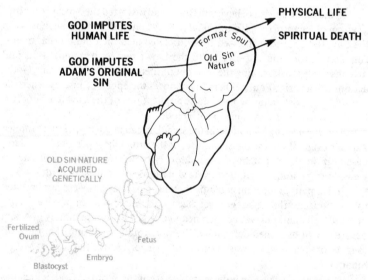

Romans 5:12 tells us not only that Adam was the original source of sin in the human race but also that sin "enters the world" for each individual when Adam's sin is imputed at birth. As Homo sapiens, we all sinned when Adam sinned (Rom. 5:18*a*) because Adam was the federal head of the human race; in fact, along with the woman, who was built from his rib and whom he ruled, Adam *was* the human race. The physical result of his transgression spreads genetically from generation to generation of his progeny, and because of the principle of affinity, the justice of God must directly impute

his sin to his old sin nature in us at the moment we are born. Thus, the formula holds true for every individual: Adam's original sin plus the old sin nature equals spiritual death. And, again, the result: the first two imputations mean that we are born physically alive but spiritually dead.

PERSONAL SINS NOT IMPUTED

We are spiritually dead, not because of our own sins, but because of Adam's original transgression. The justice of God condemns us only because of Adam. We sin personally only as a *result* of our spiritual death, never as the *cause.*

> For until the [Mosaic] Law, [personal] sin was in the
> world, but [personal] sin was not imputed when the
> [Mosaic] Law did not exist. (Rom. 5:13)

Some of the Jewish believers in Rome had distorted the Mosaic Law into a system of legalism (cf., Rom. 10:2-5). They contended that man must keep the Law to be saved or blessed by God. They held the opinion that man is condemned for failure to live up to the Law's perfect demands. But Paul disarms the legalists, taking the Law out of their hands. In illustrating God's actions toward sin, Paul deliberately chooses the epoch of history when the Law did not exist. Thus he keeps false applications of the Law from confusing the issue in our relationship with God.

The word "sin," *hamartia* in the singular, can mean one of three things: Adam's original sin, the old sin nature, or the principle of personal sin. Here, based on the development of the context (Rom. 5:16), personal sins are in view—our mental, verbal, and overt violations of God's standards.

In Romans 5:13, Paul explains that our personal sins were not imputed to us—indeed, they had not yet been committed—when we were condemned. All mankind was condemned in one fell swoop, seminally in Adam before any of us sinned personally. We were totally condemned at the Fall, long before personal sin was defined and categorized for the Jews at Mount Sinai.

The Mosaic Law is an indispensable part of the Word of God; it includes far more than the Ten Commandments.[28] It defines human freedom and morality according to the laws of divine establishment. The Mosaic Law also defines personal sin, in terms of man's failure to match up to the essence of God, and relates sin to its original penalty, spiritual death. The Law reveals man's condemnation, denounces man's resources as a means of reaching

---

28. See Thieme, *The Ten Commandments.*

God, and excludes human righteousness as a claim on divine blessing. The Law was never designed to produce self-righteousness.

The Law has a limited role; it is a minor actor that entered the stage to play a minor part (Rom. 5:20). In the role of a marriage counselor, it tells us in no uncertain terms that we have a "bad marriage" to the tyrannical old sin nature. It points the way to "divorce" and to "remarriage" to the Lord Jesus Christ by faith at salvation (Rom. 7:1-4). In other words, the Law exposes sin (Rom. 3:20; 7:7), shows us we have a problem, and reveals the solution in a detailed delineation of the Gospel. But the Law itself is not the solution to sin. Before the time of Moses, everyone sinned; after Moses, everyone still sins (1 John 1:8, 10). The coming of the Law made no difference.

Likewise, the Mosaic Law has nothing whatever to do with our condemnation. Before the Law came on the scene, we were already totally condemned. Personal sins, so clearly defined by the Law, are not imputed to man for condemnation. This has always been the case, long before and long after Moses climbed Mount Sinai.

Paul defines the Gospel specifically in terms of the nonimputation of personal sins:

> To wit, that God was in Christ, reconciling the world to himself, not imputing their trespasses unto them. . . . (2 Cor. 5:19a, AV)

David, who lived in the Age of Israel *after* the Mosaic Law had been given, rejoices in knowing that personal sins are not imputed to anyone (but Christ). This is the doctrine of unlimited atonement from the standpoint of personal sin.

> Blessed is the man unto whom the Lord imputeth not iniquity. . . . (Ps. 32:2a, AV)

When Paul quotes this verse, he doubles the negative to deny both the fact and the idea. Greek double negatives are intensive negatives, not positives. And with the verb in the subjunctive mood, this denial becomes emphatic.

> Happy is the man to whom the Lord not never imputes sin. (Rom. 4:8)

Apart from Adam's one original sin imputed to Adam himself, sins are never charged to the one who commits them. Does that sound as though people were getting away scot free? Don't worry; this is not a miscarriage of justice. It is *proof* of God's justice! In His omniscience, God found a way to save man without compromising His own integrity. Although we deserve the full fury of His wrath, His plan demands that we not be charged for our own sins. If we were, we would go immediately to hell with never a hope of salvation.

Adam's first sin falls into two categories. It is an *original* sin because it was committed by a previously sinless and perfect man. It is also a *personal* sin, committed only by Adam himself as an act of his own negative volition. We cannot commit a sin like Adam's. That is strictly impossible. Our own first sins were not original sins because we were not perfect when we committed them! We are born with old sin natures; we can commit only *personal* sins. Our sins fall into only one category, and the justice of God handles all of them in one way. But because of the uniqueness of Adam's first sin, the justice of God could handle it in two ways—a different way in each category—without violating divine integrity.

As an original sin, Adam's transgression was imputed to his newly acquired sin nature. In this way, God brought spiritual death upon the human race, which then consisted of only Adam and his already-fallen wife. As their progeny, we are born facsimiles of Adam; we immediately have the total condemnation necessary for our salvation.

As a personal sin, however, Adam's first sin is treated like all other personal sins. It was imputed to the Lord Jesus Christ on the Cross and judged. Were it not, Adam could never have been saved. If Adam's sin, as a *personal* sin, had been imputed to *Adam,* he would have gone directly to the Lake of Fire. End human race! If our personal sins were imputed to us, *we* would go to the Lake of Fire. We cannot bear our own personal sins and survive!

Only the impeccable Person of Christ, totally acceptable to the righteousness of God, totally undeserving of judgment Himself, could pay the penalty for personal sins. Only Christ could rescue us from the brink of eternal divine judgment. The genius and perfect integrity of God is revealed in the way He handled Adam's original sin. By relating it to us, and our sins to Christ, God condemns us yet preserves us alive to believe in Christ. In this way, God gives us the potential to enter with Him into a relationship of eternal blessing.

All the personal sins of mankind were set aside for the greatest moment in history, those three hours on the afternoon of the Passover in A.D. 30 when Jesus Christ bore the sins of the world and was judged in our place. As we shall see, that was the imputation that turned cursing into blessing, condemnation into salvation.

One sin, and one sin only, therefore, condemns the entire human race. If you think God condemns you for your own sins, you have listened too long to the legalist who is shocked by half a dozen kinds of overt sin. You are not that important! No human being is capable of committing a sin whose repercussions, even in his own life, can come close to matching the effects of Adam's sin. There is no need to get on your high horse about this; you must get down to what the Word of God says.

Your condemnation before God came at the moment you were born! God did not ask your opinion; He did not wait around for you to personally violate some divine norm; He did not offer you a chance to get into the act. He took the initiative and condemned you when you were a completely unremarkable infant. This hauls down your high-flying opinion of yourself, but it does more: it runs up the magnificent colors of God's wisdom.

Observe His colors. All glory belongs to God. In His plan, He does all the work, has all the merit, receives all the credit. Grace, as the policy of His justice, can be extended only to the undeserving, to the totally, helplessly, hopelessly condemned. Condemnation must precede salvation.

There are no loopholes in the plan of God. Total condemnation at birth guarantees that He treats everyone fairly. If a person had to sin before being condemned, no infant who died prior to committing his first sin could ever be saved. This becomes a major issue in how divine justice handles the human race. If God were unfair in even one case, He would not be perfect and would not possess all glory.

We might speculate as to when a human being commits his first sin. But there is absolutely no speculation as to our point of contact with God! He treats us in justice; He is always fair to every individual. Thus, the infant who dies in his first minute, week, month, year, or whatever the period might be, is already condemned; he is already qualified for grace and is taken directly into the presence of the Lord (2 Sam. 12:23). Born spiritually dead, we are born candidates for grace.

If we had to wait to be condemned for our own personal sins, there would be a period of limbo in which God could not treat us fairly: if He saved us, the natural progeny of fallen Adam, He would be inconsistent with His own righteousness; if He did not save us, He would be unfair to us. No matter what God might do for a person who died during that early period of life, divine essence would be compromised. For us to be alive for one moment as the progeny of Adam without being totally condemned would be a disaster! God could have no plan for us were there no potential for salvation. He therefore gives us the potential by immediately imputing to us Adam's sin. In condemning us at birth, not for our own sins but for Adam's sin instead, God demonstrates and proves His justice—and gives us our first break.

The repercussions of God's wisdom in this matter go yet further. God is not only able to save us before we sin, but He is also able to save anyone who dies prior to reaching God-consciousness. Gathered up in the grace of God are those who fall below a minimum level of mentality. The moron, the imbecile, the person thus unable to make a responsible decision, is automatically saved. This aspect of grace is possible only because both our condemnation and our salvation are provided by the justice of God, totally apart from any meritorious action on our part. When, for one reason or another, volition has not come into play, God is free to save us because He alone has already accomplished everything necessary for our reconciliation to Him.

You can see that the greatest thing that ever happened to the human race was to come under the umbrella of the justice of God. Love₁ could never provide salvation. Love₁ furnished wonderful blessings in an age of perfection, but love₁ is impossible (and therefore helpless) toward man after the Fall. Love₁ could only turn us over to justice. When blessings come now, they come not from the love but from the justice of God—with no strings attached.

Your own sins have nothing whatever to do with your condemnation. When you sin, all you do is manifest Adam's sinful trend which has become *your* sinful trend by a process of genetics. Of course, your volition is always involved—you sin only because you *want* to—and you are responsible in terms of divine discipline in time. But even when you express your own old sin nature in personal sin, human good, or evil, you do not add to your condemnation. Our personal sins augment Adam's original sin, but the imputation of *all* personal sins to Jesus Christ indicates that the increase of sin is more than matched by the increase of grace (Rom. 5:20). Man cannot create a problem that God has not already solved.

It is impossible to be grace-oriented if you fail to understand that Adam's original sin condemns you and that your personal sins do not. There is no room for reverse arrogance regarding the sins you have committed. There is no room for such testimonies as "I was the worst sinner in town till Christ saved me!" We cannot do *any*thing meritorious in God's economy! We are not spiritually dead because we sin; we sin because we are spiritually dead! We produce human good and evil for the same reason. Total condemnation at birth means that our personal sins are never imputed to us and do not contribute in the least to our spiritual death. In other words, we do not earn the "wages of sin" by sinning—Adam did!

Now do not go off the deep end with false applications of this point of doctrine. Do not get the idea that except for Adam we are wonderful people. We are not. Nor should you ever assume that personal sin is overlooked or condoned. It is not. You are held responsible for your sins in time in the sense that divine discipline always follows personal sin. Such punitive action from the justice of God makes sin never worth committing; no one gets away with anything. Through rebound, the discipline may be removed or reduced, or turned from cursing into blessing if it continues at full intensity. But as painful and miserable as divine discipline is, it is not the same as condemnation.

Imagine the mess we would be in if we were condemned for our own sins. The trends toward sin, good, and evil are present in each of us, but we develop these impulses in different ways. Not all of us manifest Adam's old sin nature along the same lines that Adam did. One person might lean toward asceticism. Another might have a naturally timid personality. These people would never dream of doing anything rash, so they confine themselves to mental attitude sins and sins of the tongue. Someone else might like to live it up. He would be more outgoing in the expression of his trend toward sin and would tend to produce overt sins rather than the mental aberrations of the ascetic, religious legalist.

But who is more condemned by God? Is the stuffy, self-righteous "pillar of the church" better in God's eyes than the lascivious rounder? Does God think the legalist with the shockable personality has any right to look down his nose at the person who commits obvious sins? Does He think the live-it-up type has a right to gloat about hypocrites in the church? No! Relativity of sins, variety of sins, or quantity of sins has nothing to do with our equal, total condemnation.

Some personal sins carry more severe discipline than others (Prov. 6:16–19), but that is strictly a matter between the individual and the Lord. The order of the day is mind your own business, live and let live. The principle is not to compare your sins with the sins of others but to respect the rights and privacy of others. Many churches today emphasize sin (or trying not to sin), but this emphasis is totally misplaced. God emphasizes *doctrine*—the Word of God, the Mind of Christ, the means of spiritual growth.

If you insist on sticking your nose into other people's business, trying to reform them, trying to bring them into line with your "superior" standards, you merely add human good to your sins of arrogance, judging, and bullying. This combination smacks of good and evil. By your misplaced emphasis and your preoccupation with sin, you will have put yourself in a spiritual tailspin. Neither the sins of others nor your own sins are ever an issue in condemnation. The emphasis is *never* on what *you* do but on what the justice of God has done.

And what has God done? To anticipate where Paul is leading us, the justice of God, as the function of divine integrity, condemned all of us alike for Adam's one sin, transferred all our sins to Christ on the Cross, and, to anyone who believes in Him, imputes God's righteousness and eternal life. Thus, the futility of legalism is exposed. We can do nothing to earn salvation, just as we did nothing to earn condemnation. *Keeping* the Law cannot bring spiritual life any more than *breaking* the Law brought spiritual death. These are antithetical functions, but both condemnation and salvation are handled in the same way: God does *all* the work. The justice of God is the source of both cursing and blessing. Consequently, anything we might add to simple faith in Christ in order to gain salvation is blasphemous beyond description.

The issue in condemnation is Adam's original sin; the issue in salvation is the Lord Jesus Christ. Our personal sins do not count in either area. But that does not mean that God overlooks our sins. They *were* an issue on the Cross—a terrible, agonizing issue to our perfect Savior who paid the penalty for them.

Personal sins are also an issue in our lives after salvation because they get us out of fellowship with God and temporarily cut off the filling of the Spirit. Where there is no filling of the Spirit, there can be no GAP. Where no GAP, no spiritual momentum. But the rebound technique is designed to neutralize sin as a factor even in our daily lives! The person who denounces rebound as a license to sin does so out of ignorance. God's justice provided the simple mechanics of rebound to enable us to advance in His plan despite the continued presence of the old sin nature in our bodies (Ps. 32:5; 1 Cor. 11:31; 1 John 1:9). When rebound is ignored, or buried under legalism, our status of carnality soon devolves into reversionism and evil. On the other hand, with rebound, GAP, and resultant spiritual growth, we will outgrow some sins and develop different patterns of sin. We may "refine" our sins, but we will never stop sinning as long as we remain in this body.

Sin is a factor in yet another area. Some sins are also crimes; they violate human freedom and therefore are prohibited by the laws of divine establishment. Murder, rape, theft, slander—these and others are cited in the Mosaic Law as being within the province of civil law enforcement. Where sin destroys the freedom, privacy, or property of others, or attacks divinely delegated authority, severe punishment must be meted out. But no matter what we do or fail to do, no matter in what area our sins *are* an issue, God does not impute them to us or condemn us for them.

We can only thank God that in the matchless genius of His justice He condemned us for Adam's first sin. We can only stand in awe of Him for this magnificent action in our behalf. Far from being unfair to us, God's imputation of Adam's sin to our sin natures at birth is totally to our advantage. We are qualified for grace from the start; the condemnation that must precede grace is brought down on us with our first breath.

We were in Adam when he sinned (1 Cor. 15:22), but before you disparage Adam for his failure, remember that God in His omniscience knows all iffy history. What if you had been in Adam's shoes? "Oh," you say, "I would have walked with the Lord every evening, and never, never would I have stooped so low as to eat that forbidden fruit!"

What do you take yourself for? If you think you're in a mutual admiration society with God, you are in for a little surprise: God does not share your enthusiasm. He is not impressed by your good intentions and sanctimonious promises. He knows that if you were in the Garden, eventually *you* would have done what Adam did. The action of the justice of God is fair, then, not only because you were seminally in Adam but also because you personally would have done the same thing in his place.

In His absolute wisdom, God found a way to totally condemn us as fallen, depraved mankind and yet avoid condemning us for our own sins. Indeed, He has condemned us for a sin that has already been judged on the Cross! He has thus put us in the clear to decide our own destinies—for or against Jesus Christ—without leaving any room for arrogance. By imputing Adam's sin to its genetically formed home in our bodies, God preserves us alive and gives us a chance to be saved. Thus, the Cross could have no significance apart from the doctrine of the imputation of Adam's sin.

TWO RULERS: SATAN AND THE OLD SIN NATURE

The epoch from Adam to Moses is Paul's illustration to legalistic Jewish believers of a principle that applies equally to all ages: spiritual death rules in every generation of human history.

> Nevertheless, the [spiritual] death ruled from Adam to
> Moses even over those who had not sinned in the likeness
> of Adam's transgression, who is a type of Him [Christ]
> who was destined to come [Christ's First Advent]. (Rom.
> 5:14)

Actually we are born under *two* rulers who came to power when Adam sinned. Satan is the "god of this world," ruling through a policy of good and evil (2 Cor. 4:4; 11:14; 1 Tim. 4:1); the old sin nature is the sovereign of human life, ruling through spiritual death. Under both of these tyrannies, "good and evil" is the order of the day. It is the policy of Satan; it is the function of the sin nature.

We have already been introduced to Satan. Since his powerful, multifaceted strategy has been detailed elsewhere,[29] we need draw only a thumbnail sketch of his plan. His arrogant ambition is to become, by his own efforts and great intellect, like the most high God (Isa. 14:12-14). He promotes the improvement of his kingdom, the earth. He seeks to displace God and to create a counterfeit "millennium" before Christ returns. Were Satan to succeed, he would force God to welsh on His promises regarding the true Millennium, proving God a liar with no integrity. Satan would thus win the angelic conflict by default and would avoid serving his just sentence: eternity in the Lake of Fire (Matt. 25:41).

We are not suprised to discover in the Bible that a revolutionist such as

---

29. See Thieme, *Demonism, Victorious Proclamation.*

Satan, whose world policy is both good and evil, talks out of both sides of his mouth. Satan is a brilliant chameleon, an ingenius counterfeiter, able to present himself as all things to all men.

On one hand, he favors sweetness and light and prosperity for all—a chicken in every pot. Personally, he is the most beautiful creature ever created; he is eloquent, smart, entertaining, personable, persuasive—just the kind of company you would enjoy. His attacks often come in the guise of this calm, engaging, drawing-room type of attractiveness. He knows that life depends on how people think, and he sponsors "good" anti-God thought (Isa. 47:10, 11; Micah 1:12; Col. 2:8; 2 Thess. 2:7-11).

Hence, the misery and depravity in the world is not all by Satan's design. Much is blamed on him that is not his doing. More often than not, even sin is an embarrassment to him! Perhaps never before have you understood this point, but many categories of sin only set back his utopian objectives. He spends a great deal of time in the courtroom of heaven accusing believers of sin even though he knows Christ already paid for it (Job 6:1-11; Zech. 3:1-4; 2 Cor. 2:11; Rev. 3:9, 10). Satan wants to make sure he doesn't get the blame! And he wants to use God, trying to force Him to discipline believers so severely that they will be distracted from doctrine. Man is truly a free agent; human volition and the old sin nature can prove to be just as unruly to Satan as to God.

> . . . the system which Satan has constructed includes all the good which he can incorporate into it and be consistent with the thing he aims to accomplish. A serious question arises whether the presence of gross evil in the world is due to Satan's intention to have it so, or whether it indicates Satan's inability to execute all he has designed. The probability is great that Satan's ambition has led him to undertake more than any creature could ever administer.[30]

But Satan does not appear always as an angel of light. The dark side of his strategy calls for terror, violence, confusion. If he cannot control mankind by one tactic, he always has another. No depravity or treachery is beneath him. The rules of the angelic conflict call for each man to exercise his self-determination on the earth until God removes him. But Satan never plays by the rules unless doing so happens to further his own ends. He is the original murderer, determined to destroy man's volition if unable to control it (John 8:44). The justice of God must restrain him (2 Thess. 2:7), and

---

30. Lewis Sperry Chafer, *Systematic Theology,* 8 vols. (Dallas: Dallas Seminary Press), 2:100.

periodically God judges the accumulated results of all his varied activities (Gen. 6:1-7; 15:16; Lev. 26:14-31).

Satan's antithetical methods of operation are employed not only by his human emissaries (2 Cor. 11:13-15) but also by his vast, highly organized, well-led army of angelic subordinates, known as demons (Eph. 6:10-12). Satan does not lead a mob. He understands authority; in fact, he is a tyrant who wants to superimpose his authority over God's. Satan orders some of his demons operating on the earth to be eloquent and magnetic in order to deceive people of culture and enlightenment. Many smart Germans who were not impressed—who were even repelled—by the emotionalism of Hitler's National Socialist Party were nonetheless drawn in by his demonic charisma.

Other demon organizations are charged with confusing and enslaving the simple, the emotional, the ignorant. Such people are impressed by the weird, extranatural phenomena of telepathy, mind-reading, and disembodied spirits associated with certain Hindu sects; by the voodoo victim's ritual sacrifice of himself without any symptoms of pain; by the Sudanese dervishes who with bullets in their heads and hearts continued to charge the British formations; by the human sacrifice of children in the phallic cult; by the ecstatic manipulation of the vocal cords among some modern holy rollers. Demons can unlawfully isolate the dormant faculties of those unbelievers who permit the mentality to lapse into disuse and who are therefore ruled by emotion.

Only unbelievers can be demon-possessed, in which case the demon enters and controls the body. But believers in certain categories of reversionism can come under demon influence or demon obsession in which the demon controls the soul. Satan has *ruled* the world since the Fall of man, but he has never yet succeeded in *controlling* his own domain. Whether through the drawing-room type of demon activity or through the more startling types, Satan's ultimate objective is to conquer, to control.

Believers are at a great advantage if they understand the strategy and tactics of the enemy. Unfortunately, many Christians seem to gravitate to the strange, to the weird. Any mention of the devil and demon activity risks bringing such impressionable people out of their cracks and holes. It is not wise to delve into the realm of demonism; doctrine warns us not to get involved (Lev. 19:31; 20:6; Deut. 18:10-12). We should be curious about doctrine, not about demons. The point here is that we are born enslaved to a system of good and evil more brilliant, complex, and powerful than we can possibly resist in our own energy. Our one defense is Bible doctrine resident in our souls; our only confidence lies in knowing that Jesus Christ controls history.

Satan does not control the kingdom he rules; he cannot produce perfect environment; never will he be like God. Satan and his demons are doomed to ultimate failure. The plan of God, executed by perfect divine justice, will inevitably prevail. The great demon conflict that has so ravaged human history will be won by the Lord Jesus Christ at the Second Advent (Rev. 20:2, 3). You might as well get on the winning side. Either you adjust to the justice of God or the justice of God will adjust to you—by rolling right over you! Not even the greatest intellect of the greatest creature, Satan, can compete with the integrity of the Creator. If *you* try it, you haven't a chance.

While the sin nature's trend toward sin does not always fit in with the main thrust of Satan's scheme, its trends toward good and evil are readily pressed into the devil's service. While still in the Garden after the Fall, Adam's slavery to his newly acquired sin nature was first manifested, not in an act of sin, but in a program of human good—Operation Fig Leaves.

The nakedness that had been a wonderful part of Adam's relationship with his wife was suddenly denounced by Satan as being a social problem (Gen. 3:11). The new ruler of the world insinuated that nakedness between husband and wife was wrong, that clothing was "good," that no one was going to run around naked in *his* kingdom! Adam's trend picked up the innuendo right away, and he and the woman got busy making "loin coverings" out of fig leaves (Gen. 3:7). Behind their social action, their "betterment" of mankind, their work to make everyone equal, lay the thinking of evil. They were vainly attempting to improve the devil's world, and, once clothed, they had their first evil thought. "If we are right with each other," they reasoned, "we *must* be right with God. If only we adjust to our fellow man and do well by one another, certainly God will not condemn us."

This satanic lie still caries a deadly venom. It has poisoned fundamentalist Christianity in our day and is on the verge of destroying our nation. It represents a thorough maladjustment to the justice of God. Man's good deeds cannot come close to earning the approbation of God; to assume that they do is to insult His infinitely perfect character (Isa. 64:6). Even toward man, we are required by the laws of divine establishment to respect each others' freedom, privacy, and property, not to remold society, to lift up the downtrodden, to make people equal, or to enforce the ideas of some arrogant socialist who thinks he knows what people want better than they do themselves. The many applications and examples of the "social gospel" in the world today are merely repeated evidence of our slavery under Satan's evil system. Human good always turns into evil. By following human good as national policy, both foreign and domestic, the United States is setting herself up for overt slavery to another form of evil, a more predatory form known as communism. And even communism has a "good" goal—a "new world order" of universal prosperity. But this so-called good violates all the divine institutions for prosperity in the human race. It is totally out of touch with the reality of volition and human freedom; as a destroyer, communism is merely today's most rabid brand of satanic, anti-God good and evil.

Indeed, the Soviets have adopted Satan's two-faced strategy almost straight off the forbidden tree, except that instead of "good and evil' they call it the "Hegelian theory of change": *thesis* plus *antithesis* equals *synthesis.* Their "thesis" is pacifism, peaceful coexistence, disarmament, cultural exchange, detente—anything that sounds like peace, brotherhood, goodwill. At the same time these modern Mongols feverishly pursue the "antithesis." While extending one hand in friendship, the hand behind their back has built up the greatest, most aggressive, offense-oriented military power known in human history. The "synthesis" is world conquest. Both hands are working for the enslavement of mankind to the socialist, communist ideal of governmental control.

Even in Satan's kingdom, the volition of our souls is truly free to make one choice over another, but we are not free from the influence of the old sin nature resident in our bodies. This second slavery is much more intimate and hence much more dangerous than even our slavery as citizens of Satan's domain. (For us as believers, these are both *former* slaveries since both tyrannies were broken at salvation. The former rulers are, nevertheless, still active, and they continually appeal to our free will to permit them back on the throne.) Although Satan is brilliant and powerful as the archenemy of both God and the believer, he is still only a creature. He can be in only one place at a time, and he does not have time to waste on spiritual small fry. In contrast, the old sin nature resides in every cell in your body, including every cell in your brain. More often than not, therefore, you are your own worst enemy. When you run into pressure or difficulty in life, it is not the devil after you; he does not need to intervene when you do such a nice job all by yourself.

Remember that your brain is not the same as your soul. While the soul is immaterial, the brain is part of your body, and as such, it is corrupted by the old sin nature. In other words, the sin nature resides in the brain but not in the soul.

The brain, however, influences the soul. Indeed, under spiritual death, the brain *rules* the soul since the old sin nature has its headquarters in the physical body and controls the brain as part of the body of corruption. The brain is the mechanical expression of the soul's consciousness. Note that I said *mechanical;* there is no consciousness in the brain as a physical organ. Self-consciousness is a facet of the *soul.* The self-consciousness of the soul acts as the go-between; it is where the immaterial links up to the material.

With its fantastically complicated anatomy and function, the brain is a vast physiological computer. Millions of neurons or nerve cells perform their individual roles, carrying electrical charges under highly disciplined control through blankets of gray matter, along branching connections of white matter, and throughout the entire system of the brain. But having resided in every neuron since the moment of physical birth, the sin nature uses all the brain's mechanical functions to control the soul.

In particular, the old sin nature programs the brain for good and evil; thus, the brain naturally prints good and evil tendencies into the soul. Garbage in, garbage out. The mentality operates on good and evil; the volition makes decisions for good and evil; the emotion is stimulated by good and evil. In contrast to the "newness of life" commanded of every believer (Rom. 6:4), the "oldness" of life is the computer program of good and evil which enslaves us to the old sin nature. Satan's plan also has a part in this programming. From birth, we live in the devil's world, and his ruling policy of good and evil inevitably works its way into the computer.

In spite of Christ's work in freeing us from the power of the old sin nature, many believers continue to operate on the old program. They are full of human good as they serve their sin natures and sincerely advocate the various programs for making Satan's kingdom "a better place to live." They talk about equality, brotherhood, world peace, and a deeper understanding with the communists. Although determined to "do great things for God," they fall right into line behind Satan, the greatest genius and deceiver in the world. As the only solution to this tyrannical dilemma, we are commanded to reprogram the computer.

> And stop placing your members [your physical body, including the brain], as weapons of wickedness [good and evil], under orders to sin [the old sin nature]; but place yourselves under orders to God as those who are alive from deaths [identified with Christ in His spiritual and physical deaths] and your members [your brain, for example] as weapons of righteousness to God. (Rom. 6:13)

Placing the members of your physical body under orders to God includes reprogramming your brain. At the new birth, the power of your old sin nature was broken through the imputation of God's righteousness and eternal life.[31] Add to this the simultaneous baptism of the Holy Spirit,[32] and for the first time your soul is in a position to break free from the influence of the corrupted physical computer. By the intake of Bible doctrine, new information is fed into your brain, so that it is programmed in accordance with the plan of God for your life. Only doctrine in the soul can fulfill experientially what was accomplished positionally at the moment of salvation. Through

---

31. See below, page 86.

32. See below, page 105.

perception of doctrine, you can be free from both rulers under which you were born. Doctrine makes all the difference.

Works will not reprogram the brain. Witnessing, prayer, giving money to the church—none of these will do the job. They are legitimate; indeed they are commanded—under the right circumstances, with the proper motivation, at the right time. But they do not change the computer. There is only one way to change the computer so that it becomes a weapon of righteousness to God, and that is by feeding it something greater than Satan's policy and the sin nature's modus operandi. You must consistently feed it new information—Bible doctrine.

IMPUTATION OF PERSONAL SINS TO CHRIST

GOD'S UNIQUELY BORN SON

We are born facsimiles of Adam *after* the Fall. We share his original sin by real imputation and his sin nature by genetic transmission. Thus, we share his spiritual death. His sin becomes our sin; his sin nature, our sin nature; his condemnation, our condemnation.

But Romans 5:14 tells us that Christ was born a facsimile or "type" of Adam *before* the Fall. Adam was created perfect; our Lord was born perfect, without the corruption of the old sin nature.

Like all members of the human race, however, the mother of Christ's humanity, the virgin Mary, was born spiritually dead. She was not immaculate, sinless, or perfect. Nor was she—in the most ludicrous blasphemy of all—the mother of God. Eternal God has no source, no origin, and no mother! Mary was a sinner in need of a Savior; her body was a body of corruption; her genes and chromosomes carried the old sin nature, as do everyone's. Personally, she had her good and bad points, and like all of us, she committed many sins. But because fornication was definitely not among her sins, she was truly a virgin.

She and her betrothed husband were descendants from the two branches of the royal family of David—she, through Nathan (Luke 3:31); Joseph, through Solomon (Matt. 1:6). Both were Jewish aristocrats; both demonstrated their nobility of character in the way they handled this surprising pregnancy, which undoubtedly raised many eyebrows.

Through the centuries, religion has abused Mary, elevating her far above her rightful position. She is often overrated and even worshipped as the embodiment of ideally pure womanhood (in contrast to Ishtar, Aphrodite, Venus, and others who are also worshipped—but as ideally *sensuous* womanhood). Just because religion has abused her is no reason to overlook this woman's noble character and personal integrity. True, Jesus had to reprimand her on several later occasions (Luke 2:48-50; John 2:3-5), and He deemphasized her role in His Incarnation (Luke 11:27, 28); but in many ways she was an admirable woman.

Even the finest people, however, are condemned from birth, and Mary entered the world as a carrier of the old sin nature. But as a woman, she could not transmit it to her progeny. After Christ was born, she bore at least six other children by Joseph through normal procreation (Matt. 13:55, 56). All were born spiritually dead but not because of their mother's sin nature; they received the old sin nature from their father.

In Mary, as in all normal women, approximately once a month that one egg cell was purified through meiosis. Her sin nature's presence in an immature reproductive cell had crossed over into polar bodies, leaving the mature ovum uncontaminated. In other words, the physical basis for the virgin birth can be found in any good biology textbook.

Isaiah prophesied that the virgin birth would be a "sign," a miraculous event (Isa. 7:14), but Mary herself was not the miracle. The miracle was that God the Holy Spirit provided twenty-three perfect chromosomes to fertilize her normal, pure ovum. She conceived apart from the contamination carried by the male sperm. Her pregnancy was, therefore, a virgin pregnancy—parthenogenesis—and the blastocyst, embryo, and fetus that developed within her was totally free from the corruption of Adam's sinful trend.

Even to focus on the virgin *birth* puts Mary too much in the spotlight; the virgin *pregnancy* is the true issue. And as beneficial as virginity is, even her virginity fades in importance when compared to the miraculous work of the Holy Spirit, which is the true emphasis in Christ's conception. Both the Hebrew word *almah* and the Greek *parthenos* call Mary simply a "young woman," recognizing the fact that every ovum in every woman is pure by the divine design of human physiology. Mankind gets no credit at any point in the plan of God! If God had so chosen (which He did not), He could have brought the Savior into the world as Mary's fourth or fifth son as easily as her first! Even though virginity was her actual status, God did not depend on Mary. Needless to say, this principle of grace has gone unnoticed in the glare of "Maryolatry."

At the instant when, in the Bethlehem stable, the fetus emerged from Mary's womb, God the Father imputed human life to its divinely prepared home, Christ's human soul. The result, as it would have been with any other member of the human race, was physical life. Our Lord was born true humanity, qualified to represent mankind before God.

But at the same moment, when the justice of God would normally impute Adam's original sin to a newly born infant, no such imputation was possible. Christ had no genetically formed old sin nature; Adam's sin had no home in Him. There was no antecedence or affinity between Christ and Adam's original sin because, through the virgin pregnancy, Christ was *not* seminally in Adam.

Unique, Jesus Christ was born both physically and spiritually alive. The Greek word *monogenes* in John 3:16 is not "only begotten" Son but "only born" or "uniquely born" Son. The only other perfect human beings had been *created* perfect, but the unique Person of the universe was *born* perfect in the midst of totally depraved mankind. Christ was the only free Man ever to enter Satan's world. He was free from the devil's rulership, from the sovereignty of the old sin nature, from the imputation of Adam's sin, and from the condemnation of spiritual death.

In order for the justice of God to judge our sins in Him as our Substitute, Jesus Christ had to be acceptable to the righteousness of God. He was perfect at birth, but He also had to be perfect when He reached the Cross. Thus, our Lord could not commit any personal sins during His life on earth.

Remember that Christ in His humanity could be tempted and could have sinned. In His deity, however, neither could He be tempted nor could He commit sin. If you add up these characteristics, the God-Man in hypostatic union was *temptable* but *impeccable*. In other words, through His human volition He was able to avoid sin when He was tempted as a man; in His divine essence, the integrity of God meant sin was completely out of the question. The Latin maxim is therefore true: *posse non peccare, non posse peccare;* He was "able *not* to sin and not *able* to sin."

Like perfect Adam, who could sin only by an act of negative volition toward God's prohibition of the tree, Jesus could fail only in one way, by committing an act of negative volition to the Father's plan for the Incarnation. Therefore, Satan intensified his efforts to prevent the Cross by putting the free will of our Lord's humanity repeatedly to the test (Matt. 4:1-11; Heb. 4:15). He was tempted far beyond anything we will ever face. The recorded temptations are but a few of the traps and snares that Satan ruthlessly and incessantly laid in His path. But unlike the woman in the Garden, whose ignorance of doctrine made her vulnerable to Satan's subtleties, Christ remained on positive signals all the way to the Cross.

Whereas Adam was *created* spiritually alive and through one deliberate act of *negative* volition became spiritually dead, Jesus was *born* spiritually alive and by unyielding *positive* volition remained impeccable and deliberately submitted to the Cross.

> Saying, Father, if thou be willing remove this cup [spiritual death on the Cross] from me: nevertheless not my will, but thine, be done. (Luke 22:42, AV)

THE LOGIC OF *A FORTIORI*

Condemned at birth, we are facsimiles of Adam after the Fall. But, perfect at birth and throughout the First Advent, Christ on the Cross was a facsimile or type of Adam before the Fall. This typology of the first and Last Adams is important but limited. As soon as Paul draws the analogy in Romans 5:14, he suddenly turns away from the similarities and begins to cite distinctions. The results of Adam's negative volition are completely opposite from those of Christ's positive volition.

Nor is the typology carried into the persons of the two Adams. The first Adam was unique as a perfectly created man, but Christ, the Last Adam, was unique as the God-Man. Adam fell, but Christ remained impeccable. Each was the federal head of the human race: Adam through our physical birth and spiritual death, Christ through the new birth and spiritual life. That is why we must be born again: born in Adam but born again in Christ. The first Adam brought condemnation upon the entire human race; the Last Adam brings salvation. Because of the first Adam, the justice of God condemns man; because of the Last Adam, the justice of God is free to bless man.

Still excited, still writing elliptically, Paul develops the contrast between Christ and Adam in a brilliant *tour de force* of logic. He sets up a system in the next three verses of Romans 5. He begins in verse 15 with a short *comparative clause* followed by a *conditional clause*. He repeats this pattern in verses 16 and 17: another quick *comparative clause* in verse 16 (this time expanded upon by a sentence that stockpiles doctrine) followed in verse 17 by a second *conditional clause* (which uses the build-up of doctrine to reach a fantastic conclusion).

Paul was a genius. But unlike many of genius class who are so preoccupied in their own specialized fields that they cannot match their socks or remember what day it is, Paul was always able to apply his genius to life. While still a boy, he began to harness his superior mentality through the strict academic discipline of a formal education, and his self-discipline never let up as long as he lived. Apart from Christ Himself, Paul learned and understood more doctrine than has any other human being of all time. Even Peter said that if you want to learn the most advanced doctrines, "hard to be understood," go to Paul (2 Pet. 3:15, 16). Well, that is where we are—with Paul, studying the most pivotal subject in the Bible, the integrity of God.

The two comparative clauses compare Christ and Adam. But the conditional clauses, through the inspiration of the Holy Spirit, fully express Paul's genius; in them he outlines the entire plan of God. A conditional clause has two parts: "*if* such and such, *then* such and such." The "if" portion or *premise* is known in grammar as the protasis, while the "then" portion or *conclusion* is called the apodosis.

In the first protasis, Paul sets up something well known as a basis for explaining something in the first apodosis that is virtually unknown to most believers. He goes from known to unknown in such a way as to make the unknown clear and understandable. He does the same thing in the second conditional clause. This time, however, the familiar ground in the protasis is no less than the concept just developed in the previous apodosis! He turns the "unknown" into a "known" then turns right around and launches from it into a further "unknown"! In this way, he leads us into a realm of doctrine that nowhere else in Scripture is so clearly revealed.

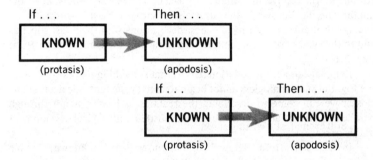

Salvation is an accomplished fact for every believer; therefore, Paul uses it as the "known" in the first conditional clause. Most of us are aware that we are eternally saved. We are at least somewhat familiar with the Cross and with what Christ accomplished there. We have a fairly good idea that it is something wonderful. What is generally unfamiliar to many believers is divine prosperity in the Christian life. Perfect happiness, occupation with Christ, grace orientation, temporal success, fame, fortune, right man or right woman, promotion, blessing to others by association, historical impact, stability under pressure—these blessings are the great "unknowns" in many believers' lives and often seem remote and out of reach. But by pure brilliance of logic, Paul makes them thoroughly understandable and familiar. Then from this new "known" of divine blessings in time, Paul strikes off into an area that is never described in specifics anywhere in the entire Word of God. It cannot be; it is beyond human comprehension. But by force of reason, he gives us an inkling of eternity's blessings, based on our knowledge of how God blesses us in time.

A person gets an eerie feeling when he drives across the Golden Gate Bridge in a dense San Francisco fog. He cannot see more than ten or twenty feet ahead—no cables, no towers, no distant shore. He's isolated on a little piece of road suspended hundreds of feet in the air. Will the road keep coming? Will he arrive safely on the far shore? He knows by the simple fact that the bridge is there that it has another end. And while he cannot see the far side, he drives along in confident assurance of reaching it.

There is likewise a "fog" that keeps us from seeing heaven. The limitations of human language and frame of reference obscure our view of the splendors of eternity face to face with the Lord. We know that heaven exists, but its special blessings can be defined in Scripture only through language of accommodation. The Bible pictures the prosperity of heaven as a tenfold or sixtyfold harvest (Matt. 13:8). From the standpoint of authority, vast estates are the mature believer's reward: ten cities (Luke 17:17), a hundred cities; Abraham will receive his unique city (Heb. 15:16). The *stephanos*—the military hero's "crown," the athlete's "victory wreath"—furnishes an analogy to the Roman Army's highest decorations with their vast stipends and to the symbol of victory and reward in the athletic games (1 Cor. 9:24; Rev. 2:10).

Language of accommodation tells us that something real exists beyond the fog, but such analogies cannot begin to convey the fantastic details. The closest we can come to describing the realities of heaven is not through parallels to life on earth but through the Apostle Paul's logical development in this passage.

In each step, from "known" to "unknown" to "unknown," divine justice is always our point of contact with God. It was our point of contact at birth and at salvation, and it will continue to be so throughout time and eternity. But Paul does more than simply go from known to unknown regarding the function of God's justice toward us; he does so using *a fortiori* logic.

A fortiori is a Latin phrase meaning "with stronger reason." The Latin is the exact equivalent of the Greek expression in our passage, translated "much more." Known in grammar as an idiom of greater degree, it is composed of the dative singular adjective *polus,* "much," plus the comparative adverb *mallon,* "more." But not simply a literal expression, "much more" becomes a technical term in the field of logic. In fact, the Latin has been brought into English as the name for a particular kind of thinking. (We will continue to italicize the phrase, however, to help you avoid confusing the Latin preposition *a* with the English indefinite article "a.")

A fortiori logic has two parts: the "greater" and the "less." What requires a greater degree of effort is used as the basis for showing what requires less effort. In our two conditional clauses (Rom. 5:15–17), the "greater" is found in the protasis and the "less" in the apodosis. *A fortiori* logic states that if God can do something that is extremely difficult, it only makes sense that He can do something that is much easier. If God has already done the "greater," it follows *a fortiori* that He can do the "less."

Let me give you an example of *a fortiori* logic in the human realm. Suppose I can do one hundred push-ups. If you had seen me do one hundred

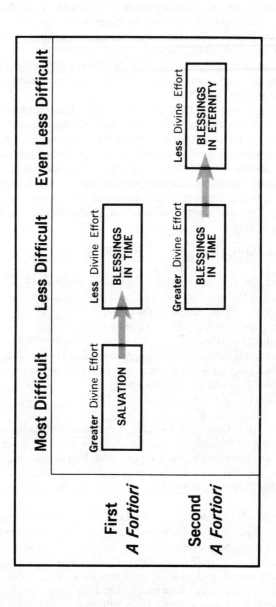

push-ups, you would know for certain that I would have no trouble at all if called upon to do ten! One hundred push-ups is the "greater"; ten, the "less." Stated in terms of *a fortiori* logic: if I can do one hundred push-ups, it follows *a fortiori* that I can do ten.

In the same way, if the more difficult function of the justice of God has already been provided, then "much more" or "with stronger reason," the less difficult will not be withheld.

Using *a fortiori* logic, Paul gets down to specifics regarding what required the greatest effort on God's part, what requires less, and what requires even less. In doing so, the great apostle sketches out the entire plan of God with a few quick strokes of the pen. Salvation, the first "known" point, is also the "greater" in the first *a fortiori*. Why is salvation so difficult for God to provide? The next two basic imputations will give us the answer. Both are part of the salvation package: the imputation of personal sins to Jesus Christ on the Cross and the imputation of God's righteousness to the believer at the point of faith in Christ.

JUDICIAL IMPUTATION AT THE CROSS

> But not as that transgression [Adam's original sin], so also is that gracious gift [the Incarnation and substitutionary work of Christ on the Cross]; for if by the transgression of that one [Adam's original sin] the many [the human race] died [and they did—spiritual death at birth], much more the grace of God and the gift of grace by the one Man, Jesus Christ, who has provided superabundance [blessings in time from the justice of God] for the many [mature believers]. (Rom. 5:15)

Jesus Christ is God's Gift of grace to mankind. Obviously, our Lord was acceptable to the integrity of God. Adam's original sin was totally foreign to our Lord and thus was not imputed to Him at birth; our personal sins likewise had absolutely no place in Him on the Cross. Thus, when the justice of God the Father imputed our sins to Him, it was a judicial imputation.

Remember that a judicial imputation emphasizes the function of divine justice rather than any connection between *what* is imputed and *where* it is imputed. There is no connection or antecedence, no home for what is judicially imputed. When God attributes or credits something where it does not rightfully belong, you might assume that He is being unfair. That is definitely not the case. Such a false assumption might arise from failing to see the complete judicial imputation (or from failing to see the total picture, for judicial imputations always travel in pairs). Each judicial imputation is incomplete until God takes action to complete it, and in order to complete it, the justice of God must render a decision. A judicial imputation is therefore always followed by a judicial verdict.

For this reason, when the sins of mankind were charged to the impeccable humanity of Christ, the justice of God had to take action: He *judged* the Lord Jesus Christ. God's judgment of our sins in Christ, including Adam's first sin, wiped our slate clean; we need only to accept this divine action in our behalf through nonmeritorious faith in the One who took our place.

God the Father loved the Son on the Cross with a love beyond anything we can imagine. Since eternity past, their love, rapport never diminished; but our contact with God is not based on His love. In relation to the fallen human race, the justice of God always takes precedence over the love of God. For our sakes, God forsook Christ on the Cross.

The Cross was an act of justice, not an act of love. Justice imputed our sins to Christ; justice judged them. The work of the Cross was therefore stronger than any act of love could ever be. Indeed, it was the greatest act that God could possibly have performed in demonstration of His matchless character.

Following the short comparative clause which reiterates the contrast between Adam and Christ, Romans 5:15 shows that God did not hesitate to do the just thing in condemning Adam and the entire human race in him. Nor did He stop short of total justice in judging His own Son on the Cross. It follows logically and in reality that His justice will *never* hesitate to execute the demands of His righteousness. Therefore, we have absolute confidence that justice will always pursue its policy of grace in blessing us whenever righteousness approves! If God did the most for us when we were His enemies, He can only do much more than the most now that we are His sons (Rom. 8:8-10). Restated in *a fortiori* logic: if God did the most difficult in providing salvation for us, it stands to greater reason that He can do what is far less difficult, namely, bless us in time.

Romans 5:15 emphasizes judgment or cursing as that which required the greater divine effort; but actually, the "greater" in this first *a fortiori* includes both cursing and blessing. The condemnation of the entire human race "by the transgression of that one" was the essential preliminary; cursing must precede blessing. But salvation is provided by a cluster of two imputations—both judicial—one for cursing, the other for blessing. The divine judgment on the Cross of "the one Man, Jesus Christ," plus the initial blessing to the new believer—divine righteousness imputed—together add up to form the "greater" of salvation.

The "less" is divine blessing to the mature believer on earth. Translated "has provided superabundance," *perisseuo* means "to make overrich, to cause to superabound." The culminative aorist tense views Christ's work on the Cross in its entirety but emphasizes the existing results: as a result of accomplishing the "greater," God is now able to provide the "less difficult." If God has already saved us, it follows *a fortiori* that He will not withhold blessings in time.

Satan thought he had scored a resounding victory when man sinned in the Garden. The devil did seize the scepter of the world, but the justice of God finessed him out of every advantage by condemning the entire human race in Adam. This was the greatest finesse in history: by it we receive "our so great salvation" and God demonstrates the remarkable, fascinating wisdom of His justice. But much more, under that same point of contact, we are now in a position to be blessed in a phenomenal way, even in the middle of the devil's world.

You should be delighted that your point of reference with God is not His love or His omnipotence or His sovereignty or His veracity or any attribute other than what it is—His magnificent justice. Everything we have studied so far concerning His justice is about to fall into place.

IMPUTATION OF DIVINE RIGHTEOUSNESS

JUSTICE CAN BLESS ONLY RIGHTEOUSNESS

Immovable strength of character backs up all God's dealings with us. Neither sentimentality, concession, nor altruism has a place in the nature of God. The inviolable righteousness of God stands guard over the justice of God, and justice protects God's entire essence from compromise when dealing with sinful man. Without exception, righteousness demands righteousness. Justice demands justice. And what righteousness demands, justice executes. Because both the principle and the function of God's integrity are immutable and impartial, His attributes are never violated.

No imperfection in us escapes ultimate judgment; no blessing comes to us apart from grace. In grace, the justice of God does all the work, carrying out the dictates of perfect righteousness. God receives all the credit while we reap the benefits in a totally nonmeritorious way. What righteousness accepts, justice blesses, but what righteousness rejects, justice condemns. Both cursing and blessing, therefore, come from the same source, and the inevitable, final result of every function of divine integrity is the glorification of God.

When we face the reality of God's integrity, we can only say with Paul, "If God be for us, who can be against us?" (Rom. 8:31*b*).

But there is only one way in which God can be "for us." Avoiding inconsistency and compromise, He acts according to a principle of doctrine that becomes an axiom: divine justice can bless only divine righteousness.

God's standards are so infinitely high that no one can meet them but God Himself. Only what God does reflects absolute righteousness. He cannot approve of or accept less than His own righteousness; certainly He cannot bless less. That is the meaning of "righteousness demands righteousness."

God designed man to be prospered and blessed and to share God's own happiness. He wants to bless us, but He cannot. From His point of view, we are totally condemned; He cannot prosper us no matter what we do. But where any opportunity remains of fulfilling His objective, God will exploit it to the last. He stops at nothing except what would compromise His essence. His genius is limitless; He never overlooks a chance to bless us. And in His genius, God found a way: His integrity demands that He *must* bless His own righteousness. So He decided in eternity past to credit or impute His righteousness to us at the moment we believe in Christ.

As that fact sinks in, it becomes an astounding revelation. The righteousness of God is the very root and center of God's essence; it is the principle behind *every* action God has taken toward *every* human being since the Fall of Adam! We now discover that *we* have this very righteousness! The function of God's integrity has imputed to us the principle of God's integrity. You should begin to sense that there must be absolutely fantastic implications. The most striking implication: at salvation you were suddenly dropped in the middle of the most exclusive relationship in the universe—the relationship within the Godhead: between the Father, the Son, and the Holy Spirit.

Each Member of the Trinity infinitely esteems His own incomparable Person and totally loves the other two Persons of the Godhead. The love *in* God's essence loves God's essence. We saw justice supersede love$_1$ at the Cross, but that does not mean love$_1$ is weak. Like all the attributes of God, His love is always maximum. The Cross showed that divine integrity is greater than even maximum love! Indeed, the integrity of God is the magnificent object of God's love. And now *we* have half of His integrity!

This is how we enter the picture, as far as the love of God is concerned. We cannot work our way in or force our way in or ever deserve entry, but once we possess God's righteousness, *He* has made us the eternal objects of love$_1$. God loves His integrity; we have the principle of His integrity; therefore, God loves us. We are amazed and comforted to know that God actually loves us. But even so, His love is never the source of our provision and blessing. Justice is the source. Justice can do much more for us than love could ever do. Love$_1$ must remain constant, but the justice of God can bless us or discipline us. Justice is stronger than love, and our point of contact with

God continues to be the acting, operating, functioning half of His integrity. Justice saves us through grace; we will always be under grace.

We never earn or deserve what God's justice gives us in grace; there is no affinity whatever between the absolute righteousness of God and our status of total depravity. What, then, is the home for this imputation? Where can it go? There *is* no home! As with the imputation of personal sins to Christ, divine righteousness is credited where it does not rightfully belong. Therefore, it comes to us in a *judicial* imputation. Indeed, that first judicial imputation at the Cross makes possible this second judicial imputation when we believe. Together they form the "greater" of salvation. This cluster of two judicial imputations might be considered an exchange: man's sins go to Christ; the righteousness of God goes to man.

Again, to complete this second judicial imputation, God must pronounce a judicial verdict; He must take action to rectify a situation where no affinity exists. He looks at us as possessors of the very principle of His integrity, and what does He do? From the bench of the supreme court of heaven, He pronounces us "justified." From one man's sin in the Garden, the entire human race is condemned; from one Man's work on the Cross, the entire human race can be justified.

JUSTIFICATION

You will recall that in one of its technical uses *dikaiosune* is applied to human beings and translated "justification." This is the judicial act of vindication that occurs at the moment of salvation when God the Judge sees His own perfect righteousness in us. Paul explains justification in Romans 5:16.

> In fact, the gift [Jesus Christ] is not like what occurred
> through the one who sinned [Adam]. . . . (Rom. 5:16a)

Remember the structure of Paul's argument. Here he gives us the short comparative clause to reiterate the contrast between the first and Last Adams. Paul then expands on this contrast, stockpiling information to be used in the second *a fortiori* which will come up in the conditional clause of the next verse.

> . . . For on the one hand, the judicial verdict came by one
> transgression resulting in condemnation, but on the other
> hand, that gracious gift [Christ's Incarnation and Atone-
> ment] because of the many transgressions resulting in a
> judicial act of justification. (Rom. 5:16b)

Because of our total condemnation at birth for Adam's one sin, plus the blotting out of our many personal sins at the Cross, the justice of God is now free to bless any member of the human race who believes in Christ. The first blessing we receive, the factor that turns everything around, is the imputation of the righteousness of God.

The last phrase in Romans 5:16, "resulting in a judicial act of justification," is the preposition *eis* plus the accusative singular of *dikaioma*. In the plural, *dikaioma* refers to "statutes, ordinances, commandments." But by using the singular, Paul emphasizes to both Jewish and Gentile believers in Rome, many of whom had distorted the Mosaic Law into a system of legalism, that Christianity is not a series of commandments. Instead, Christianity is a relationship with God based on *one* divine pronouncement; one order from God is the basis for His entire relationship with the believer.

In the singular, *dikaioma* means "a right act in the fulfillment of a legal requirement, a sentence or pronouncement of justification." From the judgment of many sins at the Cross comes one act of justification. At birth, justice acts against us to pronounce us condemned; at salvation, justice acts in our behalf to appoint us righteous (Rom. 5:19). This one judicial verdict gives us the potential for all other divine blessings.

God does not call us righteous because we obey a set of commandments or adhere to a system of taboos that supposedly honors Him. He never evaluates us as righteous because of our self-righteousness. He justifies us because we possess *His* righteousness. This is forensic justification, or justification in its legal sense. The Judge who possesses perfect righteousness acknowledges His own righteousness wherever He finds it—even in so unlikely a spot as a human being.

Justification occurs instantaneously, but its mechanics follow three logical steps. For analysis, we consider them separately although all three are actually simultaneous. According to the standard of divine righteousness we are "nothings"—less than nothings—who become "somethings" only when these steps occur: first, we believe in Christ; second, the righteousness of God is imputed to us; third, God recognizes as valid His righteousness in us and pronounces us justified.

Abraham is the model of justification. His vindication not only demonstrates the mechanics of salvation but proves as well that salvation follows the same pattern in both Old and New Testaments, both before and after the giving of the Mosaic Law. We in the Church Age receive the righteousness of God at the point of faith in Christ, but so did Abraham in the Age of Israel—and so does every believer from Adam after the Fall to the last believer in the Millennium.

> And he [Abraham] had believed in the Lord, and He [the Lord] counted it to him for righteousness. (Gen. 15:6)

Abraham had said yes to the Gospel while residing in the city of Ur, before he moved to Haran and then into the Land. Over five hundred years after Abraham's death, Moses wrote the book of Genesis and under the Spirit's inspiration, explained Abraham's salvation in context with a later event in his life. In Genesis 15, Abraham was over eighty years old; he had been a believer for more than fifty years. The account is, therefore, not chronological; instead, it describes something that occurred half a century earlier when Abraham, a Semitic, Akkadian Gentile, lived under the Third Dynasty of Ur.

The Hebrew verb *amen,* "believed," in the perfect tense, describes Abraham's nonmeritorious positive volition toward the Gospel information that God provided for him. The perfect tense indicates an action completed in the past with results that continue into the present; in this case, the results will continue throughout eternity. Faith in Christ secures salvation forever. When Paul quotes this verse in Romans 4:3, the perfect tense of *amen* is translated by the Greek constantive aorist tense of *pisteuo,* again meaning "to believe." The constantive aorist gathers into a single whole the entire action of the verb, the instantaneous act of believing in Christ.

We all enter salvation in exactly the same way, through faith in Christ. Abraham knew Him as *Adonai;* Moses writes that Abraham believed in *"Jehovah"* because that was the name by which God revealed Himself to Moses. In each case, the revealed Member of the Godhead is the Lord Jesus Christ (John 1:18; 6:46; 1 Tim. 6:16; 1 John 4:12). Whether *Iesous Christos* (as His name reads in Greek), *Jehovah* the Second Person of the Trinity, or *Adonai,* Christ is the only Object of faith for salvation.

The Hebrew verb *chashab* is translated "counted," but it means "to impute or credit something to someone." This meaning is underscored by Paul in the Greek verb *logizomai,* which was used as an accounting term meaning "to impute or credit something to someone's account." This time we have a culminative aorist; that is, the entire action of the verb is again considered, but now the emphasis is not on the action itself but on the existing results: Abraham eternally possesses one half of the integrity of God. What God credited to Abraham's account nearly four thousand years ago is the same thing that is credited to each of us today. *Tsedeqah,* as we have noted, is the same as *dikaiosune,* "righteousness," the principle of God's integrity.

God is a perfectly fair Judge. His justice must conform to the demands of His righteousness. Divine justice is, therefore, caught between the righteousness *in God* and that same righteousness *in us!* He can do nothing but declare us justified. And when the justice of God, the highest authority in the universe, calls you "righteous," that is the final word—your status can never be challenged. God Himself cannot be less than perfect righteousness; He cannot fail. You have His perfect righteousness; He cannot fail you.

Now do not suddenly forget from whence you came. There is no personal merit in placing your trust in Christ, and there is no merit in possessing God's righteousness. It is *God's* righteousness imputed to you as a gift of *God's* grace, provided by the function of *God's* integrity. None of it is your doing, and although you have it forever, never during all that time will you for one moment deserve any part of it. Both before and after salvation, the justice of God excludes

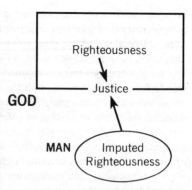

from His grace plan all categories of human righteousness (Rom. 3:20, 28; Gal. 2:16). God is not in the least impressed with us, but He is deeply impressed with His own righteousness. The righteousness of God is the one thing we have going for us.

Because justification is not an experience, your feelings are also ruled out as something that can impress God. You do not *feel* the imputation of divine righteousness or the judicial verdict that follows it. How you feel at the moment of salvation has nothing whatever to do with your relationship with God. You might feel great, but then again you might have just been jilted; you might have the flu or a hangover. Apart from being influenced by your state of health, your emotions are related to what you have in the mentality of your soul. Hence, what you feel when you believe in Christ cannot be based on more than an infinitesimal amount of doctrine. The only doctrine you then know is just what little Gospel information is needed to form the object for an instantaneous act of faith. In short, your salvation "experience" has absolutely no spiritual significance.

You become aware of your salvation only through consistent positive volition to Bible doctrine and the gradual buildup of doctrine in your right lobe. You do not (in fact, you cannot) see salvation's importance all at once. But as you fill in more and more categories of doctrine under the teaching of your right pastor-teacher, you come to understand and appreciate the implications of possessing divine righteousness. Indeed, the fact that we have His righteousness is so rich and profound a truth that we will never know all of its ramifications until we get to heaven; as long as we live and take in the Word of God, we can continually grow in our appreciation of the tremendous fact of justification.

But this critical doctrine is often taught as meaning *"just-as-if-I'd* never sinned."* The advantage of that phrase is that it has just the catchy ring that appeals to those nonstudents who want gimmicks rather than true doctrinal information. Its only disadvantage is that it is totally false. Justification is not the removal of your sins; justification is not the same as forgiveness; you were not condemned for your sins in the first place! Without them, you would still be totally condemned in God's sight.

Forgiveness is subtraction; justification is *addition*. Forgiveness is a wonderful doctrine that tells half the story. Forgiveness takes us out of the minus column by removing at the Cross our debt of sin. We are out of the hole, but we still have nothing to offer God but a big, fat zero. In contrast, justification credits to our zero account the infinite righteousness of God's personal integrity, giving us the final stamp called "justified" in recognition of our new, permanent, and total riches.

Justification is the completion of the believer's salvation and the logical consummation of the salvation work of God (Rom. 3:24, 28; 5:1; 8:29, 30; Gal. 3:24; Titus 3:7). Moreover, justification is a downpayment on the believer's ultimate sanctification in heaven where—minus his old sin nature, minus human good and evil—he will possess a resurrection body exactly like that of the Lord Jesus Christ (Phil. 3:21; 1 John 3:2).

Our resurrection comes as a result of justification. No resurrection is possible until everything related to justification is completed. That is why Romans 4:25 states that Christ was "raised again *because of* our justification." The preposition *dia* plus the accusative case is always "because of," never "for" as in the King James Version. All the work *for* justification was completed on the Cross. Although it follows His finished work on the Cross, Christ's resurrection is part of the salvation package (1 Cor. 15:1-4) because it sets the stage for us—already justified—to live on earth in the "newness of life" of spiritual maturity (Rom. 6:4-13). His resurrection also becomes the precedent or "firstfruits" for our own resurrection at the Rapture of the Church (1 Cor. 15:20-23).[33]

Justification is the solid foundation for all the *a fortiori* logic in Romans 5:15-17. It is the first "greater" that God provides. It requires much greater effort on God's part than do the blessings of time and rewards of eternity. A cluster of two judicial imputations is much more difficult to provide than are the real imputations that follow as a result. Nothing could be more spectacular than God's justice meting out cursing and blessing where they do not belong and still not violating His perfect character in the process!

Romans 5:16 states that justification is also greater than that superb demonstration of God's infinite genius, the very condemnation that made justification necessary in the first place. Our condemnation deals with one

---

33. When the royal family of God is completely formed it will be physically resurrected: all its members will receive resurrection bodies like Christ's. This event marks the end of the Church Age and is often called the Rapture.

sin while justification deals with all the sins of the world.

In a brilliant display of perfect wisdom and integrity, God has rescued man from the irreversible judgment brought on by man's own negative volition. Justification is the summit of the plan of God; all else can be only a relatively easy downhill jaunt.

THE GRACE PIPELINE

You may have noticed that God did not take you to heaven the moment you believed in Christ. Why didn't He? You were just as saved in that first instant as you ever will be. You were fully qualified. You possessed His righteousness and were pronounced justified. So, why the delay? Why are you left in the devil's world?

God has a purpose for your life. He imputed His righteousness to you with a particular goal in mind. The ultimate objective is God's own pleasure and glory, but the immediate objective is your blessing. You are alive to be blessed! Indeed, both objectives are one: God is glorified by blessing you.

Imputed righteousness is the believer's first blessing from the justice of God because it is the basis for all subsequent blessings; it is the foundation for superabundance, overriches, and advantages beyond imagination (Matt. 6:33). When God pronounced you justified, He meant, among other things, "qualified for blessing." Thus, in giving you His righteousness, He constructed a pipeline through which to bless you: its origin is His justice; its terminus, His righteousness in you. The giving and receiving ends of the pipeline are the two halves of His integrity.

The grace pipeline is completely insulated or encapsulated by the integrity of God. Even though you live in the devil's world and have the old sin nature resident in your body, the pipeline still runs through friendly territory all the way. God's justice does all the work, and divine righteousness has all the merit: you never earn or deserve anything that God pours through the pipeline. All divine blessing is a matter of grace. God does not need your help. You cannot lend Him a hand.

No human being, no angel, no system, no organization can ever break through that encapsulation and take credit for what God does. The devil and all the forces of evil cannot penetrate the screen nor can the lusts and trends of your old sin nature.

God blesses you only because His perfect standards are met; that is, only because you possess divine righteousness. He never blesses you for what you do. He does not bless you because of your scintillating personality, your talent, or your human energy. He does not bless you because you tithe or memorize Scripture or witness to ten people every day or "speak in tongues" or give up "for the Lord's sake" something that you enjoy. To do so, He would have to throw away His absolute integrity, lower Himself to the level of mankind, and stop being God. For anyone to expect divine blessing in consideration for such things would be humorous were it not so blasphemous.

When God blesses you, *He* has to do all the work. *He,* not you, must be glorified in the angelic conflict. He built the pipeline; He makes it work! When He blesses you, it is always for the same reason: you possess the principle of His integrity, divine righteousness. Divine justice is free to bless only divine righteousness.

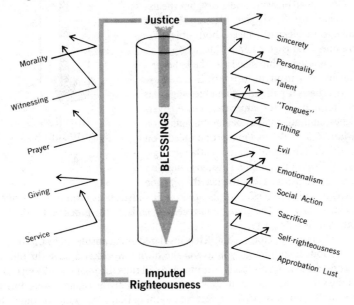

ENCAPSULATED
GRACE PIPELINE

Anything you might possibly do is outside the encapsulation and always bounces off. Legalism certainly has no place in the plan of God, but even when you do what the Bible commands—prayer, witnessing, giving, Christian service, morality—your works are still outside the channel for blessing. Not even legitimate production can earn you an ounce of divine blessing in time or eternity. True production is itself a blessing! Bona fide Christian function simply consists of the opportunities that God gives you to fulfill your royal ambassadorship (2 Cor. 5:20; Eph. 6:20).

Here we must "rightly divide the Word of Truth" (2 Tim. 2:15). Every member of the royal family of God wears two hats—he is both a royal priest and a royal ambassador; he must know when to wear which hat. Confusion on this elementary issue leads to a false modus operandi that makes spiritual advance impossible and blasphemy a way of life.

PRIEST AND AMBASSADOR

A priest is a member of the human race who represents the human race or some portion of it before God. He operates for man's benefit. Since he functions in the sphere of spiritual phenomena, he must receive a spiritual appointment. To even qualify for such an appointment, he must partake of the nature of those whom he represents, of those for whom he officiates. Hence, the Second Person of the Trinity had to become true humanity in order to become our High Priest and provide our salvation.

Christ is our royal High Priest forever (Heb. 5:6, 10). He represented us to God when He offered Himself on the real Altar, the Cross. Although he propitiated the Father on behalf of all men, all men do not belong to His priesthood (Heb. 7:14). There are three orders of priests.

Previous dispensations were characterized by specialized priesthoods (Num. 16:3; Lev. 8; 21; 22:1-16) so that most believers who lived during those periods were not priests at all. First, in the Age of the Gentiles, the patriarch of the family was also the family priest representing the members of his household before God. Second, the family of Aaron, from the tribe of Levi, represented the nation of Israel. In the functions of the Levitical priesthood God illustrates, in shadow form, many wonderful lessons regarding the future work of the coming Messiah.[34]

The third priestly order is the royal priesthood of our Lord Jesus Christ. Not limited to a few individuals, our priesthood is universal: every member of the royal family is appointed, as of salvation, to represent himself before God. In Christ, we are a kingdom of royal priests forever (1 Pet. 2:5, 9; Rev. 1:6; 5:10; 20:6). Under the perfect High Priest, the priesthood of the Church

---

34. See Thieme, *Levitical Offerings.*

Age is far superior to the former, specialized orders (Heb. 7).

On the other hand, we are also ambassadors. In the human sphere, an ambassador is a high ranking minister or member of royalty sent to represent his nation in a foreign country. As spiritual ambassadors, we represent the Lord Jesus Christ in the devil's kingdom. We are royalty, serving as emissaries of the King of Kings and Lord of Lords who is now absent from the earth. Just as we are appointed priests at salvation, we are also appointed ambassadors in the moment we believe in Christ. All Church Age believers are automatically in "full-time Christian service." No decision or dedication later in our Christian lives adds anything to our original divine appointments.

A nation's ambassador does not support himself; likewise, we are supported in Satan's domain by logistical grace from God. An ambassador has his instructions in written form; we have the completed canon of Scripture. He does not belong to the country to which he is sent; we are citizens of heaven. He does not regard insults as being personal; we, too, leave retaliation and judgment in the Lord's hands. The recall of an ambassador is tantamount to a declaration of war; soon after the Rapture recalls the royal family to heaven, overtly intensified spiritual warfare will break out in the Tribulation.

God uses ambassadors in every walk of life (Rom. 12:6-13). He has ambassadors in business, in the professions, in labor. No matter what you do for a living or in what circles you move, that is the sphere in which you represent Christ. You are to be an ambassador where you are, to make a pulpit out of your circumstances, whatever they might be. Thus, social change and the solving of social problems is not the issue in the spiritual life. In SPQR, for example, where slavery was rampant, Paul did not encourage the many slaves who had become believers to revolt or to demand a change in status; he encouraged them to remain where they were as "God's free men" (1 Cor. 7:22). Indeed, how you earn your living is an avocation. Your vocation in life is being an ambassador, a vocation to which God appointed you.

We may as well get used to the fact that we are here for a purpose. In fact, we are here for two purposes. On one hand, we are here to *glorify* God by allowing Him to bless us in the angelic conflict. On the other hand, we are here to *represent* the Lord Jesus Christ in the devil's world. These very different functions must be kept separate. If these wires are crossed, our Christian lives short out.

As our High Priest, Christ won the strategic victory in the angelic conflict (Heb. 6:17-20). As priests, our function is to win the tactical victory. The tactical victory is won when God is able to demonstrate His integrity by pouring out maximum blessings to a member of the human race. In other words, we are here as priests to learn doctrine and be blessed of God.

As ambassadors, we are here to represent the absent Christ through various categories of spiritual production commanded in the Scripture. This ambassadorial service may fall within the specialized function of our individual spiritual gifts, or it may fulfill the responsibilities common to all believers. For example, we are all charged with that type of evangelism known as witnessing whereas mass evangelism is the responsibility of prepared men with the spiritual gift of evangelist. Our job is to present the Gospel, to tell people how to be reconciled to God (2 Cor. 5:20).

PRIEST	AMBASSADOR
Represents himself	Represents Christ
Toward God	Toward man
Private	Public
Before God	Before the world
Learns doctrine	Interacts with others
Spiritual advance	Spiritual service
Receives blessing	*Gives* blessing

As priests, we represent ourselves; as ambassadors, we represent the Lord Jesus Christ. As priests, we represent ourselves to God; as ambassadors, we represent God to man. The royal priest functions in privacy before God; the royal ambassador, in public before the world. The priesthood is related to learning the Word of God; the ambassadorship, to interacting with others. The priesthood emphasizes spiritual advance; the ambassadorship, spiritual service. The royal priest receives blessings from God; the royal ambassador gives blessings to man. Divine blessings come to the believer always through his priesthood, never through his ambassadorship.

Our purpose as royal ambassadors is to produce; overt Christian production is designed to give blessing to others; thus, as ambassadors we *give* blessing, while as priests we *receive* blessing. Now, here is the important point. The blessings *we* give do not glorify God; what glorifies God is the blessing that *He* gives, the function that *He* performs, which proves *His* character and demonstrates *His* integrity. He is glorified by giving us the motivation and opportunity to produce; we produce simply as a natural result with no merit attached.

From the standpoint of our day-to-day lives, what glorifies God is not all of our Christian activity but our receiving blessings from Him. This puts our lives in perspective with the plan of God and puts our production on a true basis. Instead of running around trying to glorify God with our prayer, our witnessing, our giving, our service, we watch Him glorify Himself in our lives as we advance in the knowledge of His Word. With doctrine saturating the soul, reprogramming the brain, insulating us from satanic doctrine, our ambassadorial service becomes an opportunity, a privilege, a blessing in itself on top of many other blessings—an avenue of expressing our love for the Lord. The proper motivation from doctrine, applied under the filling of the Holy Spirit, causes us to easily and naturally represent Jesus Christ, the One we personally know and deeply appreciate.

The function of the ambassador follows only after the function of the priest. Advance in doctrine means eventual advance in production, and maximum production comes only in spiritual maturity.

The ambassadorship is inevitably related to confidence in the communication of doctrine (Eph. 6:20). Once we know doctrine, we can steadfastly declare God's plan, in both word and deed, assured that our purpose in life is upheld by the power of God. Our vocation is not jeopardized even by the most concerted satanic attacks or by the most adverse circumstances. Historical disaster, slavery, imprisonment—these things do not terminate the Lord's purpose for the lives of those who represent Him. We serve confidently as ambassadors, but since the private operation of the priest always precedes and accompanies the overt, public operation of the ambassador, the true emphasis is always on the inculcation of Bible doctrine and resultant spiritual growth. Never are the priorities reversed; never are the two categories to be confused.

I almost feel sorry for the Christian who hates to spend long hours in prayer but who forces himself to do so, hoping God will bless him for it. I pity the shy, reticent believer, embarrassed to strike up conversations with strangers, who faithfully knocks on doors to tell people about the Lord—in hopes of receiving divine approbation. Though it nearly kills him, he keeps it up, blushing all the while. These believers have been told that if they witness or pray enough God will bless them. They would simply like to have some blessing; they would like to honor the Lord. They are sincere; they mean well; but they are not read-in on God's system. Because of their ignorance, someone has sold them a bill of goods. Someone, probably also sincere, has told them that God's plan depends on man's work, saying in effect that God is sentimental and easy to please, that God doesn't mind violating His own principles, that God will go ahead and give what belongs to the priest in trade for a little work by the ambassador, that God is the author of confusion.

People spend so much time being nice to others in order to get something from them that this attitude is brought over into Christianity. But now instead of doing things for people they do not like, they are doing things for some nebulous, ethereal concept they call "God." They are going to do nice things for God, and God is going to bless them. Well, that is not true. No one can work for salvation, and much more, no one can work for blessing after salvation.

It is not difficult to understand why this blasphemy is so prevalent. We are taught from childhood that rewards come for being good, for doing good. This is human morality; there is certainly nothing wrong with it—in its proper place. We have heard that Santa brings presents for good boys and girls. We have read the stories about Rebecca from Sunnybrook Farm and the Rover Boys; these nice young people did the right thing and were always rewarded for it. Pretty is as pretty does. All our lives we have been told this, and there is nothing wrong with any of it. The problem comes when we carry this thinking across the line into the spiritual realm and try to treat God as though He were a human being.

The problem is perhaps best illustrated in the phrase "God bless you." We hear this at every turn. If you drop money in a pot at Christmastime, someone with a bell and a smile will say, "God bless you, brother." A boy scout helps a little old lady across the street and gets a "God bless you, sonny" in return. The pastor who stands at the door of the church on Sunday morning has a "God bless you" for every member of the congregation. What nerve! What presumption! How can anyone snap his fingers and call down divine blessing? What right has anyone to say that God will bless anyone else? Blessing is God's prerogative. The pastor can make it clear to his congregation *how* God blesses, but no one can actually say, "God bless you!"

Now, we might be exceedingly generous and dismiss "God bless you" as a mere idiom for "thank you," but it is a *lousy* idiom. At best, it means nothing; and if taken even a little bit seriously, it is terribly misleading.

A pastor might say "God bless you" when you give a gift to the church. Was it in the back of your mind that, if you gave twenty dollars, God might give you that business deal? Or cause your girlfriend to make up with you? If you thought so, you can forget it. You will never be blessed because you give. Giving is a function of the ambassadorship; it is an expression of worship.[35] Either doctrine is your motivation or your giving does not count. You cancel out the production with the mental attitude that hopes to get something in return. But, what's more, God never blesses anyone for any spiritual production of any kind—not even for *legitimate* production from *correct* motivation!

Do not think for a moment that production is unimportant. In a local church, for instance, many tasks must be performed faithfully, professionally, and often thanklessly. Those who do these necessary jobs are acting as ambassadors. They should understand that their eternal rewards—and their rewards in time—will come for other reasons, *better* reasons, than that

---

35. See Thieme, *Giving*.

they hustled around the church! They will be rewarded and blessed if they advance as priests; their ambassadorial production is motivated by the enthusiasm and impetus of that advance.

Our production blesses others, but God is far too smart to allow us to be blessed for blessing others. That would create false motivation from the start. He nips hypocrisy in the bud! He does not want His ambassadors running around as spiritual babies or adolescents, knocking one another over, making themselves obnoxious, trying to do good things "for others" in order to be rewarded themselves. That zealous emphasis on good works is closer to Satan's plan than to God's. God has established His plan so that production is a manifestation of spiritual progress. Production is not a cause but a result of advance. Production is not a cause of blessing; production is not even a result of blessing! Production is a result of Bible doctrine resident in the soul.

Having failed to rightly divide the priesthood from the ambassadorship, Christianity is today plagued by the idea that a believer is blessed for what he does. This is a gross error. On one hand, it violates the principle of the encapsulated pipeline, expecting God to jeopardize his perfect integrity. On the other hand, it makes believers vulnerable to spiritual bullies who con them into all kinds of "service" on pain of not being blessed by God. Such victimized Christians live under a nagging sense of not working hard enough, and they cultivate a blind arrogance concerning how important their works really are to God. This is the essence of legalism. It enslaves believers to overt activities while giving only lip service to the supreme importance of the Word of God and true doctrinal thinking. When believers attempt to conform their lives to erroneous concepts, they become disoriented toward life, divorced from reality, and maladjusted to the justice of God.

Without eclipsing or in any way dimming the real importance of legitimate production by the ambassador, the priesthood always receives highest divine priority. It is the basis for the believer's blessing: from the justice of God to the righteousness of God through the encapsulated grace pipeline. It is the basis for the Lord's glorification.

POTENTIAL DEMANDS CAPACITY

Of course, God did not take you directly to heaven the moment you believed in Christ, but perhaps you also noticed that neither did He suddenly bless you to the maximum. He did not instantly give you all the solutions to all your problems, fill you with unfading happiness, make you a millionaire, give you your right man or right woman, promote you to the top in your profession, prosper your family and friends because of their association with you, turn you into a source of historical impact and stability for your nation.

Why not? In that first instant you had the fully constructed grace pipeline as completely as you do now or ever will. God's objective is to give you such prosperity and much more besides. So why doesn't He drive straight to the goal? Again, why the delay?

As long as we remain in this life, a principle governs our relationship with the justice of God: potential plus capacity equals reality. The "potential" is justification; that is, the righteousness of God is imputed to us as a potential that demands implementation. Implementation appears on the "reality" end of the equation. The "reality" is God executing our supergrace paragraphs which He wrote into His plan in eternity past. In other words, the "reality" consists of maximum blessing imputed to divine righteousness in us in the middle of the devil's world. These blessings are the great "unknown" to most believers, but through *a fortiori* logic, Paul has put these bounties in true perspective: they are much easier for God to provide than was the "potential"—the imputed righteousness—which we already have!

POTENTIAL	+ CAPACITY	= REALITY
Imputed Righteousness	Bible Doctrine in the Soul	Blessings In Time

The reason why blessings are so often elusive is found in the "capacity" factor in the formula. Spiritual maturity gives capacity for blessing; it is the link between "potential" and "reality" in the Christian's life.

Capacity is the *missing* link for most believers in our day! Before God's justice pours out blessings, you must have the capacity for them. Without capacity of soul, blessings are not blessings at all; they only intensify adversity and misery. God is not about to promote you or make you a millionaire if you would be corrupted by these things. If what He gave you only destroyed you, He would not be fair. His integrity would be violated if He gave you certain things at the wrong stage in your spiritual advance.

You might be lonely at the moment, but there is something far worse than feeling a little blue—having the wrong mate, or even having the right mate at the wrong time! You might wish you were wealthy. It is the easiest thing in the world for God to drop a million dollars in your lap, but that would be unfair to you if the complications that always attend wealth gave you ulcers and robbed you of peaceful sleep at night. Such a "blessing" would be self-defeating. Whether you believe it or not, you would lose the advantage immediately.

However, whether you have capacity or not, God is faithful to His own perfection now residing in you. He continually pours blessings down the grace pipeline to you, beginning with the thirty-four blessings of salvation that come through in the instant the pipeline is constructed. After salvation, the blessings of grace continue in two categories: logistical blessings and special blessings.

Special blessings are the bounties of supergrace. They include spiritual blessings, temporal blessings, blessings by association, historical blessings, blessings connected with undeserved suffering, and eventually, dying blessings. These are the remarkable advantages that demand capacity of soul from the intake of Bible doctrine. God gives them when you are mature enough to appreciate them without being distracted by them. In giving you such blessings, God demonstrates His integrity to such an extent that He scores a tactical victory in the angelic conflict, exploiting the strategic victory of the Cross. God so desires to bless you in special and unusual ways that Isaiah wrote:

> And therefore will the Lord wait, that he may be gracious
> unto you, and therefore will he be exalted, that he may
> have mercy upon you: for the Lord is a God of judgment
> [justice]: blessed are all they that wait for him. (Isa. 30:18,
> AV)

Even though God cannot immediately give you special blessings, the righteousness of God in you still demands that you be blessed. During the interim between salvation and maturity, therefore, when the Lord is tapping His foot waiting to bless you, He supports and sustains you with logistical grace. Some of this support simply keeps you alive in the devil's world; you need air, food, shelter, clothing, friends, a guardian angel. But most important, you need what He provides for your spiritual advance: the completed canon of Scripture, rebound, the filling of the Holy Spirit, the prepared pastor-teacher, the local church where doctrine is taught, transportation to Bible class, perhaps a tape recorder, a radio, or some other means of hearing doctrine in the absence of a local pastor.

God supports different people in different ways. One believer might have stimulating and loyal friends; his transportation might be a Bugatti; his food, *haute cuisine*. Another might be alone; he might ride an old bicycle and occasionally splurge on a TV dinner. Whether you travel by Bugatti or bike, God gave you that transportation so you could get to Bible class!

Of course everything that God provides brings Him glory. But He is glorified to the maximum by blessing you to the maximum, not by merely sustaining you. Your positive volition toward doctrine and your growing capacity for blessings frees the essence of God "that he may be gracious unto you, and therefore will he be exalted." The justice of God cannot compromise: "For the Lord is a God of judgment [justice]: blessed are they that wait for him [choose to learn Bible doctrine]." Logistical grace does not bring the greatest glory to God because it does not require your positive volition; it involves no capacity factor. God keeps you alive as long as *He* chooses.

Through logistical blessings, God is giving us every opportunity to reach spiritual maturity. He keeps us alive at the end of the grace pipeline while we build up doctrine in our souls, preparing for the time when the promised blessings "above all that we ask or think" can begin to flow (Eph. 3:20). Some logistical blessings seem to be the ultimate in prosperity simply because we have never seen anything better. We should certainly thank God for them, but the blessings of maturity are so high above the logistical provisions that get us there that we are tempted to say that logistics are not blessings at all! You may have received some wonderful things on the road to supergrace, but keep moving: greater things are yet to come.

ENCAPSULATED ENVIRONMENT

At salvation God provides more than simply the potential for blessing. He knows that you will live your Christian life in the devil's world. He also knows that, worse yet, every cell in your body will continue to be contaminated by the old sin nature. You were born under these two rulerships, and even if God poured out blessings to you to the fullest of His ability, into what kind of an environment would they come? Satan does not exactly provide the ideal setting for God's blessings, and Adam's sinful trend is certainly no great friend and ally of God's plan!

God does not arbitrarily remove these two tyrants, however. In His justice, He is permitting the angelic conflict to run its course. Satan is given every opportunity to prove his arrogant boast that he is as good as God (Isa. 14:14), but the devil keeps proving himself to be worthy only of judgment! At the end of time, he will not have the slightest breath of an excuse for having rejected God's authority and plan. Satan would love to claim that he could have won the angelic conflict if only God had given him a chance. But divine justice *is* permitting Satan every chance to do his best. While Satan wreaks destruction, misery, and injustice, God demonstrates His own perfect integrity and proves His infinite glory through blessing believers in grace. Satan, the fallen angels, and all human unbelievers will have nothing to blame but their own negative volition for spending eternity in the Lake of Fire.

God permits Satan to operate, but God is not in the business of lending the devil a hand or of improving or whitewashing the devil's kingdom. God cannot oppose Himself! He therefore cannot simply dress up *cosmos diabolicus* and produce a little haven of perfect environment in which to bless you. There is no Garden of Eden today; its gates have been closed forever. But something better than Eden has been provided for us; we will see that in spite of Satan we now possess things of which Adam never dreamed!

But what about the old sin nature? How does God handle this dangerous tyrant? Its specific trend toward sin has already been judged on the Cross, but god permits its other two trends to continue as an issue in the angelic conflict. Since good-and-evil is the function of the sin nature, as well as being the modus operandi of Satan, God would not be permitting the spiritual battle to run its course if He simply removed the sin nature's good and evil trends. Indeed, the only way the genetic old sin nature could be removed would be by separating the body from the soul, that is, through physical death or the Rapture. If God is to bless us *on earth,* He must do so with the sin nature intact. And He does.

Even in the devil's world and in the continued presence of the old sin nature, God provides an environment that is right for divine blessings. On one hand, imputed righteousness sets up the encapsulated pipeline and becomes the potential for all subsequent blessings; on the other hand, the five salvation ministries of the Holy Spirit break the power of the two tyrants under which we were born and provide the potential for an encapsulated environment within the devil's domain. At the instant of faith in Christ, God the Holy Spirit does five things: He regenerates the new believer, baptizes him, indwells him, seals him, and distributes spiritual gifts.

Until Christ returns at the Second Advent to remove Satan and to establish His own millennial reign, the environment that God provides is primarily internal—an encapsulated environment in the soul, a spiritual setting that we carry with us regardless of our surroundings or circumstances. Certainly there are external, overt blessings, as we shall see, but what we have in our souls is far more important. Inside our own souls we have privacy from Satan, but there the ruling power of the sin nature must be broken. The five salvation ministries of the Spirit are designed to frustrate the old sin nature, to keep it from influencing and controlling the soul. These five blessings furnish the best possible environment in which to receive further divine blessings in time. The justice of God has already done more for us in the devil's world than the love of God could possibly do in Adam's world, the Garden of Eden.

Again, as with imputed righteousness, these five salvation blessings become your permanent possessions in the moment you first believe in Christ, but they are not fully exploited experientially until you reach spiritual maturity. They set you up for the advance to supergrace; they give you the potential which makes it possible for you to grow spiritually. We have portrayed the two tyrants in detail; we would be unfair if we did not explain in detail our potential for overcoming them.

As members of the royal family of God, we have privileges not granted to other believers. Believers of other dispensations, members of the family of God but not the *royal* family, receive only one of the five things we receive. This ministry common to all is regeneration or the new birth.

THE SALVATION MINISTRIES OF THE HOLY SPIRIT

REGENERATION

Regeneration is used so often today to represent the entirety of salvation that the wonderful truth of our new birth is lost in the obscurity of a cliche. "Born again" has become an abused phrase. People who have no idea of the Source, the purpose, or the results of regeneration, talk of being "born again" as though the Gospel message had no other aspects. To most unbelievers, the come-on question "Are you born again?" is either meaningless or suggestive of some kind of psychological or emotional change. Even when Christ Himself explained the Gospel from the standpoint of regeneration (John 3:3, 4), all that Nicodemus could do—typical of arrogant people faced with things they cannot understand—was to become facetious: "Can a man enter the second time into his mother's womb, and be born?" We shall see how regeneration fits into God's plan when we study the real imputation of eternal life.

BAPTISM OF THE HOLY SPIRIT

In Romans 6, the baptism of the Holy Spirit, which places us in union with Jesus Christ, is emphasized as the means of breaking the power of the old sin nature.

> Therefore, what are we to conclude? Are we to continue
> in the sin [in the sovereignty of the old sin nature] that the
> grace of God might increase? Emphatically not! We, who
> have died to the sin [the old sin nature], how shall we still
> live in it? Or are you ignorant that all of us who have been
> baptized into Christ, into His [spiritual] death have been
> baptized? (Rom. 6:1–3)

The baptism of the Holy Spirit is one of seven baptisms or identifications mentioned in the Bible (Heb. 6:2*a*). Four of these are symbolic or ritual identifications; three are actual identifications.[36] It is a sign of the apostate times in which we live that when believers see the word "baptism" they immediately think of water. Even farther off track, when most believers come across the baptism *of the Holy Spirit,* all they can imagine is the ecstatic, mindless caterwauling of the tongues crowd. Neither water baptism nor the gift of tongues is involved in the baptism of the Spirit. In fact, both of those functions served limited purposes at the beginning of the Church Age and are no longer necessary today.

The gift of tongues was a special warning to Israel of approaching divine discipline (Isa. 28:9–13).[37] With the destruction of Jerusalem in A.D. 70, the warning had no further value and was stopped (1 Cor. 13:8; 14:21). Also temporary, water baptism in the early church was a training aid, designed to help teach the baptism of the Holy Spirit to those who did not yet possess the completed canon of Scripture. The ritual training aid was no longer needed after certain New Testament passages were written and circulated (Romans 6, in particular, written circa A.D. 58). Apart from the historical record of that pre-canon period in the book of Acts, Scripture mentions water baptism only once (1 Cor. 1:11–17) and then only as being a source of argument and division among believers—as it still is today. Even while it was authorized, water baptism had no dynamics of its own; the activity itself never advanced anyone spiritually. Its only significance came from understanding the doctrine that it taught. As always, ritual without reality is meaningless.

Satan is trying with all his devious ingenuity to create perfect environment, but he continually fails. Satan's *cosmos diabolicus* is such a chronic flop that in order to bless man, God has to encapsulate an environment. What a slap in the face for Satan! It is not difficult to understand why the devil—frustrated, embarrassed, jealous, angered—seeks to obscure the baptism of the Holy Spirit by distorting it into emotionalism, hollow ritual, false doctrine, and ignorance.

In reality, with no fanfare or emotional folderol, God the Holy Spirit places each Church Age believer into union with Christ at the moment of salvation (Gal. 3:26–28; 1 Cor. 12:13). This is an *actual,* as opposed to a *ritual,* identification; we become bone of His bone and flesh of His flesh (Eph. 5:30). The baptism of the Holy Spirit is the permanent identification that distinguishes Christianity from religion. Christianity is our relationship with God by virtue of being in union with the God-Man, Jesus Christ (2 Cor. 5:16); religion is always some system of futile human attempts to gain the approbation of God (1 Cor. 15:23*a*).

The baptism of the Spirit forms the royal family of God. It is therefore

---

36. See Thieme, *Tongues,* Appendix, Doctrine of Baptisms.

37. See Thieme, *Tongues.*

unique to the Church Age. Spirit baptism first occurred on the day of Pentecost, circa A.D. 30 (Acts 1:5; 11:15-17), and will never again take place after the royal family is completed at the Rapture of the Church. Many lines of nobility and many titled families have existed in human history. But the ultimate system of royalty is unique. Established by God Himself, its members are united with the King of Kings and Lord of Lords. We are spiritual royalty through union with Jesus Christ; we share His battlefield royalty, which the Father awarded to Him for defeating Satan in the angelic conflict. Christ won the strategic victory through His spiritual death, physical death, burial, resurrection, ascension, and session at the right hand of God the Father (Col. 2:9-15). In Christ, the royal family of God is set apart from the rest of the family of God. Church Age believers are given a higher spiritual position than are the believers of all other dispensations! These unequal appointments are perfectly fair; God is perfect justice.

We are taught today to think that all people are equal, that the poor are inherently virtuous, that being a peasant is honorable, that any kind of real superiority should arouse a sense of guilt, that the successful owe a debt to the unsuccessful. These are tenets of stupidity.

We are all born *unequal*. And from birth on, the longer we live the more unequal we become. Those who demand "equality" do not want equality at all; they want superiority! Instead of diligently applying themselves in some chosen field so as to eventually earn what they want, they merely seek the power to enforce their arrogance and impose their illusions on others. We cannot be equal, but we can be free. In fact, freedom guarantees inequality. A person has the right to go as far as his abilities, circumstances, and self-discipline will take him (as long as he does not resort to crime), and he has the right to possess as private property the fruits of his labors. Equality is never the issue. Someone with a minimum of ability who keeps plugging away will go much farther in life than will a talented person who lacks self-discipline.

In complete disdain for the current popularity of Marxist-socialist "equality" and for the many evil guises in which it appears, God the Holy Spirit at the moment of salvation made you superior in position to all believers of all other dispensations. The list is awesome: Enoch, Abraham, Moses, David, Isaiah, John the Baptist, the great Jewish generals of the Tribulation, the spiritual giants of the Millennium. Yet these men, past and future, with far less spiritual capital to work with than we have, attain spiritual maturity and receive phenomenal blessings.

Never let the peasantish thinking of today cause you to feel guilty about the superiority that God has given you. You are a spiritual aristocrat! God has furnished vast resources so you can think and act and live like the royalty you are. But remember *noblesse oblige,* "nobility obligates." From the one to whom much is given, much is expected: God expects you to grow up.

Although all members of the royal family have the same position in Christ, we are still unequal in the degree to which we exploit our advantage. In other words, the baptism of the Spirit at salvation provides a second potential.

POTENTIAL +	CAPACITY =	REALITY
PRIMARY: Imputed Righteousness	Bible Doctrine in the Soul	Blessings in Time
SECONDARY: Baptism of the Holy Spirit	Bible Doctrine in the Soul	Encapsulated Environment for Blessings in Time

The formula remains the same but with different factors plugged in. The *primary* potential of imputed righteousness plus capacity from doctrine equals the reality of blessings in time. The *secondary* potential of the baptism of the Holy Spirit plus the capacity from doctrine equals the reality of an encapsulated environment. Only the capacity factor does not change: as you learn doctrine, doctrine in your soul becomes the catalyst which permits God to convert potentials into realities.

The baptism of the Holy Spirit places us into union with Christ as He is currently seated at the right hand of the Father and, retroactively, as He was on the Cross. We call this "current positional truth" and "retroactive positional truth." We are therefore identified with Christ in His spiritual death, physical death, burial, resurrection, ascension, and session.

Our position in Christ is best understood in the light of the analogy Paul draws in Romans 7:1-4. The believer is like a wife who divorces her first husband and marries another man. Now, Romans 6 and 7 are not a treatise on marriage; other passages address that subject. Paul is neither advocating nor condemning divorce. He is merely using for an illustration a familiar procedure that commonly occurred, in order to clearly explain his subject.

The first husband is the old sin nature; we are enslaved to its tyranny from the moment of birth when Adam's sin was imputed to it. According to the analogy, when we believe in Christ we divorce the old sin nature and marry the Lord Jesus Christ. The divorce involves Christ's spiritual death, physical death, and burial; the remarriage is based on His resurrection, ascension, and session.

Romans 6:3 emphasizes our identification with Christ on the Cross; we are in union with the Victim of the first judicial imputation. Your personal

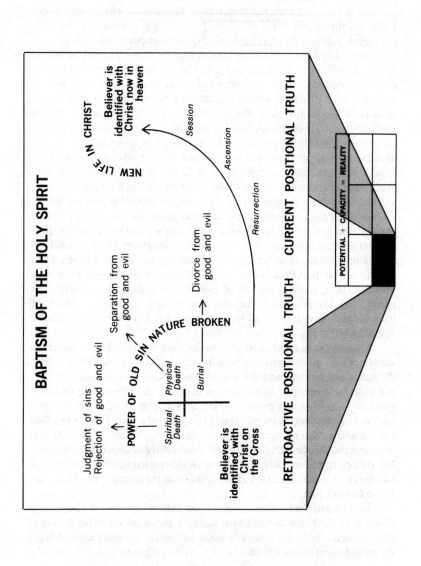

BAPTISM OF THE HOLY SPIRIT

NEW LIFE IN CHRIST

Believer is identified with Christ now in heaven

Session

Ascension

Resurrection

Judgment of sins
Rejection of good and evil

Separation from good and evil

POWER OF OLD SIN NATURE BROKEN

Spiritual Death

Physical Death

Burial

Divorce from good and evil

Believer is identified with Christ on the Cross

RETROACTIVE POSITIONAL TRUTH   CURRENT POSITIONAL TRUTH

POTENTIAL + CAPACITY = REALITY

sins and mine, along with those of all mankind, were imputed to Him and judged; this was His spiritual death.

But the old sin nature has *three* trends. Personal sin was imputed to our Lord, but the output of the other two trends—human good and evil—was not imputed. Never do we read that Christ died for our good deeds!

Christ was impeccable when He came to the Cross. He had no old sin nature, which means not only that He had never sinned but also that He had never committed a single thought, word, or deed of human good or evil. Throughout His life He totally rejected the policy of Satan and totally adhered to the plan of God. When Christ hung on the Cross and suffered spiritual death, He continued to reject good and evil. Everything He did, including His work of salvation, was divine good.[38] In union with Christ, we too have rejected good and evil, *positionally.* Even if we *experientially* produce them—even if we zealously crusade for the arch-enemy's millennium—as far as our *position* in Christ is concerned, we have rejected good and evil, both as the function of the old sin nature and as the policy of Satan.

Rejected but not judged, good and evil remain at large in the angelic conflict. But never think for a moment that they will not be judged. No production of the old sin nature ever escapes divine judgment. Good and evil will receive final judgment in the future when the angelic conflict is brought to a conclusion at the Great White Throne Judgment at the end of human history. There, unbelievers will be indicted for their human good works (Rev. 20:12-15). Sins will not be mentioned at the Last Judgment; sins have been judged once and for all in Christ (1 John 2:2). There is no double jeopardy.

A person who rejects Christ as Savior says in effect that he prefers to stand in God's final courtroom with human righteousness rather than with the Judge's own righteousness imputed to him. What a tragic spectacle! Here is a genetically corrupt, totally condemned individual depending on something he is or does. He expects some paltry system of human works and human merit to meet the incomparable standards of perfect God! When God examines the "books according to their works" (Rev. 20:12, 14) and measures the unbeliever's deeds against the standard of divine righteousness, His righteousness can only reject them. What righteousness rejects, justice condemns. The justice of God can only sentence the unbeliever to join Satan in the Lake of Fire.

In contrast, the believer will not stand before the Great White Throne (Rom. 8:1). Only rejection of Christ as Savior puts a person on the docket of that tribunal. Still, the believer's good and evil is no more exempt from divine judgment than is the unbeliever's. At the Judgment Seat of Christ, the

---

38. See Thieme, *Divine Good vs. Human Good.*

believer's human good will be cast aside and burned while he himself is saved (1 Cor. 3:15). Our Lord's spiritual death both paid the penalty for sin and rejected human good and evil, but we are in union with Him, not in His spiritual death alone, but in His physical death and burial as well.

> Therefore, we have been buried together with Him through the baptism [of the Holy Spirit] unto His [physical] death. . . . (Rom. 6:4*a*)

Christ's physical death is analogous to separation from the old sin nature, and the finality of His burial is like divorce. Similar to the woman who breaks free from the tyranny of a bad marriage, believers reject, separate from, and divorce the old sin nature. The pattern of divorce thus clarifies our retroactive position in Christ, which breaks the sovereignty of the old sin nature over human life.

In describing divorce, Paul depicts the former husband and wife as being "dead" to each other (Rom. 7:2, 3*b*). All relationship, authority, responsibility, and privilege have ceased to exist. Even though both parties are still alive, neither has any claim on the other. In the same way, we are "dead and buried" to the old sin nature (Rom. 6:5–7), though experientially our "ex" is very much alive. With his trends toward sin, good, and evil, he still resides in every cell of our bodies; his program of good and evil still controls the computer. Like an ex-husband with no personal integrity, he keeps hanging around, continually calling us up, inviting us to come over for a little social life—"just for old times' sake."

We are constantly faced with his advances, to which we can say yes or no (Rom. 6:11–13). Whenever we sin or perform acts of human good or evil, we have submitted. Our lives will never be free from personal sins as long as we live (God provides instantaneous recovery through rebound [1 John 1:8–10]); but we *can* be completely free from good and evil. This is the potential of the encapsulated environment, protected from the tyranny of Satan and the old sin nature; it becomes a consistent, experiential reality only through the advance to maturity through the intake of Bible doctrine.

Freedom from human good and evil is the subject of current positional truth, our identification with Christ in His resurrection, ascension, and session.

> . . . In order that as Christ has been raised up from deaths [spiritual and physical] by the glory of the Father, even so we should walk in newness of life. (Rom. 6:4*b*)

In union with the glorified Christ as He is seated in the place of highest honor (Ps. 110:1; Heb. 1:13; 10:12), we share all that He is and has. We share His election (Eph. 1:4), His destiny (Eph. 1:5; Rom. 8:28, 30), His sonship (Gal. 3:26; 2 Tim. 2:1), His heirship (Rom. 8:16, 17), His priesthood (Heb. 10:10–14), His sanctification (1 Cor. 1:2, 30), His royalty (2 Pet. 1:11), His righteousness (2 Cor. 5:21), and His eternal life (1 John 5:11,12).

As members of the royal family of God, we actually possess a double portion of God's righteousness and eternal life. The Father's righteousness is imputed to us, as it is to believers of all dispensations, in order to set up the grace pipeline. But in addition, through the baptism of the Holy Spirit and union with Christ, we also possess the righteousness of the Second Person of the Trinity (2 Cor. 5:21). The same is true of our eternal life. All believers must have eternal life in order to live with God forever; that is why the Holy Spirit's ministry of regeneration is for the entire family of God and not just for the royal family. But royalty receives a double portion. The Father's life is imputed to us, and the Son's life becomes ours through current positional truth (John 14:6).

Instead of living under the rulership of the ex-husband, the old sin nature, we are now in a position to live unto God (Rom. 6:8–10; Eph. 2:5–10). Positional truth demands a new way of life, compatible with the exalted relationship between the resurrected humanity of Christ and God the Father, at whose right hand He sits. This is a supernatural way of life—not in the sense of hocus-pocus mysticism, but in the sense that we depend entirely upon the resources of God. Through doctrine, we learn to harness and utilize divine resources, and by doing so, we exploit the fantastic riches of God's grace.

"That we should walk" is in the subjunctive mood, indicating potential. "That we should walk in newness of life" is the potential for the encapsulated environment. Through the baptism of the Holy Spirit, this potential is the royal family's grace provision for receiving blessings from the justice of God in the devil's world. Our "newness of life" is far greater than anything that love₁ could give to Adam in the Garden.

The grace of God is not increased by our continuing in the sovereignty of the sin nature (Rom. 6:1). It is increased when we develop capacity through doctrine so that the justice of God can convert the potentials of imputed righteousness and union with Christ into the reality of blessings in an encapsulated environment. Positionally, the power of the old sin nature has been broken; experientially, the former ruler is reduced to begging. He must wait for you to throw him a few crumbs of negative volition. I want to remind you of something: the old sin nature is no longer your ruler. When you ignore rebound and the intake of Bible doctrine and instead follow the thinking of good and evil, *you* are the culprit. *You* have placed a beggar on the throne of your life! To paraphrase James, "These things ought not be!" (James 3:10).

INDWELLING OF THE HOLY SPIRIT

As His third salvation ministry, the Holy Spirit takes up residence in the believer's body to combat the genetically resident old sin nature.

> Or do you know that your body is the temple of the Holy Spirit who is in you, whom you have from God, and you are not your own? For you have been bought with a price; therefore, glorify God in your body. (1 Cor. 6:19, 20, AV)

Since the old sin nature is dead to us positionally but not experientially, we face an inner conflict as long as we live (Rom. 8:2–4; Gal. 5:16ff). From its headquarters in the body, the sin nature seeks to control the soul. Therefore, God the Holy Spirit indwells every Church Age believer's body to provide the power needed to offset the continued activity of the sin nature. The sin nature opposes our adherence to God's plan and disrupts our adjustment to the justice of God. There exists a perpetual antagonism between our ex-ruler and the Agent who freed us, between the old sin nature and the Holy Spirit. Both adversaries are quartered in the body; the fight takes place in the soul.

> For, you see, the flesh [old sin nature] rises up in protest against the [indwelling Holy] Spirit, and the [indwelling Holy] Spirit against the flesh; for these are constantly opposed to each other, with the result that you may not continue doing what things [advance to maturity] if you desire to do so. (Gal. 5:17)

The believer's soul is the battleground in the angelic conflict, and the believer's own volition determines which side wins in his life. Here we must distinguish between the indwelling of the Spirit and the filling of the Spirit. Filling is the Spirit's control of the soul (1 John 1:9; Prov. 1:23); indwelling is His residence in the body (1 Cor. 6:19, 20; Gal. 3:2; 4:6). The old sin nature controls the soul when the believer succumbs to temptation and thus "grieves" (Eph. 4:30) or "quenches" (1 Thess. 5:19) the indwelling Holy Spirit. Grieving the Holy Spirit is carnality; quenching is reversionism. Carnality emphasizes the old sin nature's trend toward sin, while reversionism is carnality which has intensified to include the trends toward human good and evil. On the other hand, the Spirit regains control of the soul when the believer rebounds by naming his sins privately to God (Ps. 32:5). Only when the believer is thus restored to fellowship can the Spirit again provide the supernatural dynamics for executing the Christian way of life.

Unless we know pertinent doctrine, however, the inner conflict between the Holy Spirit and the old sin nature is "no contest" in favor of the former tyrant. Before we can be filled with the Spirit, we must know *how* to be filled with the Spirit! Obviously, we must learn the doctrine of rebound. Furthermore, if the filling of the Holy Spirit is to be sustained, we must understand the grace concepts behind it; we must understand the doctrine of mental attitude; we must understand the objectives of the Christian life. What is required is a doctrinal thought pattern, a system of divine thinking, a comprehensive and detailed structure of doctrine in the soul. An occasional devotional thought will not get the job done! We must understand the doctrines that the Holy Spirit uses to control the soul.

The Holy Spirit is God. He possesses all the attributes of the divine nature; thus, He personally has Self-knowledge, omniscience, and foreknowledge. But in us He does not work through His own vast knowledge; He works through the doctrine we have learned. Where there is no doctrine, there is no divine thought pattern, and therefore, there is no basis for the Holy Spirit's sustained control of the soul. The Holy Spirit completely controls the soul when we rebound, but if no doctrine resides there as a system of thinking, the Spirit's control will be short-lived and ineffectual.

"But," you ask, "can't God the Holy Spirit inject a little of His infinite knowledge directly into our minds? Why can't He just help us in that way?" If He did, He would destroy the entire system of freedom and volition in the angelic conflict. God does not magically remove all of our erroneous ideas. He accumulates Bible doctrine into our souls, not by some mystical revelation, but under the inner authority of our own academic self-discipline, which operates under the overt authority of the pastor-teacher communicating from the canon of Scripture. Only gradually can a doctrinal thought pattern, useable by the filling of the Spirit, displace the old thought pattern developed since childhood. The believer's inner conflict is as much a conflict between the thought pattern of evil and the thought pattern of doctrine as it is between the old sin nature and the Holy Spirit (Rom. 12:2).

Through the filling of the Holy Spirit and the consistent perception of Bible doctrine, the battlefield is under God's control, and He is free to provide the fantastic blessings of supergrace. Of course, the fact that all believers have the potentiality of blessings does not mean that they will ever have the reality. It is the mature believer who has exploited the victory of grace; only he glorifies God.

When we sin, we lose the filling of the Spirit, but we never lose His indwelling presence (Rom. 8:9). Hence, we are commanded to be filled with the Spirit (Eph. 5:18; Gal. 5:16)—a command to rebound whenever we sin—but we are never ordered to be indwelt; the indwelling of the Spirit is our permanent possession. Even if we are not positive toward the Word of God, we are still indwelt, but the indwelling of the Spirit is not operational apart from the filling of the Spirit.

Many Old Testament believers were filled or endued with the Spirit. He controlled the souls and empowered the lives of the prophets, the writers of Scripture, and other individuals responsible for specific, critical functions (Ex. 31:3; 35:31; Luke 1:15). But until the Age of the Royal Family, no one's body was ever permanently indwelt by the Holy Spirit. Jewish Age believers could lose the Spirit's enduement ministry (Ps. 51:11), and those who did not possess it could ask to receive it (Luke 11:13). Today, members of the royal family can lose the operational help of His filling ministry, but even then they still retain His indwelling. This is an aspect of our spiritual aristocracy. Two synonyms for the indwelling of the Spirit specifically depict His presence in us as a sign of royalty: the "anointing" or "unction" of the Spirit is because of our union with the King of Kings (1 John 2:20, 27).

The universal indwelling of all believers is unique to the royal family, but it was prophesied by Jesus Christ before the Church Age began (John 7:37–39; 14:16, 17). And what is its purpose? To glorify the Lord Jesus Christ. It accomplishes this by furnishing the base of operations for the Spirit's filling of the believer's soul. Thus, the reason the Spirit resides in us is to supersede human ability and human good; He supplies the divine power and ability necessary for us to attain every objective in the Christian life. In particular, He provides our spiritual IQ for learning doctrine, as well as our very ability to understand the Word of God (John 16:12–15; 1 Cor. 2:9–16; 1 John 3:27).

Another distinction we must keep in mind is the difference between the indwelling of the Holy Spirit and the indwelling of Christ (Rom. 8:10). The Spirit's indwelling is *functional;* Christ resides in our bodies to *manifest His glory* in our lives (2 Cor. 3:18). In us Christ provides encouragement (John 14:18–21), motivation (Eph. 3:17), and confidence (Col. 1:27). The reversionist does not benefit from the indwelling of Christ; no fellowship exists when human good and evil dominate the soul (Rom. 8:10; 2 Cor. 13:5). As long as the reversionist is out of fellowship and ignores Bible doctrine, he cannot look into the mirror of the Word and see the reflected glory of Christ (2 Cor. 3:18; Rev. 3:20).

SEALING OF THE SPIRIT

The fourth ministry of God the Holy Spirit at salvation emphasizes our security.

> Now he, who establishes us with you in Christ [baptism
> of the Holy Spirit] and anointed us [indwelling of the

Holy Spirit], is God, who has also sealed us. . . . (2 Cor.
1:21, 22*a*, AV)

The sealing ministry of the Spirit is another mark of our royalty; it is a device in our spiritual coat of arms. No one was sealed by the Holy Spirit prior to the Church Age, and the sealings which occur after the Church is removed—for example, the sealing of 144,000 evangelists in the Tribulation (Rev. 7:2-4)—serve a different purpose.

In the ancient world, seals guaranteed transactions, indicated ownership, authenticated invoices, contracts, laws, and orders. There were different seals for each of these applications.

The grace transaction which occurred when we believed in Christ is guaranteed by our sealing. We are eternally saved, members of the royal family forever (2 Cor. 1:22). We are also signified as belonging to God. As His mark of ownership, the seal declares our positional sanctification, our permanent union with Christ. Since seals authenticated documents, the sealing of the Spirit relates us to the divine decrees. In other words, the Holy Spirit ratifies the fact that God formulated a plan for each of us in eternity past, and that He has taken it upon Himself to furnish all the logistical support we need in order to fulfill it. Sealing is a downpayment or a promise to the royal family of the supergrace blessings which are written in the decrees (Eph. 1:3). Carnality, or quenching the Holy Spirit, is incompatible with our sealing (Eph. 4:30).

DISTRIBUTION OF SPIRITUAL GIFTS

The Holy Spirit's fifth salvation ministry determines how we as Christ's ambassadors are to operate during our lives on earth. Every Church Age believer receives at least one spiritual gift, sovereignly bestowed by the Holy Spirit at the moment of faith in Christ (1 Cor. 12:11). The gift involves a special ability in a particular field. Which gifts are given to which believers is strictly a divine prerogative. No one has any say as to which gift he receives, and certainly no one ever earns or deserves it. Since all five ministries of the Holy Spirit are among the thirty-four blessings that come down the grace pipeline at salvation, we cannot take credit for any of them. They come strictly from the justice of God, in this case, God the Holy Spirit.

In order to avoid the distortions and practices which have distracted so many believers from God's purpose for their lives, we must recognize that the Holy Spirit no longer gives certain gifts. Several temporary gifts, in addition to the permanent gifts which still function, were required at the beginning of the Church Age to help communicate the doctrines of the royal family or to establish the authority of those who taught (Acts 3:11, 12; 6:8; 1 Cor.

13:1, 2). But just as the gift of tongues and the water baptism of believers were made obsolete when their purposes were fulfilled, so also the gifts of apostleship, prophecy, miracles, healing, etc., were all removed by the time the canon of Scripture was completed in A.D. 96 (1 Cor. 13:8, 10).

Paul once healed the sick at will (Acts 19:11, 12). This was a super-natural calling card that established his authority in a new locale as being a communicator of the Word of God (Rom. 15:19). But as early as A.D. 62, he could not heal even his dear friend Epaphroditus (Phil. 2:25-27; 2 Tim. 4:20). By that time, Paul's reputation was well established, and the gift of healing had been removed. Likewise, in 2 Timothy 4:1, 2, the great apostle passed the colors of local church leadership to a pastor-teacher, Timothy. The gift of apostleship with its supreme authority over more than one local congregation was not perpetuated. And with the death of John, soon after he penned Revelation in A.D. 96, the function of apostleship ceased.

Many of the permanent spiritual gifts, still functional, are not explicitly mentioned in Scripture; only those which pertain to the operation of the local church are listed, plus a few others to make us realize that such additional gifts exist (Rom. 12:6-8; 1 Cor. 12:4-11; Eph. 4:7-11). Of course, no one is aware of his gift when he is saved; he recognizes it only as a result of spiritual growth. Even so, the only gifts which absolutely must be identified are those that require special preparation before they become operational. A pastor-teacher, in particular, must master many subjects before he is able to function properly. But many gifts require no concentrated preparation beyond the normal daily intake of doctrine. Even if they are never specifically nailed down, they function automatically with spiritual maturity. Your concern, therefore, is not "What is my spiritual gift?" Your only concern is to grow in grace.

The Holy Spirit gives gifts in order to provide a spiritual environment for the perception of Bible doctrine; He delegates a system of spiritual authority within, yet apart from, the devil's world. The gift of pastor-teacher carries the highest spiritual authority extant in life. One pastor rules each local congregation for two purposes: to communicate doctrine to the assembled believers and to protect their privacy and freedom to learn (Heb. 13:7, 17). The gift of evangelism functions outside the local church toward unbelievers (Acts 1:8; Rom. 15:20). Believers with the gifts of helps and government serve as deacons and accomplish the various administrative tasks delegated to them by the pastor-teacher for the efficient operation of the church (Acts 7:3).

TEMPORAL SECURITY

The five salvation ministries of the Holy Spirit provide an encapsulated environment for divine blessings in time. As long as the devil rules the world, that environment is necessarily internal, but it is not merely internal. When God blesses you, He intends that you enjoy to the maximum what He gives you. Internally, a lack of capacity from doctrine would keep you from appreciating divine blessings; therefore, God waits until you reach maturity before He imputes special blessings through the grace pipeline (Isa. 30:18). But external factors might also interfere; therefore, He insulates your blessings with temporal security. The inner capacity *for* blessings and the overt security *of* blessings are both part of the package.

Good-and-evil is the policy which characterizes the world in which we live. Obviously, we can only expect Satan's kingdom to be unfair. He has no regard for divine authority or human freedom. He attacks God's authority and seeks to curtail man's freedom in order to limit evangelism and the function of GAP (2 Cor. 4:4). He continually attempts to superimpose his own evil designs upon the nature of things decreed by God. Arrogance divorces from reality even the great intellect of the most brilliant of all creatures!

Satan's good and evil stratagems, supported by the good and evil trends of the old sin nature, inevitably build up waves of historical disaster. We should not be surprised by the fact that good and evil frequently come to a crest and break across some area of the world, destroying everything in their path. The noble-sounding "Liberty, Equality, Fraternity" of the French Revolution became the slogan of the Reign of Terror. Under the inspiring banner of "a new world order," communism spreads tyranny, slavery, and death around the world in the name of "liberation."

Modern socialism's call for "equality," "equal opportunity," and "the greatest good for the greatest number" is becoming ingrained in American thinking. Such ideas have begun to reduce the traditional aggressiveness and ingenuity of Americans to the lowest common denominator. Our national strength and prosperity have rotted from within.

It is saddening—even heart-breaking—to see our nation on the decline. But we know that Satan's kingdom is fraught with such calamities where Bible doctrine and the laws of divine establishment are ignored. Today we face the likelihood of violent historical adversity. Our economy has all but collapsed. The military power of the Soviet Union is awesome; its buildup is unprecedented. Such a military machine, strategically designed to take the offensive, must be used or dismantled—otherwise it will collapse of its own weight. The Kremlin shows no inclination to dismantle it. It continues to build strength while our military forces continue to be ignored, abused, and weakened. We live at the foot of a volcano.

God does not separate us from the trends of human history. He intends for us to live in the devil's world and to understand contemporary history in the light of the Bible doctrine in our souls. Hence, we can apply a principle of doctrine in the interpretation of history: regardless of what the Communists might do, God still blesses mature believers and guarantees that they will enjoy all the bounties that pour through the grace pipeline.

God has already provided the greater—the judgment of His own Son for our sins and the imputation of His own righteousness to us. It follows *a fortiori* that He will not withhold the less—blessings in time to us as mature believers. To bless mature believers is *much easier* for God than it was to provide the Cross. This reveals how absolute is the security of divine blessings. We can be blessed in *cosmos diabolicus,* right under the devil's nose, in spite of good-and-evil calamities. This is the tactical victory in the angelic conflict.

Justice is far greater than love₁ as a point of contact with God. The justice of God takes the devil's evil domain and, through the work of the Holy Spirit plus doctrine in the soul, creates a better environment than the Garden of Eden. Adam was given perfect environment, but in sinning he settled an issue: perfect environment does not guarantee happiness. This principle will be demonstrated once again in the Millennium when man will revolt against yet another perfect environment. At that time, he will rise up against the perfect government of the Lord Jesus Christ (Rev. 20:7-10)! Unregenerate or reversionistic man is never satisfied.

When the justice of God took over from love₁ and condemned man, the situation looked grim. The rulership of the world was allowed to pass to Satan, and the trends of the old sin nature were permitted to freely function. But we saw how Satan was finessed out of the fruits of his victory. The justice of God went to work immediately, and one of the greatest things that God has ever done for the human race was to expel Adam and Eve from the Garden and lock the gates. This was not a setback in the plan of God; God's plan is never set back. This was an advance!

There can be no looking back. It would have been a tragedy for man to live in perfect environment, which was designed for love₁, with an old sin nature which can be handled only by justice. The tree of lives was never designed for fallen man; our tree is the Cross of Christ. The Garden of Eden was not adequate for fallen man; perfect environment has no meaning for us under the old sin nature, Adam's original sin, and spiritual death. Our environment is the "newness of life."

Many psychologists, sociologists, and politicians blame environment for a myriad of neuroses and maladies and, therefore, turn to environment for the solutions to life's problems. Consequently, a large number of people in this country—in various branches and agencies of government, in disruptive activist organizations, even in Christian circles—are trying to improve man's environment. But who else is pursuing the same objective? None other than His majesty the devil. The very efforts to create perfect environment are part of the same policy that destroyed it in the first place! The tree of the knowledge of good and evil is still producing a bumper crop! The pattern has not changed; attempts to improve the world ignore or destroy everything true and worthwhile in life. Perfect environment is not the answer; encapsulated environment is.

Capacity and security are therefore related: God gives you the right blessings at the right time, and no one but God can take them away (Job 1:21). Not even the continuing activity of your sin nature destroys the security of supergrace blessings.

David is an example of this concept of encapsulation. God gave David a greater variety of blessings than has been given to any other believer in all of human history. As a mature believer, he was one of the wealthiest men in the world. His son, Solomon, *was* the richest man on earth in his day but only because he inherited his father's wealth. David was also blessed with fantastic professional prosperity as the commanding general of the Jewish army and as the ruler of the Jewish nation. He had wonderful, loyal friends; he owned palaces and ranches; he ate the best food, rode the finest horses, won decisive victories, and saw the justice of his establishment policies bring prosperity to Israel.

In spite of his spiritual greatness, David is today a target of maligning. Legalists cannot understand his magnificent rapport with the Lord because they cannot fit his energetic lust for life into their stuffy, sanctimonious molds. These believers would just love an excuse to skin David alive. So in their arrogance, jealousy, sour grapes, or simple ignorance of the justice of God, such self-righteous Christians claim that on the day David saw Bathsheba from his palace rooftop, he suddenly ceased to be a believer! "Surely," they insist, "no one could possibly commit adultery and murder and still be a believer!"

How wrong they are. Believers are human; they can commit any sin possible to an unbeliever. But the plan of God is greater than anyone's personal sins, just as it is greater than any historical disaster. To say that sin causes a believer to lose his salvation is to say that Christ's work on the Cross was not efficacious, that the divine decrees are full of loopholes, that perfect grace depends on imperfect man, that justice is unfair, that God is not God. In other words, it is blasphemous.

Once a person believes in Christ, that individual is saved forever (John 10:28). But David was more than merely a believer; he was a *mature* believer throughout the entire affair. All the fabulous prosperity that God had given him before he met Bathsheba belonged to him after the smoke had cleared. David never lost a single special blessing that had come to him down the grace pipeline.

Of course, sin is never condoned. Make no mistake, David was severely disciplined and, for the duration of his punishment, could not fully enjoy his blessings. He suffered for his sins for years to come. But he was still the king, still a successful general, still a man of tremendous personal wealth. God simply added discipline to David's prosperity.[39]

The supergrace blessings that come through the pipeline are secure, and the environment in which you enjoy them is encapsulated, insulated, protected, guaranteed. When you look at the possibilities of war coming to the United States within the next few years, you are not called upon to worry or give up. You cannot say, "Well, since the Communists will destroy my chances to enjoy supergrace, I might as well forget about doctrine." No! Face the *whole* reality. War may come; indeed, apart from the direct intervention of the Lord Jesus Christ, there is no way short of capitulation that war can be averted. But God guarantees that *whenever* you reach supergrace He will encapsulate the environment for your blessings, and give blessings He will! Now is the time to prepare for what looms on the historical horizon; you prepare by intensifying your intake of Bible doctrine.

The devil will continue to rule the world, and the old sin nature will continue to produce personal sins, but no trend of history and no personal carnality can undo what the justice of God has done. When God blesses, that blessing is permanent.

> Also, when I walk in a valley overshadowed by death, I cannot fear evil because You [the Lord Jesus Christ] are with me [mature believer]; Your rod [discipline] and Your staff [deliverance and blessing] they comfort me. You have prepared before me a table in the presence of my enemies [blessing and prosperity of maturity]; You have anointed my head with oil [security of supergrace blessings]; my cup [capacity for blessing] is overflowing. Only prosperity and grace shall pursue me all the days of my life, and I will remain in the house of the Lord forever. (Ps. 23:4-6)

IMPUTATION OF ETERNAL LIFE

God intends for the blessings of time to be permanent, and He makes them permanent by carrying them over from time into eternity. He parlays the blessings He gives on earth into even greater blessings and rewards in heaven. The real imputation of eternal life, therefore, implies far more than

---

39. See Thieme, *Rebound and Keep Moving.*

that we will live forever. *Unbelievers* will live forever! But in hell instead of heaven.

The security of divine blessings is a major principle behind the fifth basic imputation. In other words, eternal life is more than it appears to be on the surface. We are about to discover what lies behind the "born again" cliché.

God personally gives all life. We noted the biological functions that God designed as the means of passing traits and characteristics from parents to children. But human life is not simply biological. As to Adam so to all people, God personally imputes the spark of life. Even after the creation of the original parents, no human life exists until God sovereignly decides to impute it when the fetus emerges from the womb. Furthermore, no life ever exists without a home in which to live; thus, all imputations of life must be real imputations.

God gives eternal life as a real imputation because there is an affinity between eternal life and the human spirit. God the Holy Spirit sets up this affinity or antecedence when, as His ministry of regeneration, He creates the human spirit at the moment of salvation. To this home or target, eternal life is immediately and instantaneously imputed.

Just as God prepared the soul as the flawless target or home for human life, so also He prepares the human spirit as the flawless home for eternal life. In their origin, both the soul and the human spirit are creative acts of God. Both the soul and the human spirit are unchangeable, indestructible facts of existence.

Once God the Father deposits human life in the soul, that imputation is irrevocable; and obviously when He imputes eternal life to the human spirit, that arrangement is also permanent. No life can ever be separated from the home to which it is imputed. Nothing we can do will break apart a divine imputation. Satan and all his demons cannot destroy either human life or eternal life. Even God cannot undo what He Himself has done.

The unbeliever in the Lake of Fire, with his human life intact and undamaged in his soul, will be completely and constantly aware of his terrible situation. Likewise, the believer's living soul will be in full operation amid the glories of heaven. The fact that people are alive right now, both believers and unbelievers, is merely the present manifestation of the reality that they are humanly alive forever. But more than human life is required if we are to avoid the Last Judgment and live forever in the presence of God.

Two requirements must be met if we are to have an eternal relationship with God. First, we must have His righteousness; and second, we must have His life. Both are imputed to the believer at salvation. Thus, ever since the moment of faith in Christ, we have possessed two kinds of life. And again, the fact that we are alive right now, as believers in the Lord Jesus Christ, is a guarantee that we will live with God in heaven, because even now we have His eternal life. That is why, when God sees fit to call us home, it is as simple a matter as being "absent from the body, face to face with the Lord" (2 Cor. 5:8). Actually, although we possess eternal life, we are not using it now. Eternal life is what will give us the capacity to receive and appreciate the blessings of eternity. Eternal life is emphasized in eternity; human life, on earth.

Eternal life is God's life, an attribute of His essence, the very life that He is. Imputed to us, it assures us a never-ending relationship with Him. In the Garden of Eden, Adam and the woman had neither God's righteousness nor His life, but we have both. As perfect people, the original couple did not have a relationship with the justice of God; they had no security before God because their relationship with love₁ depended on their volition. In contrast, our relationship with the justice of God depends solely upon His grace. We have security in both time and eternity.

God's life in us not only implies that we will live with Him forever, but it also guarantees that we will receive a resurrection body—minus the old sin nature, minus human good and evil—when the royal family is completed at the Rapture of the Church. This is ultimate sanctification, the eternal status possessed alike by all members of the royal family of God, regardless of spiritual status on earth.

Sanctification is the greatest thing God could possibly do for all members of the royal family: He is making us like His Son. God accomplishes this in three stages. First, *positional* sanctification: when we believe in Christ, the Holy Spirit places us into union with Christ so that positionally we share all that He is and has. Second, *experiential* sanctification: as we attain spiritual maturity, Bible doctrine saturates our souls so that under the filling of the Spirit, the mind of Christ becomes our mind, displacing the good and evil of satanic thinking. And third, *ultimate* sanctification: when the royal family is complete, each of us will receive a body like His. As His resurrected royal family, we will be physically like Him, prepared to share in His triumph and coronation at the Second Advent and to become His Bride forever (Phil. 3:20, 21; Rev. 19:6-9).

Because of what *God* is doing in grace, even the most legalistic, the most indifferent, and the most antagonistic believers have an overriding security (2 Tim. 2:13). In spite of their various brands of negative volition toward Bible doctrine, they will all receive ultimate sanctification as certainly as will the mature believer. Possessing the same eternal life, all have the same guarantee. But ultimate sanctification is the minimum; it includes no special blessings, no special rewards.

Many believers fail to take advantage of their spiritual birthright. They spend their lives in reversionism. Failing to rebound, failing to consistently take in the Word of God, they miss the whole purpose of life. Their maladjustment to the justice of God makes it impossible for justice to bless them. The will of God for their lives goes unfulfilled; instead, they suffer increasingly harsh discipline until finally they die miserably under the sin unto death.

God did not give us His eternal life so we could say, "Goodbye, God, I'll see you in heaven! Until then, I'll do as I please!" Our eternal life was never meant to be placed on a shelf and admired from a distance as we go our own way. It is designed to be exploited. Eternal life is like a container, a repository, a treasure chest, a storage area into which the blessings of time are deposited. If there are no supergrace blessings in time, there is nothing in the treasure chest to be converted into the surpassing grace blessings of eternity, above and beyond ultimate sanctification.

You are undoubtedly aware that people collect things other than stamps; some collect old wines. The noble wines from the Bordeaux districts are particularly distinguished tenants in any cellar. Their famous names—Chateau Lafite-Rothschild, Chateau Latour, Chateau Margaux, Chateau Haut Brion, Chateau Mouton-Rothschild—have graced many tables over hundreds of years. Venerable and rare survivors from older vintages, still passing from collector to collector, demand prices that are noble indeed!

Not long ago, a man bought one relatively old bottle of Lafite for over $14,000. Now here is a curious thing about a bottle like that. You can bring it out and say, "Yes, this is a Bordeaux bottle," as you admire its shoulders (unlike the Burgundy bottle which merely slopes). You can identify the picture of the chateau on the label. You can note the vintage and make a comment or two about what happened that year in various parts of the world. But after a short conversation, all you can do is look at it.

"But," you say, "a $14,000 bottle of wine must be magnificent to drink!" Well, it simply is not. In the first place, if you ever opened such a bottle, its collector's value would be destroyed. But what is worse, you would probably discover that you had purchased a rather aristocratic bottle of vinegar—worse than vinegar! Having passed beyond its prime, the wine would long ago have been destroyed.

Many believers today are like collectors of old wines. At exorbitant personal cost—a lifetime of human energy: working, hustling, sacrificing, "doing great things for God"—they will end up with something that cannot be enjoyed as it was designed to be. Fine wine was made to drink, not merely to look at! Eternal life was imputed to you for you to participate in, not merely for you to talk about, no matter how glowing the terms.

Obviously, no believer will have to carry around "ruined wine" in heaven. There, eternal life will give even the reversionist capacity to have no regrets and to not be jealous or petty regarding the superior rewards of mature believers. At the very minimum, God will cause every member of the royal family to stand blameless in a perfect resurrection body, with perfect happiness and no remorse (Rom. 3:4; Jude 24; Rev. 21:4). But minimums are not the objective. God gave you the minimum at the moment you were saved! He *wants* to give you the maximum. That is why He keeps you alive on earth.

If God is free to bless you in time, you will receive rewards in heaven which will glorify Him forever—and your eternal life will provide the capacity to enjoy those rewards. If, however, He is not able to bless you in time, if you cut off His grace through negative volition or reversionism, He will not bless you in eternity. You will have no rewards, no decorations, no hundredfold harvest, no vast estates. You will be low on the totem pole in heaven. But being a comparative peon does not mean that you will be degraded or embarrassed. You will always be a member of Christ's magnificent royal family; some of its members will just be greater than others. Never forget that human equality is a myth, totally unnecessary for (and impossible in the presence of) either freedom or happiness. Just as there is no equality on earth, there will be none in heaven.

> For if by the transgression of the one [Adam's original sin], the [spiritual] death ruled through that one [Adam—and it did], much more they who receive in life this surplus from the grace of God [the blessings of time to the mature believer] and the gift of the righteousness of God [imputed at salvation], much more they shall rule through the One, Jesus Christ. (Rom. 5:17)

In one sentence, Paul spans the entire function of divine justice as God's point of contact with us. The complete plan of God is summarized: from the Fall of man, reiterated in every human birth, where the old sin nature rules by spiritual death, all the way to eternity future where members of the royal family will rule with Christ forever. In the Greek text, Romans 5:13–17 is a parenthesis; in it, the apostle stockpiles doctrine until he reaches verse 17 where he puts it all together in his second *a fortiori*.

In the King James rendering of Romans 5:17, a critical prepositional phrase has been linked to the wrong verb. It is amazing how one translator's error can completely obscure a passage! But this mistake is especially troublesome because it occurs at the very climax of Paul's great *a fortiori* argument. In the Greek, the phrase "in life" does not go with the verb "to rule" but with the verb "to receive." Believers do not *rule* in life; this is Satan's kingdom. Instead, we *receive* in life the imputed righteousness of God plus the subsequent blessings of spiritual maturity.

The "surplus from grace" is a superabundance of direct blessing from the justice of God. It is not confined to eternity; it is the current possession of every believer who cracks the maturity barrier. The primary and secondary potentials become realities *in time* when doctrine in the soul provides the capacity and security factors. Then God's righteousness in us demands that divine justice pour out supergrace blessings. Remember: what righteousness demands, justice executes. This outpouring of blessings from the justice of God, above and beyond the blessings of salvation, is eventually parlayed into an even greater abundance of grace, above and beyond the blessings of ultimate sanctification.

The inequality of blessings received by mature and immature believers will be apparent immediately after each of us returns to earth with Christ at His Second Advent. One of the few specifically stated eternal blessings for the royal family is that, with greater or less delegated authority, each of us will rule with Him during the Millennium (Rev. 5:10).

Be sure to understand that when Paul gives us an *a fortiori* glimpse of eternity as "the less" he is not talking about quantity or quality but about degree of effort. God does not give us less in heaven; He gives what is less difficult to provide! There, God does not have to contend with negative volition, the old sin nature, or Satan's evil tyranny. Therefore, where it is least complicated for Him to bless us, the blessings become so vast and wonderful that they go right off the chart of human comprehension. Any language of accommodation that represents them can only be an understatement of the facts. With our finite minds, we are unable to see beyond the fog; we cannot comprehend the specifics of heaven. But from our knowledge of how God's justice operates now, we are confident that the ultimate in blessing is as real as the bridge on which we travel.

IMPUTATION OF BLESSINGS IN TIME

TWO POTENTIAL IMPUTATIONS

It would have been impossible to explain the five basic imputations without referring to their purpose. God's purpose for our lives has been stated in some detail: blessing, blessing, and more blessing.

> Therefore, having been justified by faith, let us have prosperity face to face with God through our Lord Jesus Christ. (Rom. 5:1)

The hortatory subjunctive mood in the Greek expresses a command which encourages and enjoins voluntary compliance: "Let us have prosperity!'' This is not a simple statement in the indicative mood, as the King James translation suggests, nor is the noun *eirene* correctly rendered "peace." Like the Hebrew *shalom,* this Greek word of greeting means "prosperity."

To avoid distracting your attention from the five imputations common to all believers, I have waited until now to label the above-and-beyond blessings (John 10:10) of time and eternity for what they are. They are two more *imputations*—the sixth and seventh—from the justice of God.

Every human being is the beneficiary at birth of the first two imputations—human life to the soul and Adam's original sin to the old sin nature. Then, when anyone believes in Christ, he personally appropriates that third imputation—his personal sins to Christ on the Cross—plus, he receives the fourth and fifth imputations: God's righteousness and eternal life.

Every believer who has ever lived has been benefitted by all five of these actions from divine justice as his point of contact with God. But just as salvation carries the plan of God a stage beyond human birth and spiritual death, there is yet a stage beyond salvation. This is the realm of maximum blessing from the justice of God. For the unbeliever, salvation is merely a potential; likewise, special blessings are merely a potential for the immature believer. You are alive forever as a human being; you are saved forever as a believer in Jesus Christ; but you may or may not ever see the sixth and seventh imputations.

The sixth imputation occurs when the justice of God pours blessings through the grace pipeline to the righteousness of God in the mature believer. It is given only to the believer who, through doctrine, possesses capacity for blessings. This is a real imputation because there is an affinity between divine blessings and imputed divine righteousness.

Two *judicial* imputations were required before there could be any such *real* imputation of blessings in time. By believing in Christ, we, as it were, exchanged our sins for God's righteousness so that we actually possess half of the integrity of God. Only when we have His righteousness is there a home or target in us into which God can pour blessings when we reach spiritual maturity.

Righteousness in God demands righteousness in us. What God's righteousness accepts His justice blesses. Thus, the axiom stands unbroken even when God blesses *us:* the justice of God can bless only the righteousness of God. God is consistent and faithful; He prospers us only when, in doing so, He avoids all possibility of compromise to His character.

Special blessings in time fall into six categories: spiritual blessings, temporal blessings, blessings by association, historical blessings, blessings connected with undeserved suffering and, finally, dying blessings. We will briefly describe these categories to give you an idea of what the Word of God means by "let us have prosperity!"

SPIRITUAL BLESSINGS

All the spiritual blessings of supergrace are received by every mature believer. A person simply cannot have all that doctrine in his soul without being occupied with Christ, without having capacity for life, for love, for happiness, for blessing. The very status of maturity entails the imputation of a total appreciation for grace, of the ability to handle any disaster or tragedy that might come along, of the ability to interpret contemporary history, of freedom from slavery to the details of life, of adaptability to changing circumstances, of a sense of security regarding the plan of God for one's life.

In studying love$_2$, we noted that love for God is primarily a matter of thinking. As you reach maturity, your right lobe is saturated with doctrine; the Mind of Christ becomes your frame of reference; occupation with the Person of Christ becomes your viewpoint on life. If you were once continually petty, vindictive, implacable, jealous, and arrogant, these aberrations fall away under the very principle of focusing on the Lord. The self-induced misery caused by these mental attitude sins also disappears. You are freed from a lifetime of slavery to the "old program." Your priorities are untangled; your knowledge of the Word of God becomes a personal love for the Lord Jesus Christ. This personal love for Christ has repercussions toward people: a relaxed, impersonal love for all believers based on the strong norms and standards in your own soul. You find that you do not get upset over those with weak standards who malign you, gossip about you, and are generally obnoxious to you. You become thoughtful, tolerant, and considerate; you develop poise and common sense. You become absolutely inflexible regarding the essentials of doctrine but totally flexible on the nonessentials of application; thus, you develop true strength of soul. You can bend, but you never break.

Inordinate competition, ambition, and affections fall by the wayside. You are no longer disturbed, upset, or distracted by the pettiness and vindictiveness that you inevitably find in your daily contacts with people. You are released from the tyranny of continual mental attitude sins, and with the disappearance of these invisible chains on the soul comes freedom from slavery to verbal sins. The inner destructiveness of human good and evil is completely removed, and the damage is repaired. Spiritual blessings lay the groundwork for and continually support all the other categories of blessing.

TEMPORAL BLESSINGS

I approach the subject of temporal blessings with some trepidation. I know that I am going to overlook the particular blessing that God has in store for you. Then, when you crack the maturity barrier and receive that blessing, you will wonder what happened. Or, because you are not wealthy, or dreamily in love with your right man or right woman, or promoted above your peers, you will assume you are not mature. It is an occupational hazard of communicators of doctrine that those who listen might misapply what is taught. But we continue to press on, in spite of those few who are determined to distort and misuse the truth. For some, no amount of explaining will do.

The truth is that God treats us as individuals. His plan for our lives includes some blessing in every category but not necessarily all possible blessings, and certainly not identical blessings for every mature believer. There is no "maturity uniform." This might give you an inkling of God's disdain for the evil notion of "human equality." Some supergrace believers receive one thing, some another. One might have wealth, another just enough to pay the bills; but both are mature believers, and both are blessed in different ways in different circumstances. In every case however, there is something wonderful. God knows best what to give to whom, and God always gives the best.

Furthermore, spiritual maturity is not like Christmas morning when a person receives all his presents at once. Temporal blessings are poured out at maturity and *thereafter.* Remember that God necessarily wills the highest and the best for you; it is plain foolishness (to say nothing of blasphemy) for you to be jealous of specific blessings imputed to other believers but not to you. Do not worry if certain bounties of grace are not forthcoming to you at this particular moment; keep your eyes on the Lord Jesus Christ and save yourself some wear and tear. All the divine blessings imputed to mature believers glorify and please the Lord, and He knows how, through what He gives, to bring maximum glory and pleasure to Himself. So relax, continue to learn doctrine, and see the glory of God.

The temporal blessing prominent in many minds is wealth. Whether measured in dollars, in land, or in possessions, wealth is imputed in many cases. Abraham, David, and Solomon are Old Testament examples of men with fabulous personal riches. Imputed wealth may be received (as through inheritance) or acquired (as through moving up the ladder in business).

Although people may not consider acquired wealth to be an imputation from God, the mature believer himself sees his own situation from the divine viewpoint and knows the true Source. He knows that he can never claim to be a self-made man; even in the realm of the unbeliever's human effort, there is no such thing as a self-made man. Others are always involved in any individual's accumulation of wealth. The mature believer blessed with acquired wealth also knows that in the circumstances of life there are those variables beyond his control that might have just as easily gone the other way. Jesus Christ controls history; He controls these "variables" of life; and except for grace and the plan of God, even acquired wealth would prove elusive. When the justice of God does impute wealth to a mature believer as a blessing in time, that wealth is secure. We noted this principle in the life of David.

The mere possession of a fortune does not guarantee happiness, however. Spiritual blessing (capacity for prosperity) is what makes great riches a wonderful asset; the second category of blessings falls back on the first. This may include a special capacity for investment or for certain kinds of ownership or even a capacity for spending. When the necessary capacity develops as part of spiritual growth, the justice of God is free to impute wealth. Where capacity is lacking but wealth still exists (whether due to the free enterprise laws of establishment or as a blessing by association), the rich person is certainly not to be envied. Do not forget that there are two kinds of unhappy people in the world: the rich and the nonrich. But where capacity does exist, there are also two kinds of *happy* people: the rich and—that's right—the nonrich.

Now, there are many kinds of success, but some type will be imputed under the category of temporal blessings. Whatever it may be, it will be prominence in one's own sphere of life. If a person's sphere is growing petunias, he will become successful in the garden!

Promotion is yet another blessing for mature believers. God imputes advancement, but He never advances you beyond your capabilities. You might make an excellent office manager but a poor executive. In such a case, God recognizes that you would be out of your element and miserable in an executive position. Therefore, He will promote you into the realm of your capacity and divinely given abilities but no higher. Furthermore, you will move up without depending on "politics," without spending your time cultivating all the right people and saying all the right things.

Prosperity is a blessing that can be imputed into many spheres of life: not everyone is prosperous in the same areas. Social prosperity means having true friends. No one has more than a few real friends, but those exclusive few will usually be friends forever. We have noted that close friendships can be part of logistical grace, but with the richer capacity for life that comes as a spiritual blessing at maturity, the friendships included in social prosperity are even more wonderful and refreshing. Sexual prosperity is yet another temporal blessing, but limited to one man and one woman it is more exclusive than even social prosperity.[40]

Nearly everyone has some concept of wealth or of social and sexual prosperity. Technical prosperity, however, is not so obvious a category. It is the ability to excel in a profession such as science or engineering. Professional prosperity is imputed in the believer's profession, whatever it might

---

40. See Thieme, *Adam's Rib* and *Right Man-Right Woman.*

be: medicine, law, law enforcement, the military, teaching. One honorable profession that often goes unrecognized is that of being a waiter. Truly professional waiters are needed and appreciated, in spite of the untrue and cruel venom of the socialists who allege that it is somehow degrading to earn a living by waiting on and serving other people. I prefer the company of some of the fine waiters I know to that of many people who are so-called successful in life! Prosperity will come to the supergrace believer in his chosen professional field.

Mental prosperity is imputed as an offshoot of spiritual growth. A person cannot learn doctrine without at the same time developing his concentration and academic self-discipline. These are invaluable boons in life. Along with a widening frame of reference, they enhance the believer's ability to think, to exercise reason, to use common sense. The mental prosperity that comes with spiritual maturity raises the believer's IQ, increases his perceptiveness, and gives him an interest in many subjects in life which were previously unknown or unappealing to him.

Cultural prosperity involves maximum enjoyment of music, art, literature, drama, and history. Establishment prosperity is the protection of your freedom, privacy, and property, to include protection from crime and reprisal.

Leadership dynamics is an imputed blessing that is certainly not for everyone. The ability to lead others actually comes in various ways. It may be inherent at birth or acquired through diligent study and observation. It might also be acquired at the new birth as part of receiving one of the leadership spiritual gifts. But the ability to lead can also come as an imputation to the mature believer. If opportunities to lead, to assume authority, to take responsibility do not come your way, do not go out of your way to seek them. Inordinate ambition will only push you beyond God's will for your life. He will promote you when He is ready. If you have leadership ability, prepare, prepare, prepare! You will be given the chance to use it soon enough. And if you do not have this ability, do not feel left out; God has other blessings for you. The principle is that if God does not promote you, you are not promoted; but if God does promote you, you are definitely promoted (Ps. 75:6, 7; 1 Pet. 5:6).

Yet another sphere of blessing is good or improved health. Few people recognize its historical value. As personally important as good health may be to every individual, it has also made the difference in many strategic instances. For example, Napoleon's broken health kept him from coherently commanding the Waterloo Campaign. He lost that final battle even after winning two key preliminary victories at Quatre Bras and Ligny, which he, in earlier years and in better health, would never have allowed to slip unexploited through his hands.

Nervous energy is also an aspect of physical prosperity that few understand. Gaius Julius Caesar had a greater store of energy than perhaps anyone else who has ever lived; he was highly successful in seven or eight diverse fields of endeavor. Ranked among the greatest captains of all history, he did not even begin to devote himself to the military profession until he was nearly fifty years old. Moses was another man of prodigious nervous energy. His accomplishments were phenomenal as a soldier, a writer, an administrator, an architect, an engineer, a ruler, a composer, a man of God. When 120 years old, he ran circles around men a quarter his age! Everyone's metabolism is subject to change from time to time; how nice to have it cranked up a notch or two as a divine imputation!

The concept of temporal blessings, the second category of imputed blessings to the mature believer in time, is summed up in Paul's prayer in Ephesians.

> And come to know [maturity comes through knowledge
> of doctrine] the surpassing-knowledge love of Christ [oc-
> cupation with the person of Christ] that you might be
> filled up with all the fullness of God [the real imputation
> of blessings to mature believers on earth]. Now to the
> One, Himself being able far beyond all things to do in-
> finitely more than that which we could be asking or im-
> agining according to the power [of the Word of God] be-
> ing itself effective in us, to Him be glory [God is glorified
> by these imputations] in the Church [royal family] and in
> Jesus Christ with reference to all generations [these bless-
> ings are available to every generation of believers] forever
> and ever [blessings in time have eternal repercussions].
> (Eph. 3:19–21)

BLESSINGS BY ASSOCIATION

A great advantage of spiritual maturity is that others are blessed through association with you. Blessings overflow to those in your periphery.

Since no one in a local congregation can exceed the spiritual growth of his pastor-teacher, the overflow of prosperity inevitably begins with the pastor. The pastor continually, doggedly studies and teaches, not only so he can personally grow beyond supergrace$_A$ into supergrace$_B$ and farther yet into ultra-supergrace, but also so his flock can grow up too. If the pastor is mature, the members of his congregation will be blessed in two ways by association with him. First, directly: they will receive his faithful communication of Bible doctrine. Second, indirectly: their association with him, merely as faces in his congregation, will bring them their own blessings from God.

These direct and indirect aspects hold true of all blessing by association. On one hand, the mature believer is given so much that he can help those whom he wishes to help, or his blessings are such that they automatically spill over to his friends, relatives, and associates. On the other hand, he is blessed with the knowledge that those dear to him are prospered and protected in a special way by God personally—out of respect for the doctrine in his soul.

Let us cite some examples. The spiritual periphery is not simply pastor to congregation; mature believers in the congregation are also a source of prosperity for the entire organization. In the realm of loved ones, supergrace parents are a blessing to their children. The children will be blessed whether or not they reach spiritual maturity themselves. They will be blessed all their lives, even if they remain unbelievers. Blessing by association will continue after their parents have gone to be with the Lord. In the midst of the unfairness and uncertainties of the devil's world, the most secure inheritance that parents can leave to their sons and daughters is to personally keep taking in doctrine and to crack the maturity barrier. We cannot hope to "make the world a better place for our children." We *can* confidently entrust them to God's special care as children of supergrace heroes!

If the parents are not mature believers but the children are, blessing by association goes the other way: the supergrace son or daughter will be a cause of blessing to the entire family. Even the family pets are blessed!

If a mature believer works in a school, in a hospital, on a police force, in a military organization, in a symphony orchestra, in a law firm—in any legitimate organization that involves a number of people in coordinated activity—that organization will be blessed by association. A few spiritually mature police officers doing their jobs as unto the Lord can bless the entire force. Blessing by association can offset the effects of unrealistic department policies. This is blessing in the professional periphery.

In the business world, believers associated with a company or industry can be the basis for its prosperity. This includes investors, management, and labor. The board of directors may congratulate themselves on increased profits that, actually, God provided because of the doctrine in an ultra-supergrace night watchman! Likewise, in the social realm, one mature believer in a circle of friends can mean blessing for the entire group or club. And any geographical area—from neighborhood to city to county to state to nation—is blessed by the presence of the mature believers who live or work there.

HISTORICAL IMPACT

What can we conclude from this doctrine of blessing by association to the believer's geographical area, particularly to his nation? The natural and true conclusion is that the most significant event in the history of any generation is when a believer attains spiritual maturity.

This is not a statement made in haste. It does not overlook the truly important, world-changing events that periodically take place; nor does it ignore the trends of history. The trends of today find national liberty in a decline and Communist barbarism on the rise. Civilization is receding. The Soviets rattle the saber while talking of peace. Our backward, Communist-emboldened enemies in the so-called "Third World" bare their teeth. National leaders around the world make evil policies that affect millions. Armies march under the banners of tyranny—all while the alleged champions of freedom look the other way. But more significant to God than anything else in this tinderbox of contemporary history is a believer joining other mature believers in what is called "the remnant according to the election of grace" (Rom. 11:5). Because of this nucleus of mature believers, God stabilizes and prospers a nation.

There are many human interpretations of history. Some are patently absurd; most are built around a grain or two of truth. The Bible, however, presents God's interpretation of history. Although the Bible itself is not a history textbook, it records many historical events in order to teach spiritual lessons. It sometimes sheds the only light extant upon obscure but critical events. One man, Shamgar, for example, diverted the tide of the Greek Sea Peoples. Their mass movement disrupted the entire world circa 1200 B.C., and only the Bible explains why Israel was not inundated along with her neighbors (Judges 3:31). Likewise, the first few chapters of Genesis record events that are suggested in extrabiblical sources but are accurately presented only in the pages of Scripture.

The Word of God reveals divine viewpoint and delineates the principles of divine establishment. It thus supplies the frame of reference which is indispensable for understanding the facts of past and present history (and even of future history, called prophecy). A person may know historical facts, but to properly, accurately, and objectively interpret them, he requires a true frame of reference, a set of principles related to reality—in other words, Bible doctrine resident in his soul. A believer must understand how history is related to God, to the unseen world of the angels, and to the visible world of mankind. If his understanding of divine establishment is limited, so is his perspicacity in the field of history. He must be able to distinguish true morality from human good, sin from crime, and sin from evil. He must be thoroughly versed in such categories of doctrine as the angelic conflict, the Cross, the two Advents of Christ, the essence of God, the divine decrees, the civilizations and dispensations—to include all the specifics of the Age of the Royal Family of God. In short, he must understand history and his own place in history in the light of God's objectives for the individual and the nation.

The spiritual interpretation of history is the only accurate and true one because it alone properly relates history to the One who controls history, the Lord Jesus Christ Himself.

Our Lord controls history three ways: directly, through His divine essence; indirectly, through our voluntary compliance with the laws of divine establishment; and permissively, by allowing the angelic conflict and negative volition to run their course. According to the fourth divine institution under the laws of establishment, God has divided the human race into nations. Internationalism is never sponsored by God. Always, among the nations of the earth, one country (or more) is a center of positive volition in that generation and serves as a priest nation or client nation to God (Ex. 19:6). There, freedom is protected, Bible doctrine is preserved and taught, evangelism flourishes, missionaries are sent out to other areas of the world, and a haven is provided for the Jews. Founded upon or operating on Biblical principles, client nations have a spiritual heritage, and God watches over them more closely than over other nations. That is, blessing comes in greater abundance, but national discipline is also more rapid and severe for the generation that abuses its spiritual birthright.

When a client nation compromises the laws of establishment until reversionism and evil become the order of the day, that nation reaps divine punitive action. All nations in Satan's world eventually succumb, some lasting far longer than others. Today, the United States is in this tragic, self-created predicament. Our founding fathers developed a Constitution designed to limit government to its true Biblical functions. But after two centuries, personal freedom, privacy, and property have become the objects of governmental encroachment and attack rather than objects of governmental protection. In only a few local churches is Bible doctrine faithfully taught. We still have the freedom to evangelize, but evangelists almost universally present false issues and distort the Gospel. Our missionaries all too often export nothing but legalism or socialism. Only our relatively consistent, positive attitude toward the Jews and Israel stands in our favor, and even that seems to be wavering.

The storm clouds of divine discipline, therefore, loom above us. From horizon to horizon, everywhere we look the picture is dark. In fact, the decline of this nation has passed the point where human solutions might turn us around. The only hope for the United States and the only light in the storm is the imputation of historical blessings to mature believers.

Mature believers live in the eye of the hurricane, in the security of encapsulated environment; they are the pivot, while reversionistic believers are the spin-off. The pivot is the remnant of mature believers in any national entity. The spin-off represents believers under the influence of evil in some stage of reversionism.

If the pivot is large enough, the nation will be preserved. If the pivot is too small and the spin-off too great, the nation will be destroyed while the mature believers of the pivot are preserved (Ps. 33:17–22; Isa. 36, 37; Jer. 40:4ff). Supergrace believers are the "salt of the land" (Matt. 5:13), the preservative of their nation.

Historical blessing is imputed to mature believers in the pivot during periods of national prosperity as well as in times of catastrophe and national decline. Indeed, national prosperity reflects a large pivot: divine blessing comes to the nation because of its mature believers. On the other hand, historical disaster reflects a small pivot: the winds of personal and collective discipline rise against the client nation whose believers are in reversionism.

Thus, we as believers have the potential for far greater historical impact—either positive or negative—than do even the famous and influential leaders of our day. We may not be noticed, known, or remembered by men, but God is the One who takes cognizance. Just as He respects His own righteousness in us, so also He can only honor His own Word when He sees it in our souls. Then, not only does He implement our capacity of soul with great personal blessings but, as one category of special blessings in time, He prospers our nation as well.

In the unsettled times in which we live, it is the grave responsibility of every believer to advance to maturity. This is the essential contribution of each believer to his nation. Perhaps you have heard speakers or read books or articles on our declining momentum as a nation. Our national vulnerability has shocked you; the inevitability of a historical shake-up with all its horrifying hardships and personal tragedies has frightened you. What can you do? What can one person do? Writing letters to congressmen, casting your vote, perhaps even running for office—these are your rights and are the proper means of citizen expression in our system of government. But you have written repeatedly, and still the trends of evil have not turned around. You are certainly not to go beyond the bounds of establishment; that would merely hasten our fall. Your job is to get into the eye of the rapidly intensifying storm and stay there.

And do not worry; the storm in this illustration is different from an actual hurricane: this eye will not move. Only you can move. Only your negative volition toward doctrine can carry you out of the pivot and into the spin-off. If you stay in the pivot, you do so because you are consistently, daily, perseveringly positive to the Word of God. There, under the principle of encapsulated environment, you will be in a place of perfect blessing no matter what the historical conditions happen to be.

UNDESERVED SUFFERING

WHY MATURE BELIEVERS SUFFER

You might be surprised to find suffering on a list of divine blessings. In fact, you might be a little apprehensive! "What does God have in store for me?" you ask. "I thought He wanted to bless me! I can find plenty of suffering without going all the way to maturity looking for it!"

God does want to bless you. But even unbelievers recognize, at least to a limited degree, the relationship between suffering and blessing. A Latin aphorism says, "Misfortune does not always come to injure."

God is indeed glorified in our lives by sending special blessings down the grace pipeline, but the supergrace believer's prosperity *and* his undeserved suffering both come from the same perfect Source—the justice of God. Both come through the pipeline. Both add up to the same thing: blessing.

The difference is that blessing comes under varying circumstances; some pleasant, some painful. When blessings come to us under pleasant circumstances, we naturally tend to focus our attention on the blessings. But when difficult, painful circumstances come along, the discomfort forces us to look beyond the present and to anticipate the fantastic prosperity in store for us in the next stage of God's plan. Thus, something is provided that would otherwise be lacking. While still enjoying the pleasures and blessings of life on earth, we are given an ignition system to crank up our confident anticipation of blessings and rewards in eternity.

Romans 8:18–27 is a discourse on undeserved suffering; it is structured around three "groans." First, as an analogy, nature is said to groan (Rom. 8:18–22), innocently sharing the curse of Adam's original sin (Gen. 3:17). Second, the mature believer literally groans under undeserved suffering (Rom. 8:23–25). And finally, as a parenthesis, an anthropopathism of groaning is ascribed to the Holy Spirit in His ministry of intercession for the suffering mature believer (Rom. 8:26, 27). The "groans" of nature and of God the Holy Spirit are vital and interesting subjects, but we must pass them by in this study because we are working up to an examination of Romans 8:28. The context of that famous, often misapplied verse is the groaning of the mature believer in Romans 8:23–25.

> And not only [nature] but also ourselves [who are mature
> believers], although possessing the firstfruits from the

> Spirit, even we groan within ourselves, eagerly an-
> ticipating the adoption, that is, the resurrection of our
> body. (Rom. 8:23)

The Greek verb *echo* in this verse is a concessive participle, translated "although possessing." The "firstfruits from the Spirit" are tantamount to the real imputation of blessings at maturity. *Pneuma,* "from the Spirit," is in the ablative of source. This grammatical form implies that an original situation has contributed in some way to the present situation: here, the ind-welling and filling ministries of the Holy Spirit, as related to GAP, have brought about the state of maturity in which divine blessings are imputed to the supergrace believer.

When something is said to come first, it always suggests that something more will follow. Thus, "the firstfruits from the Spirit" depict both of Paul's *a fortiori* arguments. The "firstfruits" themselves are the six categories of blessing in time. (We are now studying category five: unde-served suffering.) These blessings are a downpayment on rewards and bless-ings which will follow in eternity. The term "firstfruits" declares the first *a fortiori* and implies the second. Mature believers who possess special bless-ings in time simply illustrate the fact that it is easier for God to bless us after salvation than it was for Him to save us in the first place. And if God can bless us in time, it follows with greater reason that He will not hesitate to bless us in eternity. Thus, blessings on earth guarantee the reality of the blessings in store for us in heaven. The firstfruits from the Spirit are the best things in life; they give the supergrace believer his first taste of what is to come.

Perhaps it never occurred to you before, but the Lord Jesus Christ is glorified by the best things in life! These wonderful things are parlayed into eternal rewards that will glorify Him *forever.*

I return to this point and dwell on it again because I want you to see the picture: whatever the mature believer receives from the Lord in time is designed to glorify Him in time, in the angelic conflict. But that is only part of the picture. In fact, that is a *small* part of the picture. Time is a mere drop in the bucket compared to eternity and, according to Paul's *a fortiori* ex-planation, the blessings of eternity will be infinitely greater than those in time. As a result of glorifying the Lord Jesus Christ now, you will be given things that will glorify Him forever and ever—after the entire angelic conflict has become ancient history, a matter long since resolved and no longer an issue.

That is what we are doing on earth. That distant future is why we are alive today, tomorrow, the next day, and the next. We are doing something now to glorify Him forever. And what are we doing? We are daily taking in doctrine under the teaching ministry of the Holy Spirit so we can gradually conform our thinking to the mind of Christ, so we can crack the maturity barrier, so we can receive blessings in time and eventually be blessed in eternity.

Now, many people do not understand that suffering is an integral part of this system of blessing and happiness. We naturally tend to associate happiness with what we consider to be pleasant circumstances. But, under God's permissive will, we experience both pleasant and unpleasant circumstances in the devil's world; this has been a characteristic of *cosmos diabolicus* since Satan took over at the Fall of man. Like a road that winds through delightfully cool mountains, descends periodically to the sweltering desert floor, then rises again into the highlands, so our life's journey takes us in and out of pleasant circumstances, in and out of suffering.

When people suffer, usually they squirm, they toss, they search for greener pastures, hoping that a change of environment will alleviate the pain and bring happiness. But God declares that the details and circumstances of life are of no consequence. Whether you suffer as an individual, as a member of a group, or as part of a national disaster, God converts even the desert experiences into great blessing. Indeed, He does not passively relegate such experiences to His permissive will. He takes a direct hand in the matter by providing undeserved suffering as a real imputation from His justice to His righteousness in the mature believer. He provides the suffering as well as the blessing in that suffering. It is fair because it is from His justice. And like all blessings that come down the grace pipeline, it is not earned or deserved.

The customary present tense of *stenazo,* "to groan," denotes what habitually occurs or what is reasonably expected to occur when the believer is given undeserved suffering. The pain is real: suffering, to be suffering, must hurt. But its purpose is not to persecute you, not to trap you, not to detract from your blessings, not to enslave you to the suffering and, being unearned, not to punish or discipline you.

We must distinguish undeserved suffering from divine discipline which *is* punitive. Only mature believers, or those being tested at the threshold of maturity, are able to receive undeserved suffering along with the other blessings of supergrace status. Both mature and immature believers, however, have old sin natures and are liable for discipline when they sin. When suffering is disciplinary, rebound is the solution to be used by both the immature and the mature believer. At the point of rebound, God may remove the suffering, reduce it, or perpetuate it at current intensity. Whatever suffering may continue after rebound is designed for the believer's benefit.

"Although possessing the firstfruits from the Spirit," we still suffer. God's purpose is to demonstrate that no circumstance of life is greater than His plan, that the power of God is greater than the power of the ruler of this world. And how does God demonstrate His power? Through your application of Bible doctrine resident in your soul. By thus sustaining you under pressure, He wins another tactical victory in the angelic conflict.

But the imputation of undeserved suffering does more than defeat Satan; at the same time it benefits the believer. The believer's function in life is spiritual growth. When the hardships and difficulties of suffering force the believer to draw upon his inner resources of doctrine, his growth is accelerated. If a believer maintains his momentum and refuses to be distracted from doctrine, knowing that the suffering comes as a blessing from God, he exercises his spiritual muscles and gains spiritual strength.

One of the growing believer's most difficult tests is to endure suffering while a reversionist prospers (Ps. 37:1, 7). The reversionist's prosperity may be blessing by association; it may be pseudo-blessing from Satan's resources as the ruler of the world. Or, it may be designed specifically by God to test the growing believer. Will he get his eyes on the reversionist and become jealous? Will antagonism or bitterness neutralize his own spiritual dynamics? Will pressure cause him to seek overt prosperity rather than continued spiritual advance? Or will he say with Job, "Though he slay me, yet will I trust in him" (Job 13:15)? Satan is keenly interested in the outcome of this testing; God, too, is certainly interested; but the believer is the winner. He develops an application of doctrine that binds him to the mast more securely than ever before!

The supergrace hero remembers that no matter what the source of the reversionist's prosperity, his lack of capacity destroys any possibility of enjoying what he has. Often, the only reason God keeps a reversionist alive is to serve as a test or a training aid for advancing believers (Prov. 16:3, 4). That is not exactly the highest Christian calling. Despite all appearances, therefore, the reversionist is certainly no one to envy.

There is yet more behind the imputation of undeserved suffering to the mature believer. Periods of suffering make periods of prosperity more wonderful by contrast. As Paul says, "I know both how to be abased, and I know how to abound" (Phil. 4:12). Both the best and the worst come to the mature believer. If he can take the worst in life, he can certainly take the best. The extremes demonstrate the capacity, stability, and confidence of spiritual maturity.

But greater yet is the contrast in the very midst of the suffering itself. The contrast between painful external surroundings and the inner wealth of divine viewpoint only intensifies the believer's occupation with Christ; it makes more vivid all of the believer's spiritual blessings. Since the mature believer's capacity insures that no disaster can trap him, God is free to impute disaster to him from time to time as a blessing that increases his appreciation for God and accelerates his spiritual growth.

To prove the sufficiency of God, to defeat Satan, to accelerate spiritual growth, to test the believer's perspective, to bless through contrast—even these are not the full story behind the believer's undeserved suffering. In Romans 8:23, "eagerly anticipating" is the Greek verb *apekdechomai,* used by Paul in the sense of confident expectation. This total confidence is the attitude of the mature believer under undeserved suffering. What is the object of thought that gives such an attitude? "Adoption" is a technical term defined in context as the believer's ultimate sanctification: "the redemption of our body." This is not to be confused with the redemption of the soul. Salvation through faith in Christ redeems the soul; resurrection at the Rapture redeems the body. Until that occurs, periodic undeserved suffering in the physical body will stimulate the mature believer's confident, eager anticipation of receiving the resurrection body in eternity.

Thus, undeserved suffering is designed to intensify the mature believer's focus on the fantastic future rewards of heaven. Such a focus, developed under pressure and carried over into periods of prosperity, stabilizes the believer in life. Indeed, the anticipation of eternity motivates the mature believer to persistently, continually pursue greater and greater knowledge of the Word of God. As contradictory as it may seem at first glance, undeserved suffering in time is actually a downpayment on eternity where suffering is impossible (Rev. 21:4): the supremely confident mental attitude that can face even maximum suffering without flinching is the closest that anyone on earth can possibly come to experiencing the mental dynamics of heaven. Obviously this is not for anyone but the mature believer with a soul saturated with Bible doctrine. God's objective in imputing undeserved suffering is definitely not to cause the believer to crack (1 Cor. 10:13). As a downpayment on eternal blessings, paid only to mature believers who have the capacity to handle it, such suffering is a guarantee of those future rewards.

Remember that undeserved suffering is one category of blessings in time. The blessings are phenomenal; they are "the things God has prepared for those who love Him." If only prosperity and pleasant circumstances were imputed to the mature believer, he might be in danger. Prosperity is a test many people cannot pass. If he received nothing but prosperity, he would become so caught up in his wealth, his promotions, his social and sexual prosperity, his blessing by association to others around him, his historical impact, that he would be in danger of forgetting from whence these blessings came. But just as God does not impute suffering to overpower and destroy a believer, neither does He design prosperity to drive a believer away from doctrine.

Here is yet another demonstration of the justice of God and, here is one further reason for undeserved suffering. In the midst of wonderful things, the pain of undeserved suffering serves as a reminder of grace. The truth dawns on you, and you say, "I'm not going to be under this pressure forever!

All the blessings I receive here on earth come from God, and He alone will be the Source of even more blessings in the future.''

You see, undeserved suffering gets your attention. Once it has your attention, it reminds you that you have a glorious future. Thus, the mature believer does not scramble to escape the pressure; he does not go on a frantic search for happiness; he does not make excuses to his friends; he does not run out and explain the situation to those who malign him. He takes the suffering as it comes, as from the Lord. Obviously, no normal person seeks suffering or enjoys the pain itself, but when even intense suffering can be only a blessing, the believer is on top of life. He is riding the crest of the wave. Such a blessing acts as a laser beam that penetrates the barriers of time and illuminates the fantastic future riches of eternity. The wisdom of God is absolutely remarkable in knowing exactly how to bless those who have the capacity for blessing!

INTRODUCTION TO HOPE

> For with reference to that hope [of future resurrection at
> the Rapture of the Church] we have been saved. . . .
> (Rom. 8:24a)

We were saved for the purpose of having a glorious future, and the believers in Romans 8:24 have their eyes on that future.

Unfortunately the English word ''hope'' often connotes ignorance. For example, if someone is asked ''Will you go to heaven when you die?'' and answers ''I hope so,'' he means that he does not know for sure. This is a pitiful status: ignorance of basic doctrine.

When the Word of God, whether in Hebrew or Greek, refers to eternity as the believer's ''hope,'' it always means cognizance, never ignorance; always confidence, never uncertainty. Several Hebrew nouns and verbs are related to hope or trust. They are best translated ''confidence; confident trust, anticipation, or expectation''; they all connote a sense of security in something greater than we are. Generally, that ''something greater'' is the integrity of God. Man counts on God for future blessings.

New Testament vocabulary for ''hope'' conveys the same meanings as the Old. In classical Greek, *elpis,* ''hope,'' expressed the popular idea that human existence was defined not merely by the present but by the past and future as well. Thinking of the past was called ''memory''; thinking of the future, ''hope.''

Paul was a genius, an *educated* genius. From his rich academic background he picked up the word *elpis,* popularized by Plato and others, and applied it to the Word of God. But whereas the classical writers had used *elpis* in one of two ways—looking ahead to either good or bad—Paul uses it only in the positive sense—anticipating good. Throughout the koine Greek of the New Testament, "hope" carries the nuance of counting on something, of looking forward to something, of expecting something wonderful and beneficial. Hope is assurance and comfort in relation to future things.

> . . . Now, when a hope is seen, it is not a hope. So who hopes for what he sees? (Rom. 8:24*b*)

This verse defines hope as a *future* prospect, as the anticipation of something not yet present. When that hope is fulfilled—when that future event becomes a present reality—it is no longer a hope.

From our study of Bible doctrine, we know that certain things are coming up for us personally in the plan of God. We know the next objective that God has designed for us to reach. The confidence that we will reach that objective if we follow the procedure laid out in the Word of God is what is meant by hope. Hope is eager anticipation in approaching a goal. As soon as we reach the goal, however, our hope ceases to be a hope. No longer confidence in the unseen future, it has become enjoyment of present experience! And where do we go from there? Do we remain in limbo? No. From that new reality, we continue to advance in the plan of God by moving toward the *next* objective. We have a new hope. God always replaces one hope with a new hope as soon as the reality comes to pass. He never leaves us "hopeless" or without an objective in life; He always points the way to greater and greater blessings. We might even describe progress and momentum in the spiritual life as being "from hope to hope to hope." This progression finally culminates in eternity when we have the ultimate as reality and no longer need a hope.

Let us get down to specifics. There are three hopes in the plan of God. We might picture them as steps in a staircase. We all started on the bottom floor when human life was imputed to our souls and Adam's original sin to our old sin natures. When we heard the Gospel as unbelievers, we had hope of salvation. We had confidence that we could be saved through simple faith in Christ. But the moment we acted upon that hope and believed in Christ, the hope ceased to be a hope; it became a reality: we *were* eternally saved. The hope of salvation was left behind; the reality had taken its place. We were permanently entered into the royal family of God, but like everyone else, we entered as immature believers.

The new hope to replace the old—the second hope to replace the first—is now the prospect of cracking the maturity barrier, of being blessed in time, of therein glorifying the Lord Jesus Christ. This second hope becomes the objective of the Christian way of life. We have total confidence

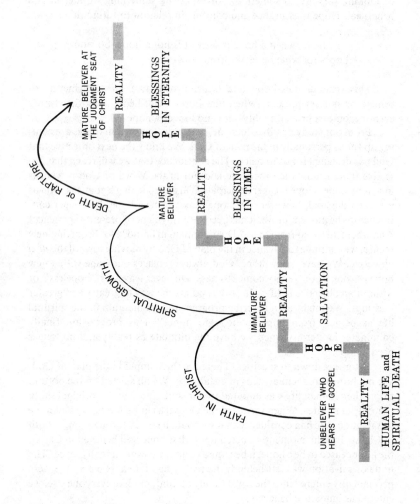

that if we persist in learning doctrine we will develop the capacity for the sixth imputation, special blessings here on earth, and as we grow, we eagerly anticipate receiving the things He has designed for us.

But once we attain spiritual maturity and begin to receive the wonderful bounties of our supergrace paragraphs, the second hope becomes a reality. Again, a hope has ceased to be a hope. What comes next in the plan of God? What is our goal for the rest of our lives as mature believers? The third hope is the confident assurance of rewards and blessings in heaven which will glorify God forever.

In explaining undeserved suffering as a category of the mature believer's blessings in time, we have come across a doctrine that lies at the heart of our relationship to the integrity of God. Unless we understand the doctrine of hope, we cannot orient to the plan of God: hope anticipates the function of God's integrity. As our study of divine integrity continues to unfold, we will develop a complete doctrine of hope which will become a touchstone of confidence in life.

> Now, if we hope for what we do not see [and we do],
> through fortitude we stand in eager anticipation. (Rom.
> 8:25)

The question is, Of the three hopes in the plan of God, which is in view here? The answer, hope₃. Undeserved suffering is a category of blessing imputed to the *mature* believer to act as a supercharger on his anticipation of future reality.

Romans 8:23-25 is not a description of just any believer. Since most believers of the present generation are tragically immature, Romans 8:25 actually describes only a relative few. The immature believer has no bulwark of doctrine in his soul to give him fortitude under pressure. His suffering is self-induced misery, divine discipline for reversionism, or the simple inability of his human resources to cope with the vagaries of the devil's world. He has no capacity to weather the storm, let alone to be blessed by it. But the mature believer not only benefits from undeserved suffering, he periodically requires it. Otherwise he might allow the fantastic blessings of time to eclipse eternal issues. The mature believer maintains his momentum in both prosperity and suffering by drawing upon the categorical doctrine in his soul. The mature believer alone has fortitude in time of crisis. And more than fortitude, he has eager anticipation of the yet unseen rewards and blessings which he knows will be imputed to his resurrection body in heaven. He is totally, unshakeably confident. As painful as his undeserved suffering might be, it merely causes him to rejoice in the fact that life on earth is not permanent. He knows unequivocally that his divine blessings in time guarantee that he will be phenomenally blessed in eternity.

DYING GRACE

Dying grace is the sixth and final category of blessing that God imputes to the mature believer in time. The curse of death with its fear and pain is completely removed; death itself becomes a blessing worthy to conclude a life of blessings. Death for the mature believer is not the desert but the dessert of life. Indeed, dying grace finds the supergrace believer standing confidently atop the vantage point of tremendous blessings in time with his eyes on the wonderful prospects of eternity; he then crosses the high golden bridge into heaven—from one prosperity to the next! You can see why death holds no terror for him.

I have elsewhere addressed in detail the subject of dying grace;[41] but, briefly, it is God's final opportunity to bless the mature believer on earth, an opportunity that God always exploits to the maximum.

> Precious in the sight of the Lord is the death of His godly
> ones. (Ps. 116:15, AV)

The mature believer has the best in life, better in death and even better in eternity. God chooses the time and manner of death for every believer, and in every case His decision is perfect, not to be maligned or doubted by those left behind.

For the top echelon of supermature believers, God sometimes combines categories five and six of imputed blessings in time: undeserved suffering plus dying. In this connection, the highest honor He can bestow upon a Christian in the devil's world is the transfer from time to eternity via martyrdom. Such a combination of blessings can be given only where great capacity of soul exists.

Indeed, the imputation of martyrdom to the ultra-supergrace believer is even more rare than are ultra-supergrace believers themselves! On this point we have become sloppy in our interpretation of history. For example, those first-century Christians who were thrown to the lions or burned alive to provide outdoor lighting for Nero's garden parties are all traditionally called "martyrs." In the technical sense of the word, many were not martyrs at all.

As is well attested in the New Testament epistles, the early churches were seedbeds for some of the worst imaginable distortions of doctrine. In passage after passage, false doctrine is refuted and this or that brand of legalism or antinomianism is exposed. Most of the so-called martyrs were simply reversionists receiving maximum divine discipline—the sin unto death. This is the alternative to dying grace. Instead of being "precious in the sight of the

---

41. See Thieme, *Dying Grace.*

Lord," it is an unpleasant task for God to have to administer final discipline to the reversionistic believer. No high golden bridge for him: he transfers to heaven via the low road of maximum pain and misery, the thousand-yard low crawl over ground glass. Judging by their rejection of Bible doctrine, most believers prefer this route, at least most believers in this generation.

In all of Church history the number of believers who have been honored with martrydom is much smaller than is commonly assumed. Paul was certainly one of that elite fraternity. From the day he first realized that this time he would not be released from prison in Rome, he enjoyed the stimulation of knowing that he would soon be with the Lord. During those final few weeks of confident anticipation, he wrote his second epistle to Timothy, a great man's last words. In that book, he expresses no panic, no loss of capacity for life, no regrets for past failures, no mental attitude sins against those who had just committed perjury against him (2 Tim. 4:14-16), no complaints that he had been condemned before being tried (2 Tim. 2:9). He does not advocate demonstrations or call for the overthrow of the government that treated him unfairly. Instead, he recognizes the importance of establishment; he knows that even in history's most unjust and evil moments, Jesus Christ is still in control. Paul remembers his friends; he sends for his favorite books and for his warm coat so that he can be as comfortable as possible. He issues instructions for the continued spread of doctrine and relaxes in his intensified hope that is about to be fulfilled.

Then, on the appointed day in the spring of A.D. 68, he was escorted through the gates of the Mamertine prison and out along the Via Appia toward the coast. Stopping somewhere between Rome and the bustling seaport of Ostia, Paul watched the lictor unbind the ax from the fasces. Then Paul knelt and was beheaded.

Decapitation is painless. The nerves are simply cut—cleanly, quickly. The only possible problem is mental anguish in anticipation, but that was no problem to Paul. The greatest apostle, the man who had "fought the good fight," "finished the course," and "guarded the doctrine," departed from the body with highest honors to be face to face with the Lord.

IMPUTATION OF REWARDS IN ETERNITY

THE FINAL EVALUATION

When the Lord Jesus Christ evaluates the lives of believers and rewards them accordingly, He does so as a Judge, as the Chief Justice of the supreme court of heaven (John 5:22). He functions as a Judge because all divine blessings, in fact all imputations, come from the *justice* of God. God is glorified in demonstrating His ability to bless man totally without compromise to divine righteousness. He is glorified to the ultimate by what He will give in that final imputation.

In all real (as opposed to judicial) imputations, two factors are required: factor one, what is imputed; factor two, its home or target. In the seventh imputation, the mature believer's hope becomes reality when eternal rewards and blessings—factor one—are credited to his resurrection body—factor two. His hope in time has a double focus: toward his surpassing-grace blessings and toward his resurrection body. Each of these two factors is called a hope (Eph. 1:18; Acts 23:6).

In order to anchor his confidence in this future reality, the mature believer must be familiar with the sequence of events leading up to and immediately following his final evaluation. No matter when he dies, he will not be evaluated until he receives his resurrection body. The real imputation of rewards and blessings cannot take place until a home or target has been prepared for them. No Church Age believer will be evaluated until the entire royal family has been formed. Only then will the resurrection or Rapture take place. In that moment, each member of the royal family receives a body exactly like Christ's resurrection body, free from the old sin nature, free from good and evil.

But if resurrection will not occur until the end of the Church Age, what happens to Church Age believers who die prior to the Rapture? Remember that the believer's real self is his soul and human spirit. The body is simply a house or temporary residence for the real person. The departed Church Age believer's soul and human spirit, with human life and eternal life intact, dwell in heaven with the Lord (2 Cor. 5:1-6; 1 Thess. 5:23). Each individual is fully conscious; indeed, no longer limited by the mortal body, his perceptive ability is enhanced. He is completely recognizable and perfectly happy—but as yet minus a resurrection body.

At the Rapture, these billions of Church Age believers, called "the dead in Christ," will accompany the Lord from heaven to a rendezvous in space

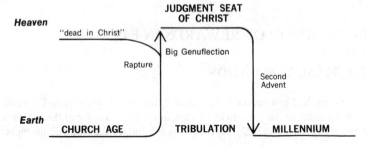

above the earth, where they will be joined by the living generation of believers. There they will receive their resurrection bodies (1 Thess. 4:14–17; 1 Cor. 15:51–54).

Immediately after the Rapture, there will be a period of fantastic happiness and celebration, a "reunion" of the entire royal family, assembled for the first time in spontaneous mass recognition of Christ. I call this the big genuflection.

> For it stands written, as I keep on living, and by myself I
> have sworn: every knee shall bow to me [Christ], and
> every tongue shall confess to God [the Father]. (Rom.
> 14:11)

This time of worship and of breaking into song will culminate as Christ leads the entire royal procession back to heaven. With the Church Age completed, the interrupted Age of Israel will resume for its final seven years, known in eschatology as the Tribulation. While the Tribulation unfolds on earth, Jesus Christ will prepare His Bride to accompany Him in His Second Advent. "The Bride of Christ" is the title for the royal family in heaven (Rev. 19:7–9; 22:17), just as "the Body of Christ" is one of its titles on earth (Col. 1:18). At the Second Advent, the King of Kings will return to overthrow Satan and to establish His personal thousand-year reign over the devil's former kingdom.

In this future sequence of events, an almost shocking contrast comes when the initial celebration and maximum esprit de corps of the big genuflection suddenly gives away to grave solemnity. The Lord Jesus Christ will convene court.

> So then every one of us shall give account of himself to
> God. (Rom. 14:12)

In this life we plug along, we plod, we become involved in routine, we take in doctrine today, tomorrow, the next day, and the next (or we should). We meet all kinds of tests, distractions, and problems, but we keep going, keep concentrating, "keep on keeping on" one day at a time. There is no flash in the pan, no special recognition, no fanfare. The years pass, and suddenly life is over. Then comes the big question: What did we accomplish?

Just as salvation has an issue, What do you think of Christ? (Matt. 22:42), so life after salvation has an issue, What do you think of doctrine?

> For as [a man] thinks in his heart [right lobe], so is
> he. . . . (Prov. 23:7*a*)

What we think is what we are. The plan of God has seen fit for us to share the thinking of Christ and to utilize His divine orientation to reality in our walk through this life. If Jesus Christ is important, then what He thinks is more important than anything else in life. But what has been important to us?

When we come to the end of our road and look back, we will see a switchback—from positive to negative to positive—as we have fluctuated in our attitude toward the Word of God. No human being with an old sin nature will have a perfect record; no one will have followed a straight path. But the question will be, What has predominated? Have we been positive toward doctrine or consistently negative? How far has our positive volition carried us? Have we cracked the maturity barrier? Have we advanced beyond maturity? Have we persisted in learning doctrine one day at a time, day after day? We have been given doctrine, the grace apparatus for perception, logistical grace, and—except in special cases which we will note later—sufficient time to grow up spiritually. How have we handled these assets?

I cannot emphasize enough the gravity of this question. When I stop to think of how easy it is for people to get away from doctrine and of how difficult it is to be consistent in GAP, the importance of this issue becomes emphatic.

God's plan is simple, the issues and objectives are clear-cut. But life can become very complicated when we manufacture our own problems, when our friends manufacture problems for us, when life itself adds problems and distractions of its own. For example, many Christians have spotted on the horizon our fast-approaching historical crisis, and they are scared to death. These believers have been distracted from the most important thing in life by a situation that is also very critical but far less so. Doctrine must be given first priority. With doctrine in your soul, you know who controls history, and you know your place in it. Doctrine keeps even historical disasters in perspective and enables you to think instead of panic under pressure. Whatever may occur in the future, you must assign politics and warfare and world affairs as well as your own ambitions, your family life, your social life, your business life, all to lower priorities than you give to the Word of God. As legitimate and important as these other things may be, doctrine is the eternal issue. And that doctrine must be in *your* soul.

At the Judgment Seat of Christ you will be on your own facing the Lord of Glory. "Each one" in Romans 14:12 means that Christ will handle each case separately. Christianity is personal, and you must answer for yourself. In life, you may have evaded the responsibility for your own decisions; you may have found others to blame or to lean on; you may have developed a prodigious ability to make excuses. But in front of the omniscient King of Kings, you will not be able to evade, to compensate, to laugh it off, to find any excuse. He has all the facts. The evidence is all in the mind of Christ: He knows your every thought during your every moment on earth, and if doctrine resides in your soul, He recognizes His own thoughts in you. He knows your true attitude toward His Word. The invalidity of every excuse you ever made for declining to learn doctrine is no secret to Him. You are standing in front of the Person who provided the means of overcoming even *legitimate* excuses! More than ever before, when you face Him, you can only say, "No excuse, Sir." Perhaps for the first time, you will accept *full* responsibility for your own decisions.

Does this make you feel uncomfortable? Be sure to understand that I am not talking about your sins. They were judged on the Cross and will never be mentioned again. The thoughts, decisions, and actions for which you must give an account actually have nothing directly to do with sin. Sin is not the issue; the issue is your attitude toward doctrine. You will render a report about all the time you wasted in human good, in social action, in attempting to compensate for a guilt complex. Your sincerity will cut no ice with God—you will have been sincerely wrong. Ignorance will be no excuse—it will be the problem.

The Son of God will add together all the facts and come up with a final "efficiency report." In those exceptional cases in which an individual did not have enough time to reach maturity—a new believer in the Rapture generation, for example, or a person who died in childhood, or who was a moron, or who was taken home "early" in order to glorify the Lord in a special way—Christ in His omniscience will simply extrapolate beyond the actual into the possible. He will add up both the known and the unknown. In other words, God knows "iffy" history. He knows what that person *would* have accomplished had he been given sufficient time, and He rewards him accordingly! Even if our Lord Jesus Christ must call upon His certain knowledge of what to us is speculation, He will be totally fair with each of us. God is fair now; He will certainly be fair then.

By the time you reach the Judgment Seat of Christ (in fact, as soon as you die), it will be too late to do anything about your evaluation. There is no way to sway the Judge, no way to obscure the facts. Your efficiency report will cover the period of time between your salvation and your departure from the earth. The time to learn doctrine is now.

At the Judgment Seat of Christ, only the believers who received the sixth imputation will receive the seventh imputation.

> For we must all appear before the judgment seat of Christ
> that each one may be rewarded for the things he has done
> by means of the body [that is, during his life on earth] face

> to face with what he has accomplished, whether good or
> worthless. (2 Cor. 5:10)

If you did not grow up spiritually and thus did not permit God to bless you in time, your evaluation will be very simple: "worthless." The zero imputed to divine righteousness in time will be parlayed into a zero imputed to your resurrection body in eternity. The only other possible efficiency report is "good." This is the fulfillment of God's plan for your life. According to this report, the blessings that were imputed to God's righteousness in time will be converted into utterly fantastic blessings and rewards which will reflect the glory of the Lord Jesus Christ forever.

The criterion for eternal rewards will not be what you produced but your attitude toward doctrine. You will be judged according to your function under GAP while a believer on earth.

> But the one having looked into the perfect law of freedom
> [the Bible when taught] and having persisted [the func-
> tion of GAP], that one having become not a hearer of
> oblivion but a doer of assigned occupation [one who
> fulfills God's objective for the believer—the advance to
> maturity], that one [the believer] shall be happy in so
> doing. (James 1:25)

Logistical support and confident anticipation of blessings in time will make the growing believer happy en route to maturity, and divine blessing plus his new hope of greater blessings in eternity will make him happy after he arrives.

> So keep speaking and so keep doing as they who through
> the law of freedom [the Bible when taught] are about to
> receive evaluation [the Judgment Seat of Christ]. For
> evaluation without mercy [no special rewards in heaven]
> for those not having produced the mercy [those who fail-
> ed to receive blessings in time from God]. Mercy [bless-
> ings in time], on the other hand, has esprit de corps at the
> evaluation [the Judgment Seat of Christ]. (James 2:12,
> 13)

Bona fide, properly motivated production is a natural consequence of a mental attitude renewed by doctrine, oriented to grace, and occupied with Christ. But our Lord as Judge goes straight to the heart of the matter, rewarding the cause, not the results.

Obviously, all human good is rejected at the Judgment Seat of Christ. What the righteousness of God rejects, the justice of God condemns. No production of the old sin nature escapes judgment: personal sins were judged at the Cross and human good and evil are judged at the Judgment Seat of Christ. They are burned like wood, hay, and stubble (1 Cor. 3:11-15).

> If anyone's work which he has built remains, he shall receive a reward; if anyone's work is burned, he shall suffer loss [no rewards at the Judgment Seat of Christ], but he himself shall be saved, yet as through fire. (1 Cor. 3:14)

The justice of God is the source of divine blessing, all of which comes through the grace pipeline. The integrity of God encapsulates that pipeline. Any attempt to earn, deserve, or work for blessing from God is human good, which not only fails to penetrate the encapsulation in time but is totally destroyed in eternity.

Loss of reward, however, does not imply loss of salvation. Paul emphasizes this point by quoting a few lines from a doctrinal hymn popular in the early church, entitled "Faithful is the Word" (cf. 1 Tim. 1:15; Titus 3:8).

> Faithful is the Word. For you see, if we died with Christ [and we have, through retroactive positional truth], at the same time also we shall live with Him. If we endure suffering [the mature believer under undeserved suffering], we shall rule with Him [as a sign of maturity, undeserved suffering is a guarantee of reward in eternity]. If we [the reversionist, negative to doctrine] repudiate the Lord, the same one [Jesus Christ] will also refuse us [no reward at the Judgment Seat of Christ]. If we are unfaithful, He remains faithful [salvation is secure]; for you see, He cannot deny Himself. (2 Tim. 2:11-13)

We permanently possess one half of God's integrity; therefore, for God to deny us salvation would be to deny Himself.

The *a fortiori* approach to the Judgment Seat of Christ merely turns around what we studied in Romans 5:15-17 and views it from the standpoint of its final result. Parlaying the blessings of time into blessings of eternity is much easier for God to accomplish than providing those temporal blessings in the first place. And furthermore, blessing us in time is far less difficult than purchasing our salvation. In other words, we are able to appear before the Judgment Seat of Christ instead of before the Great White Throne—the place of the unbeliever's final judgment—only because of the Cross.

Whether evaluated "good" and given rewards or "worthless" and given none, we are still saved.

DESCRIPTIONS OF ETERNAL REWARDS

BUMPER CROPS AND LARGE ESTATES

All the Biblical descriptions of rewards at the Judgment Seat of Christ are drawn from the ancient world. Following a basic principle of hermeneutics, the science of intepretation and explanation, we must understand these descriptions in the light of the times in which they were written.

Judea had an agricultural economy in the days of Christ. The wheat farmer, or the sower he hired, broadcast seeds by hand from a sack slung under his arm. The seeds sown fell on different types of soil and therefore produced different yields. Some soils produced "thirtyfold, some sixty, and some an hundred" (Mark 4:3–21), while others produced only what withered in the sun and died. Likewise, there will be wide variations in the eternal rewards and blessings imputed to believers at the Judgment Seat of Christ based on their response to the Mind of Christ in time.

The Bible also mentions cities as rewards (Acts 7:20; Heb. 11:16). In the ancient world city-states were familiar political entities. Among them, Athens (or Attica) is probably best known to us, but there were many others. Sodom and Gommorah were two cities of a five-city Canaanite confederacy in the Arabah Valley (Gen. 13). The five city-states of the Philistines, founded as Greek colonies on the coastal plain even prior to Abraham's arrival in the Land, figure heavily in the history of Israel. Rome, too, began as a city-state which, like Athens, absorbed everything around it and eventually became an empire.

A single ruler might control several cities, as did Herod the Great. When he died, and after Augustus confirmed his will, many city-states of the Levant were bequeathed or imputed to his heirs. Several of these cities are known in Scripture, such as Gadara and Caesarea Philippi.

A city represented great authority and wealth for its ruler. Thus, the mature believer who is given ten, twenty, or a hundred cities at the Judgment Seat of Christ is depicted as receiving immense wealth. The Lord Jesus Christ will grant him a personal estate measured in billions of light years. Vast tracts of space will become his eternal domain, entailing unheard of riches and the rulership over those believers who, minus rewards of their own, will live within his realms (Heb. 11:10, 16; 13:14).

MILITARY DECORATIONS

As another expression of the variations in eternal rewards, the Roman army's system of decorations is adapted to the Judgment Seat of Christ. We are at least somewhat familiar with modern military decorations. The Medal of Honor is awarded by the President in the name of Congress as our highest award for valor in combat above and beyond the call of duty. The Victoria Cross with its claret ribbon and brass medallion (still individually struck from cannons captured at the battle of Sevastopol in the Crimean War) is England's supreme military honor. In France, Napoleon founded the Legion of Honor with many orders, both military and civilian. Before Germany became a nation, Frederick the Great of Brandenburg-Prussia instituted the *Pour le Mérite* or "Blue Max," which was perpetuated after Kaiser Wilhelm united Germany. Wilhelm II offered it as the highest decoration of the German Empire. Hitler despised the old system and was livid when his generals wore the Blue Max in his presence. He replaced it with the Knight's Cross which had several ascending classes. Each nation's top decoration caps an entire hierarchy of lesser awards.

Military decorations in ancient Rome were a little different from those of today: they were far more remunerative! And Paul knew all about them. As a prisoner in daily contact with Roman soldiers, he learned a great deal about their personal and professional aspirations. But that is not where he first learned about the army's crowns. It required no special experience to know their significance; what they meant was common knowledge throughout the Roman world. Not only Paul, but Peter, John, and James as well, found it natural to illustrate surpassing grace with Roman crowns.

Most Christians today are aware that crowns are mentioned in the Bible. "Will there be any stars in my crown?" is a line from a hymn, long on enthusiasm but short on accuracy. A king's crown, called a *diadema,* might be embellished with a star or two, but our eternal rewards are depicted as the *stephanos,* the "wreath" worn on the heads of Roman heroes.

The several grades of wreaths were the supreme military decorations. They were worn uppermost on the body; they signified the highest personal valor and symbolized the highest glory of SPQR. Lesser awards were worn lower: medallions suspended from the neck, brass or silver bands around the arm, medals sewn to a leather sash across the chest.

In chronicling the Punic Wars, the historian Livy gives us the name of one of the most highly decorated heroes in Roman history. Spurius Ligustinus was a professional officer, four times the senior centurion of his legion. In twenty-two years of service he actually won thirty-four decorations, including six civic crowns! His uniform was magnificent, but even more magnificent was the combined stipend attached to his awards. He probably drew a quarter of a million dollars annually as long as he lived, along with extra rations and the proceeds from the large tracts of land awarded to him. Some of the wealthiest citizens of SPQR earned their wealth on the battlefield. Knowing this and imbued with the honor of the legion, soldiers were inspired to train hard and to perform feats of unusual valor in battle.

There were at least six categories of wreaths. The highest order was the *corona obsidionalis* made of golden strands of grass. It was also called *corona graminea,* and awarded only for rare deeds of supreme valor, it was almost never seen. Next in order came the *corona civica* made of gold oak leaves. The "civic crown" is roughly equivalent to the Medal of Honor or Victoria Cross. The third category was the *corona navalis,* the highest decoration in the Roman navy, usually awarded to the first marine who boarded an enemy ship or to a commander who destroyed an enemy fleet.

Corona muralis, the fourth crown, was awarded to the first soldier to scale the wall of a besieged city. The fifth order, *corona castrensis,* was usually awarded to the first soldier to reach an enemy fort or camp in a charge. The sixth *stephanos* was the *corona triumphalis,* given to army commanders after a victorious campaign; it is comparable to our Distinguished Service Medal.

Gaius Julius Caesar won a wreath woven of golden grass, which carried with it the title "Imperator" and demanded that all, regardless of rank, salute the wearer. His grandnephew Octavius, called Augustus, was rummaging through Caesar's effects one day and discovered the wreath. He put it on his own head and said, apparently to a mirror, "Hail, Imperator!" From then on, Imperator became a title of the emperor, as had Caesar's family name, so that Octavius' full imperial title was Augustus Caesar Imperator. Even the title of the emperor himself came partly from the system of military decorations that was so familiar to Paul.

The writers of Scripture created an almost startling picture when they borrowed the concept from the Roman army and outlined a system of Christian wreaths, to be awarded in the future by the Lord Jesus Christ. Wreaths were highly coveted and were held in awe. When first-century believers actually saw one of those rare soldiers wearing a crown, they knew very well that here was a man of fabulous wealth. Now they were to picture themselves in his shoes!

Paul distinguishes three "crowns." Let us roughly align them with the stages of maturity and call them the "Alpha Cross," the "Bravo Cross," and the "Ultra Cross" to coincide with supergrace$_A$, supergrace$_B$, and ultra-supergrace. These three decorations for "spiritual valor" do not express everything that mature believers will receive at the Judgment Seat of Christ; they represent a system of awards that carry with them a wide variety of eternal blessings.

The Alpha Cross, or "wreath of righteousness," is available to anyone who fulfills the potential of imputed righteousness by attaining spiritual maturity. Paul mentions it in the final chapter he wrote before his execution.

> I have fought that honorable fight [advancing through every stage of spiritual growth]; I have finished the course; I have guarded the doctrine [resident in the soul]. In the future [eternity] a wreath of that righteousness [*dikaiosune*, the total fulfillment of all spiritual progress] is reserved for me, which wreath the Lord, the righteous Judge, will award me on that day [the Judgment Seat of Christ] and not only to me but to all those who love His appearing [mature believers who, from the detailed system of doctrine in their souls, eagerly anticipate the Rapture, which will precede the Judgment Seat of Christ]. (2 Tim. 4:7, 8)

Next, and perhaps a somewhat higher decoration, is the Bravo Cross, or "wreath of life."

> Blessed is [happinesses to] the man who perseveres under testing [the mature believer receiving the imputation of undeserved suffering]; he will receive the wreath of life which God has promised to those constantly loving Him. (James 1:12)

The believer's occupation with Christ is crystallized and stabilized in the "no man's land" of testing in supergrace$_B$, through which the mature believer must advance en route to ultra-supergrace. The Bravo Cross is awarded specifically for using and applying doctrine in the midst of undeserved suffering.

> Do not fear those things which you are about to suffer [undeserved suffering]. Behold, the devil is about to cast some of you into prison that you may be tested. Also, you will have pressure and affliction ten days. Become faithful unto death and I will give you the wreath of life. (Rev. 2:10)

Always, the pastor-teacher is more spiritually mature than anyone who sits under his teaching for any length of time. No believer can exceed the growth of his right pastor-teacher. The Ultra Cross, or "wreath of glory"—the highest decoration—is therefore related to the gift and function of the pastor, even though all believers can win it by attaining ultra-supergrace. The pastor is delighted that those who listen to his teaching day after day, year after year, are motivated by an enthusiasm for doctrine that parallels his own. He will receive, as it were, an "oak leaf cluster" affixed to his own Ultra Cross for every member of his flock whom he leads to ultra-supergrace. He thus anticipates the pleasure of presenting the mature members of his congregation at the Judgement Seat of Christ and of watching them receive fantastic riches, vast sections of heaven, and untold eternal blessings.

> Therefore, my brethren, loved ones, deeply desired ones, my happiness, my victory wreath [the Ultra Cross], in this way keep on being stabilized by the Lord, ones worthy of love [mature believers]. (Phil. 4:1; cf., 1 Thess. 2:19, 20)

> And when the Chief Shepherd [Jesus Christ] shall appear [the Rapture], you [in this context, pastors only] will receive the unfading wreath of glory. (1 Pet. 5:4)

ATHLETIC WREATHS

Paul often alludes to the Roman military wreaths, but a different kind of wreath was the prize for victors in the ancient Games—whether the Olympic, the Pythian, the Nemean, the Isthmian, or one of a host of less illustrious contests. Every city of any importance in the Greek or Roman worlds sponsored its own games.

Paul uses this connotation of *stephanos* in several passages. Like the military crown, the athletic crown was more than a mere garland of grass or leaves. It was the coveted badge of victory, and it symbolized the very substantial rewards which were bestowed upon the champion runner, wrestler, pentathlete, boxer, or chariot owner.

A gala celebration feted him even before he left the site of his victory, but the real reward came when he reached his home town. The crown of leaves and other honors bestowed at the games were like the strong believer's blessings in time; the rewards at home like his blessings of eternity. The mere wreath was parlayed into something wonderful and permanent at the place where he held his citizenship.

To begin with, the common road into town was not good enough for so great a hero. A section of the city wall was torn down for his entrance then rebuilt and sealed with an inscription of his name. The chariot of the city and the entire population awaited him inside the wall, and his victory parade surged through the streets. The revelry was so unrestrained that Cicero complained that the parades for hometown winners of the Olympic Games outshone the triumphal processions of Rome's conquering generals.

The athlete was given a cash award of from $10,000 to $50,000 and a lifetime pass to the games. A poet lauded him in an ode; a sculptor was commissioned to erect a statue of him competing in his event. Greater yet, his children were fed and educated at public expense; but best of all, he was exempted for life from all income taxes.

Only the winners were so rewarded. A winner must train, and train hard. A person with natural athletic talent cannot step onto the track, luck out, and take home a wreath. Nor can the believer luck out in the Christian life. *Losers* depend on luck, on tripping over a pot of gold, on just falling into divine blessings. A winner works hard, and the Christian must, as it were, train rigorously by diligently taking in the Word of God. That is the only way to be a winner at the Judgment Seat of Christ.

In two passages, Paul compares the Christian way of life to athletic training.

> Now if anyone really competes in the athletic games, he
> does not receive a winner's wreath unless he trains ac-
> cording to the rules. (2 Tim. 2:5)

Strict rules governed the ancient games, and every athlete had to follow them all just to get into the competition. Likewise, we cannot train in any way we please. Our lives are governed by the impartial, unbendable rules laid down for man's spiritual growth by the absolute justice of God. In every athletic rule, we can find parallels for the believer who is striving to crack the maturity barrier and is seeking to win the wreath of eternal blessings from the justice of God.

The athlete had to register and enter a state gym—a large, walled area of tracks, workout areas, fields, and buildings. To enter he had to be a citizen of Greece, of pure hellenic descent, or, later, a citizen of SPQR. Likewise, the justice of God requires that a person be a believer in Christ before he can begin his spiritual training.

There were two kinds of athletes in the ancient world. The *agonistos* went to the local gym to keep himself in shape with an occasional workout and to throw his opinions into the discussions constantly kept up by the other idlers there. He is analogous to the believer negative toward doctrine. Perhaps he leisurely exercised once or twice a week, but he was not a true athlete and was not qualified for the games. The *athletos,* on the other hand, lived at the gym, followed its rules, and trained for the competition. He is like the positive believer.

The athletes had to live in the gym for ten months prior to the competition; the believer has to identify himself with his right pastor-teacher and enter the long-term (life-long) academic discipline of the local church. The athlete was disqualified if he went outside the walls; the believer cannot afford to run from pastor to pastor. He must recognize his right pastor's authority, settle down, and learn the Word of God through his own pastor's particular system of categorical development. Bits and pieces from a dozen different sources do not a system make!

During those ten months of intensive training, the athlete was required to answer all trumpet calls, both the warning calls and the assembly calls. There was no such thing as sleeping in. The warning calls can be compared to rebound as the means of recovering the filling of the Spirit, mandatory for the intake of doctrine. The assembly call brought all the competitors together just as the pastor's communication brings together all those in the congregation. Both on the training field and in the local church, self-discipline—to concentrate—and group discipline—to avoid distracting others—are demanded if anyone is to advance in his training.

At the first trumpet call, the trainers rubbed down the athletes with oil and fine African sand. This was the only "clothing" permitted the athletes on the training field, whether the temperature was 10° below or 110° above. The oil warmed up the muscles, comparable to the filling of the Spirit which causes GAP to function; the sand, though abrasive, was as much a part of the warm-up routine as academic self-discipline is a part of any learning situation.

The exercise master supervised the gym's training schedule. All athletes, no matter what their special events, had to exercise under his direction. If the schedule called for a five-mile run, everyone went the distance, including the discus throwers and shot-putters. If a weight workout appeared on the schedule, the sprinters were right there along with the weight men.

A distance runner who bucked authority and complained that power exercises would ruin his stride would be allowed to practice his precious stride right out the front gate of the gym, leaving the victory wreath to men of better character. In the local church, every believer-priest listens with the same self-discipline and continuity of positive volition to every subject that comes up in the passage being taught, no matter how dull or seemingly irrelevant. He cannot pick and choose doctrines that suit his fancy at the moment and at the same time maintain stability or grow spiritually.

Some believers who seem to be positive (and who think themselves to be positive) have the tragic flaw of basing their intake of doctrine on their personal problems. They concentrate only on the points that apply to their immediate difficulties or that can be distorted to apply. Instead, under the filling of the Spirit, we should practice a neat little trick when we come to Bible class: leave personal problems at the door (Rom. 12:3; 2 Cor. 10:5).

It is essential that we concentrate on everything taught if we are to orient to the authority of the pastor and the passage at hand. Doctrine itself—not some current, unstable situation in our lives—must be allowed to sort out the essentials from the nonessentials. If we fail to set every doctrinal brick required by divine blueprint, we will have no structure at all! If we as Christian athletes work out only for one favorite event, we are arrogant for assuming that we know better than God what must be learned, and subjective for insisting that everything center around our own standard of thinking. We divorce ourselves from the reality of what a passage teaches by bending it to our current problems. As a result, we fail to learn doctrine and fail to advance spiritually—no matter how much time we log in Bible class. In other words, positive volition is more than mere attendance. We must come prepared to set aside our problems for an hour or so; we must be ready to learn anything and everything that comes up. There is plenty of time to apply what we learn; sooner or later, *every* subject taught will be required for application. We must learn them all.

As a further rule at the gymnasium, the competitors were forbidden sex. All contact with the opposite sex was prohibited during the ten-month regimen. No distractions were allowed, and although this particular prohibition is, of course, not pertinent to learning doctrine, the principle remains. Sooner or later, every believer faces distractions from the one he loves. If (to take the man's point of view) she is more important to him than doctrine, if he fails to incorporate his love for her into the big picture which gives supreme importance and first priority to the Word of God, he will never enjoy her to the fullest. It is tragic that people simply fail to realize that doctrine in the soul is the foundation for any relationship; doctrine gives the wonderful capacity, wisdom, and sensitivity that make a person a great lover. With no capacity of soul, a man cannot treat the one he loves with both the strength and the tenderness that she requires, nor can his inevitable unhappiness from ignorance of doctrine be dispelled even by this person he loves. An athlete needed self-discipline, and there was no greater self-discipline than in refraining from the wonderful company of the opposite sex when true capacity for love existed.

The rules of training included diet as well. Only wheat, lean meat, cheese, and figs were served; wines and desserts were off limits. The young man who loved mother's home cooking had to lay aside his preferences and follow the dietary program of the gym. When doctrine is taught, we too must lay aside the preconceived ideas and legalistic prejudices from our background. Objectivity in learning is mandatory. We cannot expect to advance spiritually if we sit and vibrate every time the pastor teaches a doctrine that tramples our pet area of self-righteousness. When the student of doctrine is in conflict with doctrine, he is wrong. Doctrine is always right.

Finally, the "training according to the rules" that Paul mentions was enforced by the governor of the gym, called the *gumnasiarchos*. His was an honored profession. He enjoyed high standing in the community, and his badges of authority—the white sandals and purple robe—were recognized everywhere. Retired generals often held such posts and dedicated themselves to producing athletes who would bring renown to the city and to the gym. He delegated authority to judges and marshals who enforced the rules. When they discovered an infraction, they disqualified that athlete from competition. For the believer, disqualification is divine discipline for reversionism: lack of blessings in time means a lack of rewards in eternity. You as a believer must regulate your own life in the light of divine objectives, or God will regulate your life for you through divine discipline. Either you adjust to the justice of God or the justice of God will adjust to you.

> Do you not know that those who run in the race all run,
> but one receives the prize [that although all believers live
> on earth, few exploit their spiritual potential and receive a
> reward]? Run in such a way that you may win. And
> everyone who competes in the games exercises self-
> discipline in all things. They do it to receive a perishable
> wreath, but we do it to receive an imperishable wreath.
> Therefore, I run in such a way as not without a goal. I box
> in such a way as not to hit the air [miss my blows]. And I
> discipline my body, and I keep it in training [consistent
> GAP], lest having proclaimed [preached] to others, I
> myself should be disqualified [from eternal rewards].
> (1 Cor. 9:24-27)

What has been "proclaimed" in our study so far? Let us summarize. The holiness of God is comprised of His righteousness and justice—His *dikaiosune*—which we have identified as His integrity. Righteousness is the principle of God's integrity; justice, the function. God loves His integrity. He loves it so much that on that basis alone (not even considering the fact that He is immutable!), He could never turn around and love something so *un*righteous as a sinful, human-good, evil man who "comes short of the glory of God." When we assume that God loves us, we take a great deal of credit upon ourselves, exhibiting, whether intentionally or not, a presumptuous self-righteousness that is itself offensive to Him.

Even if God *could* love what is totally repulsive to Him (which He cannot), He could never allow His love to sway His justice; that is *not* how He saves us! God's perfect plan and perfect actions toward imperfect man are not and cannot be the functions of His love; they must be and are the functions of His integrity. Our salvation is based on God's inviolable essence, not on a compromise of His essence.

The righteousness of God is the sum of His perfection. God accepts only what meets this perfect standard; He rejects anything that falls short. The justice of God either blesses or curses; it is never neutral, doing nothing. What His righteousness *accepts,* His justice must bless; what His righeousness *rejects,* His justice must curse.

Man's first sin brought down divine cursing. Condemnation came as a simple matter of fairness, of God's impartial justice executing the demands of absolute righteousness. But the God-Man, Jesus Christ, was acceptable to the righteousness of God and worthy only of blessing. In grace, the justice of God made an exchange: God transferred our guilt to Christ and judged our sins in Him on the Cross so that, with the debt against us paid in full, God can now credit His own righteousness to anyone who believes in Christ. We now *possess* God's righteousness! Through Christ, *we* are now completely acceptable to God's righteousness! When we believe in Christ, the justice of God *must* bring down salvation blessings upon us—a simple matter of fairness.

God turned the tables completely—from cursing to blessing—all as a matter of justice and total Self-consistency. Our standing with God is as strong and permanent as His own integrity.

What we possess because of Christ is not a result of partiality, of sentimentality, or of condescension to our sincere good deeds. How can we understand the superiority of what is ours through Christ? Only by comparing it to something known to be exceedingly wonderful: we have something *now* which is far more stable, far more secure, far more valuable than anything possible in the idyllic perfection of the Garden of Eden! The fact that God loved Adam and the woman was the sum total of their relationship with Him; the fact that He loves us, possessors of His righteousness, is icing on the cake. And how can we see the superiority of justice over love as our point of contact with God? Initially through language of accommodation. "For God so loved the world" is one anthropopathism designed to shed light on the magnificent action of God's justice in giving us our Savior.

Through the system of five basic imputations, of which every believer is a beneficiary, the justice of God has solved the problems connected with the Fall of man and has elevated us far above Adam's original created state. And the justice of God *continues* to be our point of contact with Him; salvation is only the beginning! Now we, like the athletes of antiquity, registered in the gym, can concentrate on the goals that God desires us to reach. God's goal for us in time is that we be blessed to the maximum—the sixth imputation. And His objective for us in eternity is literally beyond description. The Scriptures are limited to using analogies and *a fortiori* logic to even hint of the high quality of blessings that will fill out the sequence of events outlined in prophecy: the Judgment Seat of Christ, the Second Advent, the Millennium, and beyond. By our nonmeritorious positive volition toward doctrine now, we acquire capacity for blessing and permit the justice of God to impute these above-and-beyond blessings to us. This is how we glorify and please Him forever.

The doctrines we have studied so far have pointed out the course we are to run in order to win the prize of the plan of God. We must learn these doctrines in detail, study them, restudy them, "renew our minds" with them, in order to have a basic frame of reference as to where God is leading us. But we have covered so much ground that it is perhaps difficult to picture the entire course in one panoramic view. Perhaps we are lost in the details. What we need, as a guide to our further intake and application of doctrine, is some means of seeing in a glance all the prominent features of God's plan. In the doctrine of hope, which is the context for Romans 8:28, we find just such a spiritual map.

3
Integrity and Hope

THE CHRISTIAN'S CONFIDENCE

THE INTEGRITY OF GOD, working in our behalf through seven imputations, is what makes life wonderful. Imputations are the outline of our lives. When we understand this system, which is totally consistent with God's perfect essence and through which His justice blesses us, we gain confidence in the plan of God. We are motivated to move forward; we eagerly anticipate the next imputation. This confidence in the future is what the Bible means by "hope."

We have noted that there are three hopes in the plan of God. Hope$_1$ belongs to the unbeliever who hears the Gospel and knows that if he simply believes in Christ he will possess eternal life. Hope$_2$ is the motivation of the growing believer who knows that if he persists in learning doctrine he will receive the sixth imputation. Hope$_3$ is the attitude of the mature believer; he confidently looks beyond the barriers of time to his indescribably valuable rewards at the Judgment Seat of Christ.

As we advance in the Christian life, we move from hope$_1$ to hope$_2$ to hope$_3$; from one objective to the next to the next. Once a goal is reached, we move on from there; we do not slow down or stop. We keep our eyes up and our focus on where we are going in God's plan. We do this by continuing to learn the Word of God. For example, after we believe in Christ, we would be squandering the time on earth that God has allotted to us if we continued to seek salvation. As believers, we need more than to hear the Gospel again and again; we need to hear the whole realm of doctrine systematically taught. There is something better than to anticipate salvation, and that is to anticipate blessings in time after we *have* salvation. But there is something even greater than to look forward to the many categories of prosperity in time, and that is to eagerly anticipate the blessings of eternity while *enjoying* blessings of time!

> With reference to the hope [in this case, the third hope],
> keep on rejoicing. . . (Rom. 12:12*a*)

God is the Author of hope—which means that the justice of God gives our lives meaning, purpose, definition.

> In the hope of eternal life which God, who cannot lie,
> promised before times eternal. (Titus 1:2)

God authored hope in eternity past, in the divine decrees. But there are three hopes. Which one is in view in Titus 1:2? Hope₁. God is said to have promised *salvation* "before times eternal." That is why, as unbelievers, we were able to have total confidence in the Gospel. Only an unbeliever can have a *hope* of eternal life; everyone else *has* eternal life. Remember the definition of hope in Romans 8:24: "Now, when a hope is seen it is not a hope. So who hopes for what he sees?" Doctrine in the soul is more certain than what we might see through the eyes (2 Pet. 1:15–21); we "see" through doctrine that we already have eternal life. Hence the confident anticipation of receiving eternal life can only belong to the one who does not yet possess it. God is the Author of hope₁. But God is also the Author of hope₂ and hope₃.

> To whom God decreed to make known what are the
> riches of His glory [the sixth and seventh imputations] of
> this mystery [God's glory as manifested in the royal fami-
> ly, not revealed until the Church Age] in the Gentiles
> [Gentile believers—the Church Age has interrupted the
> Jewish Age], which is, Christ in you, the hope [confident
> anticipation] of glory. (Col. 1:27)

Not only is God the Father identified as the Author and Originator of hope, but so is the Lord Jesus Christ. "Christ in you" is the indwelling of Christ which belongs exclusively to the royal family of God. Christ indwells every Church Age believer. Hope of glorifying Christ belongs only to those who are advancing in the plan of God.[42] Thus, the hope in view in Colossians 1:27 includes both the second and third hopes.

---

42. See above, page 115.

Our objective is to develop the capacity that frees God to bless us; it is the imputation of blessings that glorifies the Lord Jesus Christ.

Many believers quote "Christ in you the hope of glory" without knowing what it means. It simply identifies the origin of glory after salvation. Christ is the origin of glory; He is the One who is glorified; He is our hope, our confidence. His personal residence in us intensifies our confidence. His Person and His saving work on the Cross form the object of hope$_1$, and after salvation He is the basis for our hope of blessings, both now (hope$_2$) and forever (hope$_3$). We develop capacity through learning the Mind of Christ; our first blessing in the sixth imputation is occupation with Christ; and, in the seventh imputation, the very Christ who indwells will place on our heads the wreaths of tactical victory.

God is the Author of hope, but doctrine is the source of hope. God does not provide hope in any other way. Another well-known but poorly understood passage explains the relationship between doctrine and hope.

> In fact, doctrine is the reality from which we keep receiving the hope, the proof of matters not being seen. (Heb. 11:1)

In its English translation, Hebrews 11:1 is commonly mistaken for a definition of faith. But the word for faith, *pistis,* is used in its objective sense; it means "what is believed, the object of faith, Bible doctrine." Bible doctrine reveals the plan of God. Under His plan, He glorifies Himself by blessing us. He can bless us only because of a series of basic imputations. These imputations, especially the imputation of divine righteousness, create a potential for blessing. But our potential remains unknown to us apart from learning doctrine. If unknown, unfulfilled. If we are ever to use our God-given volition to adjust our thinking, our actions, our lives to the plan of God, our ignorance must become cognizance; our uncertainty, confidence; our potential, hope. Hebrews 11:1 is actually a definition of hope.

Having a hope is based on having a potential; true hope is based on reality. Hence, just as we have three successive hopes, we also have three successive potentials. And just as each hope, when realized, is replaced by a new hope, each potential, when fulfilled, is replaced by a new potential. We never run out of room in which to grow. When one potential is fulfilled, we acquire an even greater potential whose fulfillment then becomes our next objective in life.

We are born with our first potential. God has a plan for the *entire* human race. He demonstrates that fact, first of all, by imputing life to each of us at birth, and secondly, by simultaneously imputing to us Adam's sin for the purpose of our immediate, total condemnation. Condemnation must precede salvation, and He condemns us as fast as we *can* be condemned! The justice of God is shown immediately to be our point of reference. That's how strong our first potential is: all the work has been accomplished—at our birth and on the Cross. God in His perfect integrity desires that all of us be saved (2 Pet. 3:9); we need only believe in Christ. Our second potential is acquired at the moment of salvation: the justice of God imputes the righteousness of God to us. Since God's righteousness in us is the receiving end of the grace pipeline, we are eligible for blessings in time. Finally, our third potential—the potential for blessings in eternity—is established when we possess blessings in time, imputed at maturity and thereafter. One category of blessing guarantees the next.

Hence, there is one potential for the unbeliever, one for the immature believer, and one for the mature believer. But having a potential is simply grace; it is not an advance in the plan of God. Every hardened unbeliever and every reversionistic believer has a potential, but he has no hope and no advancement. Only the intake of doctrine moves us ahead. Bible doctrine reveals the plan of God, points out our objectives, and assures us that we actually can reach them. Doctrine alone converts potential into hope.

Hebrews 11 presents a series of case histories that illustrate how doctrine makes the difference between potential and hope. Man's entire confidence in life—in everything he thinks, decides, or does as a believer—is based on the fact that he has learned Bible doctrine.

> For by means of it [doctrine in the soul], men of old gained approval [cracked the maturity barrier and received the sixth imputation]. By means of doctrine, we learn that the dispensations have been put together by the decree of God with a result that what is being seen [the unfolding of history] has not come to pass from those things which are visible. By means of doctrine resident in the soul, Abel offered to God a greater sacrifice than Cain. . . . By means of doctrine, Enoch was transferred. . . . (Excerpts, Heb. 11:2-5)

In each case, doctrine made the difference. It converted each one's potential into hope, and that hope gave him the confidence which led him to maturity and beyond. Each person expressed his maturity in the various courses of action recorded in this lengthy honor roll.

> And without doctrine resident in the soul, it is impossible to please [God]; for when one is occupied with God, he must be convinced that He is [the doctrine of divine

> integrity] and that He becomes a Rewarder of those who
> diligently seek Him. (Heb. 11:6)

In Hebrews 11:6 we read the whole story. Seeking God is the persistent, consistent, academically disciplined—"diligent"—intake of the Word of God. We seek because we have a hope of finding; and God has provided that we find Him in the pages of Scripture. God "becomes a Rewarder" when, from the doctrine now resident in our souls, we have the capacity to receive rewards; that is, when we are occupied with the Giver. In so blessing us, God is pleased and glorified.

> This I recall to mind [remembering what has been
> taught]; therefore, I have hope [hope₂]: the Lord's grace
> functions never cease [logistical grace], for His compas-
> sions never fail [He forgives us every time we rebound],
> they are new every morning [God gives us a day at a time
> to advance to maturity]. Great is your faithfulness [in-
> tegrity]. The Lord is my portion says my soul, therefore, I
> have hope in Him [hope₂]. The Lord is good [blessings in
> time] to those who wait on [trust in] Him, to the soul who
> seeks Him [perpetuated positive volition toward doc-
> trinal teaching]. (Lam. 3:21-25)

As we concentrate, under the filling of the Spirit, on what the pastor teaches, the body of doctrine in our souls continually grows (even when we seem to be making no progress). We develop a doctrinal frame of reference; we build a technical vocabulary that accommodates Biblical concepts; our standards gradually line up with God's standards. Renewing our minds is not an overnight process. The Bible is not a mystery novel; we cannot turn to the last page and find all the answers. Doctrine must be inculcated a little today, a little tomorrow, day after day. As we grow in our knowledge of doctrine, our confidence becomes stronger—it is confidence in the facts. But until we become conversant in the facts of spiritual reality, we stand on another confidence which I call the first stage of "faith-rest."

Faith-rest is a three-stage procedure that we will describe later,[43] but the first stage is limited to claiming the promises specifically stated in the Bible. Immature believers must rely on these promises without having mastered the doctrines upon which the promises are made. Once we learn a point or two and begin to claim doctrines, our confidence moves into the realm of being a hope. Then, our complete assurance as to the future comes from knowing

---

43. See below, page 212.

pertinent doctrine; understanding, for example, that our point of contact with God is His justice and that His justice is the very wellhead of the grace pipeline.

> By means of doctrine resident in the soul, Noah, having been warned about things not being seen [destruction of the earth by water] . . . constructed an ark . . . [Noah met the historical crisis with the doctrine in his soul]. By means of doctrine resident in the soul, when Abraham was called he obeyed . . . [he, too, had confidence from doctrine when the Third Dynasty of Ur was about to fall and God instructed him to depart for an unknown land]. By means of doctrine, he [Abraham] lived as a temporary resident with reference to the Land as in a foreign land, dwelling in tents . . . for he himself kept waiting with anticipation for a city having foundations whose Designer and Builder is God. (Excerpts, Heb. 11:7–10)

God promised Abraham a city as part of his seventh imputation, and Abraham knew so well that he would receive it that, although he had grown up in a great city, he lived out his life in a tent. God prospered him so that he became a millionaire many times over; he could have built his own city. But he expressed his hope$_3$ by refusing to live in permanent buildings, happy to wait for those eternally permanent buildings from the Lord. To Abraham's mind, if the first and second hopes could become reality, so could the third, especially since each successive reality—salvation, blessings in time, blessings in eternity—is easier for God to provide.

Hope is the momentum factor in the plan of God; it is the motivation to move ahead. Hope looks *forward* with the same certainty we have in looking back. This absolute security regarding the future, whether near or distant, gives us our confidence in the present: the same God who blessed us with salvation in the past, and who will bless us with eternal rewards in the future, will never permit more pressure or prosperity to come into our lives than we are doctrinally prepared to handle.

The hope$_3$ of the mature believer has special ramifications. We have seen that, unlike hope$_1$ and hope$_2$, its impetus comes not from doctrine alone but from doctrine plus undeserved suffering. Furthermore, it focuses on God's ultimate objective in creating man—the seventh imputation; hope$_3$ is therefore the highest motivation in life.

The believer's confidence in the plan of God properly relates him to historical circumstances; the third hope overflows from the individual to the nation. When a nation has declined beyond a certain point (Ezra 10:2), it has only one remaining hope. Too far gone for the laws of establishment to have effect, its hope is the hope, that its mature believers carry in their souls. The hope of the nation resides—literally—in the pivot of supergrace and ultra-supergrace believers. Their eagerness to stand before the Judgment Tribunal of Christ leads that same One, who controls history, to preserve their nation, or to preserve them if their nation must be judged. In the eyes of the Lord, the entire nation is carried on the shoulders of its mature believers.

In contrast, reversionistic believers are a curse by association; they are the spin-off which tears their nation apart. Reversionists always have a hope, but their hope is useless and powerless. They place their confidence in things that are no basis for confidence; their hopes always prove false.

> So are the paths of all who forget God [reversionists who neglect doctrine and hence forget God's essence, justice, policies, grace, plan]; therefore, the hope of the godless [the believer with false doctrine or no doctrine] will fail, whose confidence is fragile and whose trust is a spider's web. (Job 8:13, 14)

To take an example, the believer who allegedly speaks in tongues has confidence in what he does. He assumes that his emotional activity is a spiritual advance; he is certain that he has broken through into some higher spiritual realm. He'll tell you all about it, and listening to him, you'll realize that he has a hope. The tragedy is that he has placed his hope in a satanic modus operandi. Satan's good-and-evil strategy is hopeless in the face of God's plan, and this apostate believer's hope is just as hopeless. It is as weak as the spider's web.

When a believer rejects the modus operandi set forth by the integrity of God, he builds his confidence on something immeasurably weaker. Neither tongues, nor tithing, nor sacrificing, nor "discipleship," nor good deeds, nor any Biblically commanded Christian service—nor *any* humanly meritorious activity—gives us a basis for expecting salvation, approval, or rewards from God. The basis for hope is our knowing what God does, not His knowing what we do.

Because of what God has done in salvation, even the reversionistic believer has the reality of a permanent relationship with God. Even the believer who nurtures false hopes on earth will live in heaven forever. But the unbeliever goes through life "having no hope and without God in the world" (Eph. 2:12). Having rejected hope, he has no blessing relationship with the integrity of God. There is no other source of permanent blessing and no other basis for true hope. When the unbeliever's life on earth comes to a close, the potential, which he refused to convert into a reality, is extinguished forever.

When a loved one who is a believer dies, we grieve—certainly—but we do not grieve "as do the rest [unbelievers] who have no hope" (1 Thess. 4:13).

God's will is *not* that people fail, especially not in that endlessly horrible way of rejecting Christ as Savior. He desires that we succeed in reaching spiritual maturity. The doctrine of hope keeps us pointed in the right direction, a direction sketched out in Romans 8:28.

PROFILE OF THE MATURE BELIEVER

> And we know that all things work together for good to
> them that love God, to them who are the called according
> to his purpose. (Rom. 8:28, AV)

Among Christians, Romans 8:28 has become a household phrase, as familiar as aspirin in a medicine chest. Many discouraged, disillusioned, despondent believers take Romans 8:28 as though it *were* a spiritual aspirin! Somehow it makes the hurt go away. But is that the purpose of this verse? Is it meant to be a cure-all for the complicated symptoms of a doctrine deficiency in the soul? No, it is not.

We must approach the Word of God with utmost care. Never are we to indiscriminately lift a phrase here and a verse there and apply them to suit our fancy. We must always analyze the Scripture in the light of certain principles of interpretation. In studying "cities" and "crowns," we were richly rewarded by adhering to one such principle: the Bible must be interpreted according to the times in which it was written. Now, to avoid misinterpreting "all things work together for good," we must follow yet another principle of hermeneutics: every passage must be interpreted in its context.

By integrating Romans 8:28 with its context, we discover to our surprise that most of the "comfort" derived from this verse is illusory. In its strict interpretation, Romans 8:28 does not apply to all believers; it belongs only to the mature believer! In analyzing this passage of Scripture, I am not trying to deprive any "suffering saint" of his only consolation in life! Far from it! I am interested in the true meaning of a vital passage. When accurately interpreted, this verse contains a power, an encouragement, a wealth of doctrine that has not been properly explained in this generation.

You will recall from our study of undeserved suffering that the context of Romans 8:28 is Romans 8:23–25. (Verses 26 and 27 are parenthetical.) This context describes the mature believer.

In Romans 8:23, "possessing the firstfruits from the Spirit" reveals that the category of believers in view is those who have already developed the necessary capacity from doctrine to receive supergrace blessings in time.

Which category of believers is that? Mature believers. These "firstfruits" are merely a taste of far greater blessings in heaven that will come to the believer who trained and persevered and disciplined himself on earth to cross the goal of spiritual maturity.

Further, undeserved suffering, described as a "groan" in Romans 8:23, is the fifth category of blessings in time—imputed to the mature believer. This temporary pain is a guarantee of blessings in eternity; it is the ignition system that sparks his hope. But which hope is in view? His is not the first hope, the anticipation of future salvation. (He is not still an unbeliever.) Nor is it the second hope, since he already possesses the sixth imputation—blessings in time. (He is not still an immature believer.) His hope is the third hope, the confident anticipation of blessings imputed to the resurrection body at the Judgment Seat of Christ. This hope belongs to the supergrace believer only.

The next verse, Romans 8:24, reiterates the fact that only the mature believer is in view. God's ultimate objective in saving members of the human race (even in imputing human life in the first place!) is that He might also impute fantastic rewards and blessings to our resurrection bodies. The only ones who have fulfilled this divine objective are mature believers, whose blessings in time will be parlayed into blessings in eternity. These are the people who glorify God both now and forever.

Again, in Romans 8:25, the *mature* believer under undeserved suffering has "fortitude"; a believer minus doctrine who comes under pressure grasps at straws, goes in for self-deception, reacts with a frantic search for happiness—in short, falls apart. Furthermore, the mature believer's stability is not a matter of gritting his teeth. The pain of imputed suffering is real, but it focuses his attention on greater blessings yet to come and causes him to "stand in eager anticipation." Pressure intensifies the doctrine in his soul and makes it a vivid reality. That cannot be said of anyone but the believer with maximum orientation to the reality of God's plan.

Now, from these verses we see that Romans 8:28 does not suddenly appear out of nowhere, shed its context, and throw itself open to all believers no matter now reversionistic or ignorant of doctrine. Anyone can memorize and quote Romans 8:28, but it is the legitimate property of the mature believer only. The immature believer or reversionist has little or no ground for claiming this verse. All things do *not* "work together for good to them who" are negative toward Bible doctrine!

> And if you will not for all this harken unto me, but walk
> contrary unto me; then I will walk contrary unto you also
> in fury. . . . (Lev. 26:27, 28*a*, AV)

It cannot be said, merely because all believers end up in heaven or because divine discipline often convinces the reversionist to recover, that "all things work together for good" even to the reversionist. Reversionistic believers *do* go to heaven. Discipline *can* correct the errant member of the royal family. But the context of Romans 8:28 is undeserved suffering—a category of blessing—not deserved punitive action. "All things work together for good" cannot be construed as a description of the sin unto death! "All things" do not include cursing from the justice of God.

THE EQUATION OF HOPE

What makes Romans 8:28 clear is the third hope. The mature believer has left behind the first and second hopes. For him, the first hope was long ago replaced by the reality of salvation. His second hope has likewise given way to the reality of blessings in time. His sights are now set on the next objective in the plan of God; he eagerly anticipates the rewards and blessings that await him in heaven.

Romans 8:28 describes the supergrace believer, who is looking forward to the seventh imputation. He knows that God's purpose in giving things to us is that they work together toward the ultimate imputation which will glorify Him forever. "The good" *is* the seventh imputation. The believer's third hope is the absolute confidence that "all things" are working toward that goal.

All things   work together for   the seventh imputation.

The "all things," which in the mature believer's life add up to the glory of God, began at birth and continue until he departs from the earth via death or the Rapture. Romans 8:28 gives us the basis for a simple formula that maps out God's plan for man from birth to eternity.

We can write out this formula in the form of an equation. "All things" can be broken down into three basic parts, categories, elements, or radicals. We will define a radical as a basic fundamental, something which forms part of an overall concept. Let us label the three "basic fundamentals" in the plan of God as "X radical," "Y radical," and "Z radical." Hence:

X + Y + Z   work together for   the seventh imputation.

Or, more concise yet:

X + Y + Z   equals   the seventh imputation.

Now possibly math was not exactly the highlight of your school days. Perhaps, even yet, your most vivid memory of graduation is of waving good-bye to the geometry teacher and of leaving behind—finally and forever—those unruly little imps called axioms, postulates, theorems, and equations. If so, do not let our mathematical format frighten you off. I am simply laying out concepts already familiar to us so we can clearly see them all at once.

$$X \left[\begin{array}{l} \text{Human} \\ \text{Life} \end{array} \begin{array}{l} \text{Adam's} \\ + \text{Original} \\ \text{Sin} \end{array} = \text{Potential}_1 + \begin{array}{l} \text{Doctrine} = \text{Hope}_1 \\ \text{(The Gospel)} \end{array} \right] +$$

$$Y \left[\begin{array}{l} \text{Judicial} \\ \text{Imputation}_1 \end{array} + \begin{array}{l} \text{Judicial} \\ \text{Imputation}_2 \end{array} = \text{Potential}_2 + \text{Doctrine} = \text{Hope}_2 \right] +$$

$$Z \left[\begin{array}{l} \text{Eternal} \\ \text{Life} \end{array} + \begin{array}{l} \text{Blessings} \\ \text{in Time} \end{array} = \text{Potential}_3 + \text{Doctrine} = \text{Hope}_3 \right]$$

$$= \text{The Seventh Imputation}$$
$$\text{(Blessings in Eternity,}$$
$$\text{the Plan of God,}$$
$$\text{the Glory of God)}$$

In effect, this formula is a map of God's plan for each individual, a framework to which all categories of doctrine will attach, a guide by which doctrine can be properly applied, a tool for objective thinking even under pressure. Each radical represents a segment of the plan of God.

X [life as an unbeliever   ] +

Y [life as an immature believer] +

Z [life as a mature believer   ] = the seventh imputation

The X radical covers that part of each person's life spent as an unbeliever. Many members of the human race never advance beyond this stage; others live most of their lives here before believing in Christ; yet others become believers at an early age and log only a few childhood years in the X radical. The Y radical is the life of the immature believer. Unfortunately, most believers never advance any further than this stage in God's plan. But that does not alter His plan; the Z radical is still God's objective for mankind on earth. It is the life of the mature believer.

Each radical contains a hope. The X radical includes hope$_1$, or the anticipation of salvation. The Y radical, hope$_2$; the hope of future blessings in time. The Z radical, hope$_3$; confident anticipation of eternal blessings imputed at the Judgment Seat of Christ.

In each case, hope anticipates the function of the integrity of God. And how does the integrity of God function? By now you should understand perfectly. God's integrity functions through imputation! Blessing is *anticipated* through hope; blessing is *realized* through imputation.

The first six imputations are clustered into three pairs. Each pair sets up a radical. Two imputations provide the basis for each hope, and each hope anticipates the next two imputations.

X   [Imputation + Imputation→Hope$_1$]⌐

Y ⌐→[Imputation + Imputation→Hope$_2$]⌐

Z ⌐→[Imputation + Imputation→Hope$_3$] = the seventh imputation

This pattern continues up to the third hope, which looks forward to the unique seventh imputation. That imputation stands alone as the final glorification of Christ.

God's plan for man begins with the real imputation of human life to the soul at the moment of birth. Clustered with this first imputation is the second: the simultaneous imputation of Adam's original sin to the old sin nature.

Remember that divine justice is man's point of contact with God. This is always true for all men—whether Adam at the Fall or the last person born before the end of the Millennium, whether the reversionist or the ultra-supergrace believer, whether the believer in heaven or the unbeliever in hell. Justice always does one of two things; it either curses or blesses. The policy of God's justice in blessing undeserving mankind is called grace. Because man can take no credit and can steal no glory for what God does, every person must be totally undeserving, totally condemned before he is qualified for grace. Were we not totally condemned, we could not be saved! The justice of God provides this condemnation at the instant of birth by condemning us for Adam's sin. Thus, the two real imputations at birth immediately create the potential for salvation. This is man's first potential; we will abbreviate it P$_1$.

HL   AOS
↓   +   ↓   = P$_1$ (potential for salvation)
Soul   OSN

A potential is worthless, however, if an individual is not aware that it exists. This fact brings into the equation the very first sentence in our book:

early in your life you became aware that God exists. When you reached God-consciousness, you already had the potential for an eternal relationship with Him! If you responded with positive volition, God was obliged to furnish Gospel information so that your potential might be realized. The Gospel made you aware that you *could* be saved. When you heard about and understood some of the basic blessings of salvation and the mechanics of obtaining them, you had confidence that if you believed in Christ you would in fact be saved. This is what motivated you to believe. Of course, you should recognize this confidence: it is $hope_1$.

Here the equation gives us a frame of reference for the presalvation and salvation ministries of God the Holy Spirit. Only the Holy Spirit can make the Gospel understandable to the unbeliever; the Holy Spirit alone enables the unbeliever to have $hope_1$. Theologically, this is called "common grace." The unbeliever takes action on his divinely provided confidence in the Gospel when he believes in Christ. We call this "efficacious grace": his act of positive volition results in the reality of salvation. In that moment of faith in Christ, the five salvation ministries of the Spirit—along with the rest of the thirty-six blessings of salvation—become a permanent reality.

Thus, the *potential* for salvation is converted into the *hope* of salvation, which itself is converted into the *reality* of salvation. Potential, hope, reality. Hope becomes a reality through faith in Christ, but what caused the potential to become a hope? Bible doctrine; pertinent Bible doctrine—in this case, the Gospel.

$$P_1 + \text{Bible doctrine (the Gospel)} = Hope_1$$

Now if we combine these last two short equations, write them on a single line, and enclose the entire result in brackets, we will have the complete X radical.

$$X [HL + AOS = P_1 + BD = H_1]$$

This is a picture of God's plan for the unbeliever. God gave him physical life and spiritual death, thus creating the potential for salvation. When the Gospel is made clear to the unbeliever and he is positive, this potential is converted into hope or confident expectation that he *will* be saved if he believes in Christ. This first hope may last a few seconds or several years, but as soon as the unbeliever does believe, he closes out the X radical, puts a plus sign after it, and moves on to the Y radical.

$$X [HL + AOS = P_1 + BD + H_1] +$$
$$Y [\text{life as an immature believer} \quad]$$

The "plus" represents the fact that reality has replaced the first hope; this is salvation adjustment to the justice of God. Remember that blessing is anticipated through hope, but blessing is realized through imputation. The imputations—again a cluster of two—that realize or fulfill hope₁ are found at the beginning of the Y radical. Indeed, the Gospel describes these two imputations! They are among the blessings upon which the unbeliever sets his hope when he believes in Christ.

I hope you are beginning to see things fall into place. If not, go back to the beginning of the equation and review again what we have brought together so far. This formula is a panoramic view of God's integrity in action. If you learn it well, it will serve you faithfully in times to come.

The Y radical follows the same pattern as the X radical: imputations, potential, doctrine, hope, reality. But here we begin with the two judicial imputations. When a person believes in Christ, he accepts Christ's work on the Cross on his behalf. There, all the personal sins of mankind were imputed to the perfect Person of Christ and judged. Because our sins were judged (and our human good and evil were totally rejected), God is free to judicially impute His own righteousness to anyone who believes in the Lord Jesus Christ and to declare that person justified. One judicial imputation removes our debt of sin while the other credits to our account the most valuable treasure in the universe—God's righteousness, the very principle of His integrity.

By exchanging our sins for God's righteousness, a cluster of imputations has once again created a potential.

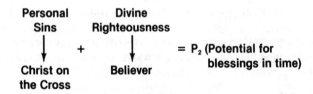

As the receiving end of the grace pipeline, divine righteousness resident in us means that we are qualified for blessings in time. Imputed righteousness is a potential that demands implementation.

We have already studied the conversion of this potential into reality under a more simplified equation: potential plus capacity equals reality.[44] What is it that builds up our capacity to appreciate divine blessings, to enjoy them, and to benefit from them? Knowledge of Bible doctrine, of course. Our function under GAP creates the capacity in our souls that enables God to bless us in time.

44. See above, page 101.

But en route to maturity, we must be motivated—to keep up and even to increase our spiritual momentum. This motivation comes from knowing certain doctrines. Whereas pertinent doctrine in the X radical was limited to the Gospel, pertinent doctrine here in the Y radical includes the whole system of truth related to the believer's life on earth. Especially applicable are those New Testament doctrines concerning the status and modus operandi of the royal family. We are motivated by knowing where we are going in the plan of God and by our eager expectation of receiving blessings when we get there. In other words, our motivation to continue developing capacity for blessings is no less than hope$_2$.

P_2 + Bible doctrine = H_2

This hope is the firm knowledge that if we continue to take in Bible doctrine, we will receive the sixth imputation and will thereby glorify the Lord Jesus Christ. In the Y radical, just as in the X radical, pertinent doctrine converts potential into hope. But for the growing believer knowledge of doctrine does not simply create hope, it builds his capacity as well.

In writing out the growing believer's radical, I want to emphasize the unique and utterly dramatic nature of the two imputations involved. We will abbreviate them J_1 and J_2 as a reminder that these are the only *judicial* imputations.

$Y [J_1 + J_2 = P_2 + BD = H_2]$

Here, then, is God's plan for the believer between salvation and spiritual maturity. The reality of salvation, which closed out the X radical, includes two factors. First, the judgment of our sins and, second, our possession of God's own righteousness. The *principle* of divine integrity resides at our end of the pipeline, and the *function* of divine integrity operates at God's end. Only capacity from doctrine is needed before our potential for blessings in time can be implemented—above and beyond all we could ever ask or think.

As we learn doctrine, we become aware of God's essence, of His decrees, of the fact that His objective is to bless us even in the devil's world. We learn that in so blessing us, He will win the tactical victory in the angelic conflict just as He won the strategic victory on the Cross. (And we learn that He won that strategic victory through the very judicial imputation — J_1—that, for each of us, opened up the Y radical in the first place!)

Doctrine tells us that nothing can stop the plan of God and that the function of GAP is God's stated procedure for giving us capacity for blessing. Doctrine teaches us the lesson of *a fortiori:* if God has already accomplished the most difficult thing at the Cross, He will not hold back in the much easier task of blessing us in this world. In other words, despite difficulties, pressures, disappointments, and distractions along the way, doctrine creates in the growing believer an unshakable confidence that the next stage in God's plan *will* come to pass. This hope becomes stronger as capacity increases, until finally the believer hits his stride as a mature spiritual athlete running for the final prize.

Once again, reality replaces hope. As soon as the reality of blessings in time replaces hope$_2$, the Y radical is closed out and the plus sign is added. The "plus" signifies maturity adjustment to the justice of God; the now-mature believer has moved into the Z radical.

Y [J$_1$ + J$_2$ = P$_2$ + BD = H$_2$] +

Z [life as a mature believer]

In the Z radical, we once again find a cluster of real imputations. The real imputation of eternal life to the human spirit at salvation, plus the real imputation of special blessings to divine righteousness in the mature believer, creates the third potential: the potential for blessings and rewards in eternity.

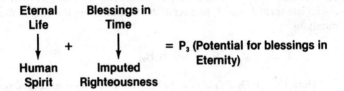

We possess eternal life now, but eternal life will be fully operative only in the resurrection body. The imputed life of God will provide the mature believer with capacity for the endless rewards he will receive in heaven. Imagine, we already possess the capacity factor for the reality of blessings in heaven! The only factor that must be filled in is blessing in time. The blessings of time are themselves what will be parlayed into blessings of eternity. Again, two imputations have set up a potential. Actually, here and in the X and Y radicals the *second* of the two imputations—Adam's sin, divine righteousness, blessings in time—sets up each potential.

The third potential is transformed into the third hope by knowledge of pertinent doctrine. Particularly relevant are certain doctrines related to future events. The mature believer knows about the resurrection body and about the eternal blessings that will be imputed to it. He is thoroughly briefed regarding the Rapture, when he will receive his new body, and regarding the Judgment Seat of Christ, where the seventh imputation will take place. Of course, these facts of eschatology are part of the frame of reference which the believer develops as he progresses through the Y radical. But in the Z radical, they are moved out to the launching pad of his soul to become the object of his third hope.

The XYZ equation is in perfect balance. Each radical contains a cluster of imputations, a potential, a body of pertinent doctrine, and a hope. But let us remember something before we get caught up in the nicety of a clean, symmetrical equation. The context of "all things" in Romans 8:28 is a delineation of undeserved suffering.

Romans 8:28 is strictly a description of the mature believer in Z radical. For him everything in the equation is already a reality, except the seventh imputation. For him "all things" are thoroughly familiar—from the first imputation at his birth to the imputation of his most recent blessing in time—and he knows exactly how they "work together for the purpose of the good." Indeed, "the good"—the plan of God, the glory of God, the final imputation—is the object of his confidence and motivation in life.

The mature believer eagerly anticipates the seventh imputation, and he does so "with fortitude" because he has come to know the pain of undeserved suffering. Undeserved suffering is a category of blessing that belongs to the sixth imputation, already included in the equation as part of "BT," blessings in time. The context places special emphasis on this special type of suffering as the factor which stimulates the third hope.

If surrounded with nothing but luxury and faced with no challenge to apply doctrine, we might grow fat and sloppy, accustomed to prosperity and forgetful of the plan of God. We might become so wrapped up in the present that we would forget where we are—in the devil's world—and forget where we are going—on to glory. We cannot afford to be like the schoolgirl, in love for the first time, who wishes that this moment could go on forever. Life does not stand still for anyone; we must move on. Undeserved suffering is what snaps us out of dream world and keeps us moving. It establishes—and strengthens—the third hope in the soul.

Therefore, we must understand that the Z radical includes undeserved suffering; it is the factor, in addition to pertinent doctrine, that converts the *potential* of eternal rewards into the *hope* or eager anticipation of those rewards. For emphasis, therefore, we will write this portion of the Z radical to include undeserved suffering before we return again to the proper symmetry of the overall equation.

$$P_3 + BD + \textit{Undeserved Suffering} = H_3$$

Let us now complete the Z radical.

$$Z\ [EL + BT = P_3 + BD = H_3]$$

Eternal life plus divine blessings in time create the potential for eternal blessings. Knowledge of eschatological doctrines, which foretell the Rapture and the Judgment Seat of Christ, make the mature believer aware of this third potential. Such a briefing prepares him for the future and allows him to face with total confidence what looms ahead in the plan of God, while periodic undeserved suffering is what drives him to focus on the Lord and eagerly hope for that final goal!

The Z radical is definitely not the property of the reversionistic believer. He is negative toward doctrine and will therefore never receive special blessings in time or eternity. He will never have a hope beyond $hope_1$. His ignorance of doctrine prevents him from looking forward to blessings in time. Although he has as great a $potential_2$ as does any other believer, $hope_2$ is a washout for him. $Hope_3$ is completely out of the picture.

But the reversionist does have a hope—of sorts. From hearing the Gospel (and perhaps he attends a church on Sundays where he is evangelized every week!), he has learned something about heaven. Therefore, in the midst of warning discipline, intensive discipline, and dying discipline, he looks forward to receiving the resurrection body. And somewhere along the line he has picked up some information about the Rapture so that when he hurts enough, he longs for the Rapture. He fervently wants it to occur *right now!* He selfishly distorts the prayer at the end of Revelation into a pitiful, agonized plea: "Even so, come Lord Jesus!"

To him the Rapture is not part of the "all things" working together for "the good." To him the Rapture is just another big aspirin!

Now, he has volition, and he is free to be disinterested in the Word of God. If that is what he wants to do, he can go ahead and try to replace God's system of hopes related to time and eternity with his own desperate hope for the super aspirin that will end it all. But to prefer that course of action, that disorientation to life, is blasphemous—not to mention idiotic. God keeps us *alive* for a purpose!

It is interesting to note that undeserved suffering focuses the mature believer's hope on the resurrection body, whereas *deserved* suffering and all the systems of divine discipline force the reversionist to focus on that same resurrection body. Despite this common focus (as "common" as is possible to believers at such opposite ends of the maturity spectrum), the reversionist does not live in the Z radical.

The Z radical is the realm where the mature believer both enjoys supergrace blessings and confidently anticipates his guaranteed surpassing-grace blessings. Thus, the Z radical brings Paul's second *a fortiori* argument into the XYZ formula. To bless a believer who has an old sin nature and who lives in the devil's world requires much greater effort on God's part than is required to bless a believer who has a resurrection body, who lives in heaven, who knows all doctrine, and who has perfect rapport with God. But if God has provided the blessings of time, which the mature believer enjoys every day, it follows *a fortiori*—"with greater reason"—that He will bless that same believer in eternity. The believer living in the Z radical looks forward to eternity, but he continues to take in doctrine, always advancing in the plan of God. He continues to glorify God in *cosmos diabolicus* until God sees fit to call him home.

When the third hope is fulfilled at the Judgment Seat of Christ, there is no new hope to replace it. Hope ends at that final evaluation. From then on, there is only reality forever.

We now have the complete equation.

$$X \text{ [HL + AOS} = P_1 + BD = H_1] +$$

$$Y \text{ [}J_1 + J_2 = P_2 + BD = H_2] +$$

$$Z \text{ [EL + BT} = P_3 + BD = H_3] = \text{the seventh imputation.}$$

I hardly need to emphasize how important this equation is as a tool for systematizing your knowledge of Bible doctrine. But the equation is only as good as your understanding of what it represents. So let us create a short index to all of its terms and abbreviations.

X radical: the unbeliever's life from birth to salvation.

HL: human life imputed to the soul at birth.

AOS: Adam's original sin imputed to the old sin nature.

P_1: potential for salvation for totally condemned mankind.

BD: pertinent Bible doctrine, specifically the Gospel.

H_1: hope of salvation upon believing in Christ.

+ : hope$_1$ being replaced by the reality of salvation.

Y radical: the believer's life from salvation to maturity.

J_1: judicial imputation of sins to Christ on the Cross.

J_2: judicial imputation of God's righteousness to the believer.

P_2: potential for blessings in time imputed to righteousness.

BD: pertinent Bible doctrine.

H_2: hope of blessings upon reaching maturity.

+ : hope$_2$ being replaced by the reality of blessings in time.

Z radical: the believer's life from maturity to death or Rapture.

EL: eternal life imputed to the human spirit at salvation.

BT: blessings in time imputed to divine righteousness at maturity.

P_3: potential for blessings and rewards in eternity.

BD: pertinent Bible doctrine, including eschatology.

H_3: hope of blessings in eternity at the Judgment Seat of Christ.

$=$: culmination of the plan of God at the final objective.

The seventh imputation: blessings in eternity imputed to the mature believer's resurrection body; "the good" of Romans 8:28; the eternal glorification of God.

THE EXEGISIS OF ROMANS 8:28

The *context* of Romans 8:28 is a discourse on the mature believer enduring undeserved suffering. The *concept* of Romans 8:28 is expressed in the XYZ formula. Now for the *exegesis*.

The first thing we must recognize is that this well-known verse deals with something extremely important: here are the believer's emergency rations for the crisis of undeserved suffering. Thus, the Greek particle *de* is here more emphatic than usual. As a transitional conjunction, it is often correctly rendered "and," as we find it in the King James Version, but that is too tame for Romans 8:28. The intensive use of the particle must be translated "in fact." In this way we seize upon the concept of fortitude and eager anticipation from the end of verse 25 and move into an emphatic application.

Next comes the verb *oida,* "we know." The perfective present tense indicates a fact which has come to exist in the past but is emphasized as being a present reality. The believers in view already understand $X + Y + Z$ and already hope for the seventh imputation. Pertinent doctrine for them is no longer the Gospel, nor are they still building basic doctrine. This verb implies that they have already passed through the X and Y radicals. Again, Romans 8:28 is the property of the mature believer.

"We know in fact that. . . ." From the Greek, we discover immediately that the King James Version has misplaced a phrase. What comes next in the original word order is not "all things" but the present active participle of *agapao,* "to love, to delight in, to esteem."

This participle and its definite article are in the dative case, indicating two things. First of all, the dative case points out whose interests are at stake; we call this the dative of advantage. The action of the verse—all things working together for good—is being performed for the believer's benefit. Secondly, the definite article is used here as a demonstrative pronoun, "to those . . . ," calling special attention to mature believers. "To those who love the God" identifies mature believers as those who are occupied with Christ, one of the spiritual blessings included in the sixth imputation.

Growing believers—in the Y radical—are in the process of learning to love God, but no one actually loves Him before cracking the maturity barrier. He loves us, but we do not love Him. Now do not puff up your self-righteousness and insist that you do too love Him! Only at maturity do we have enough doctrine to *know* God; only with maximum doctrine do we possess the *capacity* for love which enables us to be occupied with Him. We need to keep growing, not assume we have arrived.

The generic definite article with *theos,* translated "the God," emphasizes the uniqueness of the divine attributes, the origin of the unique plan of God. Here, in effect, Paul has inserted the doctrine of divine essence. The sum of God's attributes, revealed in Bible doctrine, engenders awe, respect, and ultimately love.

"We know in fact that to those who love the God. . . ."

Having long ago memorized the Authorized translation of Romans 8:28, we expect at this point to find the familiar heart of the verse. We glance at the Greek text—and get a shock! We look back and forth from the Greek to the King James English and wonder how this could be? As if misplacing a phrase were not bad enough, the next two words were inexcusably mistranslated by the dons of 1611.

No one can become an expert in Greek grammar overnight, but to see what Romans 8:28 teaches, you must first know a thing or two about how Greek sentences are put together. In a standard Greek sentence, as in an English one, there is a subject, a verb, and an object. The subject produces the action of the verb; the object receives the action of the verb. Knowing which is which is absolutely essential to the correct interpretation of God's Word.

The subject and object are nouns, and in these nouns Greek shows its versatility. An English noun can appear in only one or two forms (singular or plural), but a Greek noun can take on a variety of forms. With its many suffixes, it can show not merely singular or plural but other things as well, including what part it plays in a sentence. We can quickly identify the subject because it is in the form of the nominative case; the object, in the accusative case. It makes no difference at all where the word appears in a sentence—first, second, or so on; we can always discover by checking its case what role the noun plays. Subject: nominative case. Object: accusative case. So far so good.

With this rule firmly in hand, we turn back to the statement translated, "all things work together." These four English words represent only two Greek words: *panta sunergei. Panta* is a plural form of the adjective *pas,* meaning "all." This adjective is used here as a substantive—like a noun—and because it is in the neuter gender, it is correctly translated "all *things.*" But what role does "all things" perform in this sentence? Is it the subject or the object? We immediately pull out our rule: check the case. *Panta* is the *nominative* neuter plural of *pas.* But then, the *accusative* neuter plural of *pas* is also *panta!* Which is it? Our rule is no help at all. Obviously we must look further.

The verb comes to our rescue. *Sunergei* is a form of *sunergeo,* "to cooperate, to work together with." When we analyze *sunergei,* we can list a wealth of information. The tense: present. The voice: active. The mood: indicative. The person: third. The number: singular. Sifting through this analysis, we finally hit upon something useful in solving the problem of whether "all things" is the subject or the object.

A basic rule of Greek and English grammar states that the *number* of the *subject* must agree with the *number* of the *verb.* A singular verb must have a singular subject; a plural verb, a plural subject. What is the number of the verb *sunergei?* Singular. What about "all things"? Plural!

No singular verb ever takes a plural subject. That would be like saying, "They has a problem," or "Young pups is smart." But for some reason, despite their brilliance, the King James translators chewed up this tremendous verse in just that illiterate way. They said, in effect, "All things work*s* together for good." That is poor English; it would be terrible Greek.

What then is our conclusion? "All things" can only be the object, not the subject, of "works together." A singular verb *can* take a plural object: "He (singular) has (singular) problems (plural)" is perfectly acceptable. That seems to settle the matter—until we suddenly realize that we have only a verb and an object. Where is the subject? We look again and find nothing; there are only two words here: *panta sunergei.* Someone or something must be producing the action of this verb; verbs do not appear out of the blue. We have another mystery on our hands. Where do we look for the solution?

Fortunately, Greek is a more expressive language than English. Greek verbs have built-in subjects. Where we would have to supply a separate subject, the Greeks could leave it out, knowing from the verb's suffix who was producing the action. There is no equivalent of this system of suffixes in English, but in the verb *sunergei,* the suffix *-ei* points to the subject we have been seeking. We have already identified this suffix in our analysis: it is the third person singular. In other words, the subject of "works together" can be "he," "she," or "it." How do we determine which is correct here? The immediate context tells us.

> . . . to those who love the God,   (he, she, it)   works
> all things together. . . .

The antecedent is a masculine noun; the correct translation is obvious. "He *[God]* works all things together for good!" Indeed, several ancient manuscripts actually fill in the blank with *ho theos,* "the God"—in the nominative singular to indicate that God is the subject.

With or without the specific reference to God, however, the Greek syntax is unquestionably clear. "All things" is not the subject; "He" (God) is. All things do not necessarily work together for our good. Instead, *God* works all things together for good for mature believers, for those who are adjusted to His justice, for those who are so oriented to Bible doctrine as to know and love Him.

Why only for mature believers (and for those approaching maturity)? God continually works all things together for His *own* glory; *that* is the objective of His plan. It is because we have adjusted to His unswerving justice that He can, at the same time, work things together for our good. He never for a moment compromises or departs from His goal; we simply adopt His goal for our own as we renew our minds with divine viewpoint. God's plan moves on, and the mature believer has come on board. God does not adjust to us in blessing us; we adjust to Him and reap what He has sown.

Now that we have straightened out the translation, we can pick up the more detailed interpretation of *panta sunergei*. "All things" includes more than the blessing of undeserved suffering in context (Rom. 8:17-39); it emphasizes the great variety of supergrace blessings which characterize the life of the mature believer in the Z radical. But even special blessings of the sixth imputation are only one piece of the overall puzzle. "All things" include every factor in God's predetermined plan for mankind.

This plan expresses God's desire for everyone to whom He imputes human life and Adam's sin. The plan of God begins at birth; no one is ignored. The justice of God provides all the pieces to the puzzle; our nonmeritorious positive volition toward the Gospel and all subsequent doctrine puts them together. The pieces include the first six imputations, the three potentials, all pertinent doctrines, and all three hopes, as well as the surroundings and circumstances of the individual's daily life in which these factors occur. For the mature believers in Romans 8:28, the puzzle is completely assembled; "all things" are in place.

Mature believers do in fact possess that final, total confidence in their future rewards, hope$_3$, and everything leading up to it. For unbelievers and immature believers, however, some of the pieces are not yet fitted into the formula. The phrase "all things" does not yet apply to those still in X or Y radical.

Sunergeo, in the present active indicative, is a compound verb, composed of the preposition *sun,* "with, together with," and the verb *ergazomai,* "to work." The customary present tense indicates what habitually occurs or what may be reasonably expected to occur. Because of the infinite faithfulness of God, the mature believer can be confident regarding everything that happens to him: it is for a divine purpose. This means that he can expect suffering from time to time as the ignition system for the third hope. Undeserved suffering fulfills the purpose, amid divine prosperity within the devil's world, of causing the mature believer to remember the plan of God and to anchor his confidence only in the Lord.

Once you begin to understand the XYZ formula, it dawns on you that undeserved suffering will not cause misery or detract from your blessings; it will *add* to your blessings. In fact, Paul was so advanced a believer that God gave him perpetual suffering, which the great apostle carried on his shoulders like a cloak of honor (Rom. 8:18, 35; Phil. 4:12). Moses, too, was given just such an ultra-supergrace mantle, which kept his eyes on the Lord and on future rewards (Heb. 11:24-26).

The key to Romans 8:28 is the prepositional phrase "for the good." The preposition *eis* is often used with the accusative case to express purpose; thus, the phrase is correctly translated "for the purpose of the good." The phrase lacks a definite article, in which respect English and Greek are exactly opposite. In English, we add a definite article to create emphasis—"*the* good"—whereas the Greeks dropped the definite article for the same effect. If a Greek article had appeared with *agathos,* "good," it would have pointed out the *identity* of the good, but the anarthrous construction which we actually find here emphasizes the high *quality* of the good. *Agathos* itself means "good of intrinsic value."

Therefore, the highest quality of the most intrinsically valuable blessings and rewards comprises God's ultimate purpose for you. "The good" is the summation of all that God has ever intended for the human race. It *is* the plan of God. In time, "the good" is the object of the third hope; in eternity, it is the reality of the seventh imputation. "The good" is maximum blessing; it will be received from the hand of Jesus Christ Himself; it is awarded to the mature believer in resurrection body. Above all else, "the good" is the glory of God. God is glorified in blessing us.

Paul next takes up the "how" of God's plan, and he continues to describe these divine mechanics through Romans 8:29, 30. How does God cause "all things" to work together for "the good"? In whichever way He does, it must not coerce man's volition. Man must be free to believe in Christ or remain unsaved, to rebound or remain carnal, to learn doctrine or remain spiritually immature. God never violates your free will. But along with freedom goes responsibility, and God holds you personally responsible to conform to His plan by progressing from X to Y to Z.

Your volition and God's plan come together in the divine decrees, set up in eternity past (Eph. 1:11).[45] Since you were in God's thoughts billions of years before you were born, He knew that you would be receptive at God-

---

45. See Appendix B.

consciousness and that He would subsequently provide Gospel information. But the Gospel sets up a choice: *you* must decide.

In eternity past, God knew in precise detail what would happen to you if you refused to believe in Christ, just as He knew what would happen if you believed. Way down the line in the twentieth century, which alternative would be the actual reality? God certainly did not make the choice for you! He did, however, have the good sense to know which way *you* would decide. God knew in eternity past that, given the opportunity, you would say, "Yes, I believe in Christ as my Savior." (I assume that anyone who has come this far in a study of God's integrity either was a believer from the outset or has become one by now.) Knowing that you would say yes to the Gospel, He decreed that *your* positive volition would actually exist, and because it would, He did something else for you which He does for every Church Age believer.

The noun *kletos* means "called to privilege" and is a technical term signifying the doctrine of election. Election, like foreknowledge and predestination (or foreordination), is a result of the divine decrees. Based on your decision to believe in Jesus Christ, God elected you into the royal family with fantastic potential for blessings (P_2 leading to P_3). There can be no greater security than to realize that your entrance into Y radical was known and guaranteed billions of years before human history began.

"To those who are the called ones" is also a dative of advantage describing those in whose interest God works the X, Y, and Z radicals together for the good. Since all Church Age believers are called or elect effective the moment of faith in Christ, this description obviously applies to the mature believers in context. But growing believers and even unbelievers can take heart from knowing that those who are now so far advanced were themselves once back at the point of entry into the royal family. There is a hope for every human being alive on the earth! In fact, the Greek noun *prothesis*, "predetermined plan," covers all phases of the plan, from X to Y to Z to the final glorification of God in the seventh imputation.

In corrected translation, Romans 8:28 now stands:

> We know in fact that to those [mature believers] who love the God, He works all things [X + Y + Z] together for the purpose of the good [the seventh imputation], to those who are the called ones [the elect to privilege] according to the predetermined plan [X + Y + Z = the seventh imputation]. (Rom. 8:28)

USING THE EQUATION

THE EQUATION AND ADJUSTING TO THE JUSTICE OF GOD

Not only does Romans 8:28 depict the integrity of God working constantly in our behalf, not only does it build the framework on which we construct a true, systematic theology in our souls, but it also maps out where we have been, where we are, and where we are going in life. The XYZ equation helps us integrate new doctrines and remember those we have already learned; it is a tool that organizes our thinking. To become skillful in the use of this doctrinal tool we must practice applying it. The remainder of this chapter therefore is devoted to using the XYZ equation. We will see various categories of Bible doctrine pulled together under the organizing principle presented in Romans 8:28.

The XYZ panorama of God's plan sets forth the principle to which we have alluded ever since we saw the Athenians adjusting themselves to the unalterable *dikaiosune* of Solon. Infinitely more unbending than the justice of Solon, the justice of God is immutable; it goes on, with or without us. Our adjustment to God's justice is His freedom to bless us.

ADJUSTING TO GOD'S JUSTICE

	X	Y	Z
Salvation	✔		
Rebound		✔	✔
Maturity		✔	✔

What is the practical application of this point of doctrine? What must we do to free God to bless us? We must make three adjustments: first, salvation adjustment; second, rebound adjustment; and third, maturity adjustment. The first is required of those in X radical. The second is required in the Y and Z radicals. The third is the objective of the Y radical and the reality of the Z radical. Salvation and rebound are instantaneous adjustments: salvation, once and for all; rebound, as often as necessary. Maturity is a gradual adjustment. Therefore, rebound and the advance to maturity (and beyond) become the basic functions of life after salvation.

We have studied salvation adjustment in some detail, all the way from the Fall of man (reflected in the second imputation), to the Cross (the third imputation), to our awareness of our potential (P_1) through hearing the Gospel (pertinent BD), to anticipating salvation (H_1), to actually believing in Christ (+) to receiving the righteousness of God (the fourth imputation) and eternal life (the fifth imputation).

What is our part in salvation? None. How do we make this adjustment? Entirely without merit. Salvation comes totally free of charge; we contribute *nothing*. But since God's integrity can never be compromised, someone had to pay for our salvation. That Someone is our matchless Savior, Jesus Christ.

Salvation is perfect; we cannot improve it. It is complete; we can add nothing to it. We receive it in a moment of time through faith in Christ, and it can never be taken from us. If we had something to do with earning salvation perhaps we could lose it. But since it is exclusively the work of God, it depends on God alone, and He will never reverse Himself. Once we leave the X radical, we can never return.

Each adjustment to the justice of God has a corresponding maladjustment. Salvation maladjustment is rejection of Christ as Savior: negative volition toward the Gospel or toward God-consciousness. Negative volition takes many forms, from outright antagonism to any of the subtle ways in which people try to add human works to the work of God. If we refuse to meet God exclusively on His terms—simple nonmeritorious faith in Christ—we do not meet Him at all. In order to be saved, no one must walk an aisle, raise a hand, renounce sins, publicly confess, "speak in tongues," join the church. The reason is that we do not come to God; God comes to us. False issues muddy the water. The Word of God makes it clear that a person who believes in Christ is forever saved even if he never tells another soul about it![46]

A person can believe and immediately thereafter become involved in erroneous doctrine so that he credits his salvation to some false system. Regardless of what he might now claim, he was saved through mere faith in Christ. But if someone accepts false doctrine *as an unbeliever* and tries to be saved by works, promises, penance, or reform, he is not saved at all. The third imputation is sufficient, efficient, efficacious, complete; salvation can come by faith only—by accepting what Christ has done. God has integrity; God's integrity accepts no human being but Christ; God cannot acquiesce to

---

46. Romans 10:9, 10 is frequently taken out of context and misinterpreted.

even our most sincere good deeds though He fervently desires that we all be saved.

"But," you ask, "if an evangelist or someone in personal witnessing presents a mixture of true and false information, what is the poor unbeliever to do?" God anticipated the problem and solved it long before we thought to worry about it. God never lowers His standards, but He does guarantee to everyone a fair opportunity to trust in Christ.[47] God the Holy Spirit works through doctrine, not falsehood; therefore, acting in place of the human spirit, He extracts the true from the false and illuminates only what is accurate. Hence, in spite of false concepts, the unbeliever is able to face the true issue. The Gospel stands; unbelievers are being saved; the plan of God goes on; God has integrity—in spite of human distortions and apostasy.

"But," you ask, still worried, "how much faith is required for a person to be saved?" Only a little more than no faith at all. If at any time, for even a moment, a person believes Christ is his Savior, that person has freed the justice of God to save him and to move him from X into Y radical. He has made his first adjustment to the justice of God. Permanently.

Salvation maladjustment, however, eventually results in unbeliever reversionism (2 Pet. 2:20–22; Rom. 1:18–32).[48] The unbeliever who rejects what is true fills the void in his soul with what is false and tries to adjust to life on that basis. This explains much of the misery and tragedy of human history. Ultimately, salvation maladjustment results in spending eternity in the Lake of Fire (John 3:18, 36; Rev. 20:12–15). The human citizens of Satan's kingdom who refuse to accept free citizenship in the kingdom of God will share the fate of their good-and-evil ruler.

It is either ignorance or impudence for people to ask, "How can a loving God send His creatures to hell?" This complaint (first registered by Satan—a fact that speaks volumes) attacks God's very basis for bringing anyone to *heaven!* Undeniably it is a disaster when anyone is cast into hell. There is no question about that. But God is free to judge unbelievers without violating His perfect character; in fact His perfect character obliges Him to judge them. It is right and just.

God exhausts every possibility in seeking to save us (Rom. 2:4), leaving eternal condemnation as the only alternative to eternal salvation. Justice either blesses or curses, and if a person of his own volition refuses to adjust to the justice of God, the justice of God must adjust to him—with cursing. If God did not remain consistent in this (Rom. 2:11), He would not be God. He would have no integrity. And lacking integrity, His absolute guarantee of our salvation would be worthless; there would be no eternal security.

---

47. See Thieme, *Heathenism.*

48. See Thieme, *Reversionism.*

Believers who react to the self-determined eternal judgment of the unbeliever by blaming God do not realize that they are laying siege against the walls of their own salvation. Happily, the walls are impregnable.

Following salvation, our second adjustment to the justice of God is part of the inner conflict between the old sin nature and the Holy Spirit. After we have permitted the sin nature to gain control of our souls through some personal sin, we need a means of recovering the filling of the Spirit and of being restored to fellowship with God. I have coined the term "rebound" for the technique by which a believer bounces back from carnality into spirituality again. We get out of fellowship when we sin; we return to fellowship when we cite that sin privately to God. This essential and basic technique of the Christian life is taught extensively in other publications;[49] here we will quickly show its relation to divine justice, our point of contact with God.

> If we confess [cite, name, admit] our sins, He [God] is
> faithful [He always does the same thing] and just [it is
> consistent with His justice] to forgive us our sins and to
> cleanse us from all unrighteousness. (1 John 1:9)

Why is this simple procedure consistent with the justice of God? The context of 1 John 1:9 gives us our frame of reference. First, the old sin nature remains an active part of our physical bodies as long as we live (1 John 1:8). And second, throughout our lives we will continue to use our volition to commit personal sins (1 John 1:10). All our *sins* have already been judged (1 John 1:7*b*); they are no longer an issue in our *eternal relationship* with God. But our *volition* is always an issue in the angelic conflict: we cannot make wrong decisions with impunity. The negative volition which yields to temptation and places us under the old sin nature cuts off our *temporal fellowship* with God. After we sin, we exercise positive volition again by citing that sin to God as one that His justice has already handled. We are identifying that sin with the Cross. In effect we are citing the court case in which that sin was brought to trial, imputed to Jesus Christ in our place, and judged. Although the justice of God has dealt with all our sins once and for all on the Cross, we too must deal with them via our own free will as we commit them in time.

> If we would judge ourselves [adjust to the justice of God,
> ie., acknowledge that we have committed a sin which was
> judged at the Cross], we should not be judged [divine
> discipline is cancelled]. (1 Cor. 11:31)

---

49. See Thieme, *Rebound and Keep Moving, Isolation of Sin, Prodigal Son,* and *The Plan of God.*

Always, justice is our point of contact with God. As long as a believer thinks that God's love is our point of contact, he will never appreciate rebound. The very fact that we are not perfect and do sin is part of the reason that God's love *cannot* be His point of contact with us. Love₁ can love only what is perfect, and Adam's original sin (which was a sin of negative volition) destroyed any possibility of blessing from love₁. Divine justice blesses us—with salvation, with instantaneous recovery from sin, with every divine blessing.

Does rebound seem too simple? Even as we accepted the Gospel by faith, so also we must accept rebound by faith. In the Gospel, God promises that if we believe in Christ who was judged on the Cross for our sins, we will be saved. In rebound, God promises that if we acknowledge that the particular sin we have committed was judged on the Cross, we will be forgiven. The same imputations which form the basis for our salvation also form the basis for our return to temporal fellowship. Rebound is simple for a purpose: God wants us to be in fellowship with Him.

In rebound, as in salvation, we meet God on His terms, not on ours. We name our sins to God—period! That is what perfect justice demands; we add nothing to it. When we try to include anything else in rebound, we are telling God that our standards are higher than His.

Believers want to get into the act by feeling sorry for their sins, by promising God to never commit them again, by performing some type of penance. If only we can stir up a feeling of remorse within ourselves, if only we can confess our sins publicly or tell a clergyman or priest about them, then we *feel* cleansed and forgiven. Somehow it *feels* more like we are back in fellowship if we do something to earn it. But rebound is not some kind of psychological catharsis. In rebound, the question is not how we feel about our sins but what God has done about them. His righteousness and justice have been completely satisfied by the work of Christ on the Cross. The whole idea of rebound is to adjust to what divine justice has already accomplished. Integrity's grace system is: name it, forget it, and move on. Anything else is rebound maladjustment.

We do not need to feel remorse, because a guilt complex is itself a mental attitude sin. God does not require that we sin as part of recovering fellowship! Nor does He require that we wait until we experience some kind of emotion; emotion is never a criterion in the spiritual life. Furthermore, we cannot promise God never to sin again; a promise is only as good as the person who makes it—in our case, no good (1 John 1:8, 10). And when the particular sin is our area of weakness, promises become ludicrous. We are helpless to do anything but accept grace.

Penance, too, is ridiculous. God does not want people to grovel. He wants us to grow up so He can bless us! Besides, nothing we can possibly do could ingratiate us with God; Christ alone was qualified to suffer efficaciously for our sins. We insult the Lord when we compare our works to His. And when we confess to a clergyman instead of directly to God, we are telling God, "Thank you very much, but we prefer to ignore our position in Christ." It is *not* okay to violate God's system! Both the clergyman who listens and the parishioner who confesses are royal priests; neither can do more than the other. But worse, in confessing our sins to a pastor, we destroy the privacy that God designed to protect us. When that pastor stands up to teach the Word of God, we can no longer be objective.

Since the filling of the Spirit is essential to all aspects of the Christian life, the mechanics of rebound by which we recover the filling of the Spirit become a vital issue. We must master this technique as soon after salvation as possible. The fact that we need only admit or name our sins is not a license to sin. Rebound is a license to grow up! Adding our own personal touches to the simple grace procedure is not a demonstration of sincerity, love, and dedication to the Lord; it is maladjustment to the justice of God.

Salvation is instantaneous and permanent. Rebound is instantaneous and effectual until we sin again. But maturity adjustment to the justice of God is a gradual process. The Y and Z radicals explain this process: through the faithful intake of Bible doctrine we fulfill the phenomenal potential for blessings which God gave us when He imputed to us His righteousness. Doctrine creates confidence in future blessings, and that confidence or hope becomes our motivation and momentum in life. As we conform our thinking to God's thinking, we eventually free the justice of God to impute those promised blessings to us, first in time, then in eternity. God provides every factor in our advance, and the result is His glorification.

Maturity maladjustment, on the other hand, is the rejection or neglect of doctrine, resulting in reversionism and the thinking of evil. Indistinguishable from unbelievers, reversionistic *believers* are often among the worst misfits on earth. They not only contribute in large measure to the world's ills, but their personal reward, as we have seen, is divine discipline in time and a lack of special blessings in eternity. For them, due to their own negative volition, God certainly cannot work all things together for the good! Nevertheless, God's grace guarantees that there will be no remorse or embarrassment in heaven—not even for reversionists (Rev. 21:4).

Lest we wander too far afield, let us reorient ourselves to the ground we are covering. We have just practiced using the XYZ equation to clarify our spiritual responsibilities before God. From the first imputation at birth to the final imputation after death, God's plan for our lives is that we adjust to His justice. By seeing ourselves in the light of His overall plan, we have been able to understand what is essential and what is nonessential. Faith in Christ, rebound, and GAP are essential, or, reduced to utmost simplicity, what is essential is Bible doctrine. Everything else in life, to a greater or less degree, is nonessential. Many things which are thought to be important in the Christian life simply are not. Misconceptions can thrive under partial, unclear, or false ideas of what God's objectives really are. Perhaps some of these misconceptions have been exposed by XYZ as never before.

Let us try the equation again, using it once more as a tool for clarifying our thinking, for integrating and recalling categories of doctrine. How does God sustain us? Until we learn His Word, the manner in which God treats us remains a mystery, but the X, Y, and Z radicals give us a basis for categorizing His policy for our sustenance and protection. In all cases, as long as we live, we require special care.

THE EQUATION AND DIVINE PROTECTION

God protects us throughout our lives in whichever radical we live. In X radical, we are supported, sustained, and protected—and the human race perpetuated—by the laws of divine establishment. God designed these laws for both believers and unbelievers. Therefore, every citizen has a duty to his nation. Patriotism, not internationalism, is incumbent upon all. The nation has the authority to protect the freedom, privacy, and property of those who live within its borders, and such freedom is necessary for evangelism. God is not the author of confusion; He has ordained the laws of establishment to provide the modicum of orderliness needed for human prosperity and survival, and for the furtherance of the plan of grace in human history. The laws of divine establishment require the use of our volition. If a nation does not adhere to them, the alternate laws of divine discipline go into effect against that nation (Lev. 26:14–31). Thus the importance of rendering unto Caesar the things which are Caesar's.

$$X [HL + AOS = P_i + BD = H_i] +$$

$$\boxed{\text{ESTABLISHMENT}}$$

When we are evangelized and freely decide to move into the Y radical, we continue to live under establishment (all believers should be paladins of establishment freedom, grateful for its part in their salvation). But, for believers, additional divine protection is added. Logistical blessings from God keep us alive in the devil's world and enable us to advance in the plan of

God. Different from the laws of establishment, logistical grace does not depend on our volition. God keeps us alive as long as *He* chooses.

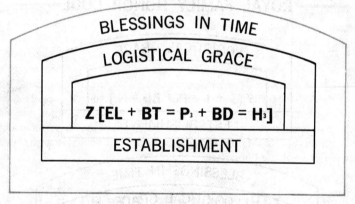

When we break through the maturity barrier into Z radical, we still live within the bounds of establishment; we still relax in logistical grace; but simple logistical grace is now parlayed into the sixth imputation. God shifts gears from merely sustaining us into giving us special blessings. In Z radical, we are both sustained and blessed.

But as we exercise positive volition in Y and Z radicals, we need more to sustain us, protect us, and guide us in the use of our free will than just the principles of establishment. To use our volition properly, whether long-range in planning what we are going to do in life or short-range in making day-to-day decisions, we must have accurate information. The immediate objective of God's plan is that we *have* that information—Bible doctrine—and from it line up our volition with God's volition. As under establishment, here too, freedom and authority meet. We are under God's authority: we do not make policy; we follow policy. Our decisions must conform to His.

God has a purpose for each of us, and we must understand as soon as possible—at least in generalities—what is His will and desire for our lives. We must become familiar with God's plan, with God's objectives for us. We must see that learning Bible doctrine has the highest priority. Doctrine renovates our thinking, displaces evil, neutralizes the sin nature, converts potentials into hopes and hopes into realities, and glorifies God in the angelic conflict. Therefore, God's policy is to insure for each believer the greatest possible opportunity to learn doctrine—to mature spiritually (Y radical) and to continue growing beyond maturity (Z radical). Freedom, authority, and *blessing* meet in spiritual growth!

The common objective of all believers in both the Y and Z radicals is spiritual maturity and the glorification of the Lord Jesus Christ. God sustains and protects us and enables us to keep moving toward this goal by giving us a series of principles to follow. These practical guidelines constitute an honor code for the royal family of God.

The XYZ equation is the principle of the plan of God; the royal family honor code is the function. Indeed, the honor code *is* the Christian way of life.

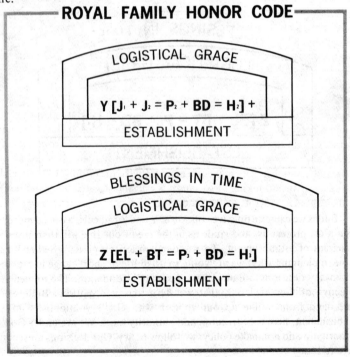

ROYAL FAMILY HONOR CODE

LOGISTICAL GRACE

$$Y [J_1 + J_2 = P_2 + BD = H_2] +$$

ESTABLISHMENT

BLESSINGS IN TIME

LOGISTICAL GRACE

$$Z [EL + BT = P_3 + BD = H_3]$$

ESTABLISHMENT

It is of course beyond the scope of this book to teach the Christian life in all its detail, but the equation allows us to at least summarize some of the basic concepts of how we are to conduct ourselves as believers under the justice of God. By following the honor code, we not only pursue our relationship with God's integrity but we also develop integrity ourselves! The circle is complete. Justice demands justice, but justice also *fulfills* justice.

THE EQUATION AND THE ROYAL FAMILY HONOR CODE

HIGH STANDARDS FOR ROYALTY

We are spiritual aristocrats, born again into the royal family of the King of Kings and Lord of Lords. We come from vastly different human backgrounds, but as believers in the Lord Jesus Christ, all of us must learn to think like royalty, to be motivated like royalty, to make decisions like royalty, to act like the royalty we are.

Liberals and socialists would have us believe that royalty is evil; that members of the nobility should feel guilty about having privileges; that the thinking of aristocrats is arrogance, greed, insensitivity to others, tyranny. But the opposite is true. *Socialism* is arrogance. Socialism refuses to admit the existence of the old sin nature, yet it champions sin, human good, and evil. As a means of gaining power for a few, it encourages and foments the sins of jealousy, greed, and violence in those who arrogantly presume themselves to deserve something for nothing. To those who do not understand human freedom or appreciate the proper function of man's soul, socialism sounds good: equality and prosperity for all! Intoxicating words make perverse ideas popular, but words do not change facts. Socialism crushes volition and individuality. It divorces people from reality. It systematically robs them of capacity for life. It turns them into dependents of the state, and therefore makes them maleable to the tyranny of their leaders. The peasantish thinking of socialism is evil; the elevated doctrinal thinking of spiritual aristocrats is "the good."

In both the spiritual and the temporal realms, aristocracy is a wonderful word. It denotes achievement. The aristocracies that exist in all countries (even the United States has eschewed only the overt titles) indicate that someone rose to meet a crisis or accept a challenge and accomplished something far above the common activities of his contemporaries. He established his achievement within a certain area or over a certain group of people and earned the privilege of being called an aristocrat. Aristocracy is aristocracy, not for having blue blood, but for having superior standards—standards of thought, courage, leadership, achievement, responsibility.

Ultimately, all lines of human nobility decline. The sons and daughters are frequently weaker and less brilliant than their great forebears. Some turn their inherited positions to evil ends. In many cases power corrupts. But as long as high standards are passed from generation to generation, the responsibilities and obligations of aristocracy can be fulfilled and the line maintained. In succeeding generations, the standards take the form of a code, a code of honor.

How is a young heir different from a commoner? It is the young nobleman's long and arduous training in the family's (or the upper class's) honor code. His training begins almost at birth. He is drilled and drilled in everything from etiquette and deportment to moral courage and personal integrity. When finally he steps into public affairs, perhaps in his late teens or early twenties, it is not by accident that he is a self-composed, courteous gentleman trained to think fairly and prepared to assume his public responsibilities.

We are aristocrats not through our own achievements but through grace, based on the achievements of the Lord Jesus Christ, the Prince-Ruler of the Church. During His First Advent Christ earned the royal title of King of Kings and Lord of Lords (1 Tim. 6:15) just as military commanders throughout human history have been awarded titles of nobility for their victories. Of Napoleon's marshals, for example, Murat was made King of Naples; Davout, the Duke of Aurstädt and Prince of Eckmül; Bertier, the Prince of Neuchâtel; even Ney, the Duke of Elchingen and Prince of Moscow. Britain's Admiral Nelson became Lord Nelson for his bold successes against Napoleon's fleets.

Our Lord Jesus Christ defeated Satan at the Cross. For winning the strategic victory in the angelic conflict, God the Father gave Him the title above all titles and caused the humanity of Christ to be seated in the place of highest honor, the right hand of God. Our Lord's victory over Satan is the source of our royalty; it was the founding of the royal family. Christ's royalty is eternal, and whereas the titled houses of Europe have all but disappeared, our aristocracy in Jesus Christ will be sustained forever.

As members of His endless spiritual dynasty, we too have an honor code to guide our lives on earth in the Y and Z radicals. "Right thinking results in right motivation," says the royal family honor code. "And right motivation results in right action." Always, *thinking* is the great issue in aristocracy. The Christian way of life is not so much what we do as what we think. Doing *follows* thinking. Right thinking, right motivation, right action all depend on the Bible doctrine resident in our souls and on the filling of the Holy Spirit. Therefore, nothing must distract us or prevent us from learning doctrine, and we must do nothing that would hinder others in their intake of the Word of God. The honor code is designed so all of us can move from spiritual infancy to spiritual maturity.

THE SUPERIORITY OF THE ROYAL FAMILY HONOR CODE

An honor code is necessary because no man is an island and because it is human nature to be arrogant, self-righteous, vindictive, deceitful, thoughtless, and small. Human nature is the old sin nature! Everything we do as we advance toward the Z radical is done elbow to elbow with other members of the royal family. Each of us is imperfect in his own way, and no two of us are at exactly the same level of spiritual growth. This diverse and often unlikely crowd must be able to gather together and listen to the teaching of the Word of God without subjectivity, schism, and strife. We must be objective in learning doctrine; the honor code therefore requires thoughtfulness, flexibility, and understanding toward each other. Nor can this tolerant objectivity among believers stop at the church door; it must carry over from Bible class into the wider realms of Christian fellowship. And each believer must carry it even beyond Christian relationships into the realm of *all* contacts with *all* other people. As we live in the devil's world, each of us with his own old sin nature, we must regulate our lives by the fact that spiritual growth is our most pressing concern.

What are some basic characteristics of a good honor code? An honor code must be specific enough to instill a sense of what should be done and what should be avoided. It should not be so general as to lend itself to rigid, legalistic interpretations that insist on inconsequential details. In some ways the famous honor code at West Point encourages tattling and pettiness in the corps of cadets. The code's flaw is that essentials are not distinguished from nonessentials; pettiness is a bad trait in a future officer. But a practiced eye in spotting the essentials in any situation would be a boon not only during a cadet's training at the academy but even more so in facing real-world pressures and decisions once he dons the Army blue. A good code of honor faces reality.

None of us is perfect; therefore, the code must recognize the existence of the old sin nature. In this way an honor code does not permit appearances to be substituted for reality. A poor code would permit lip-service to pass for genuine integrity; people could manipulate the system while still claiming to be honorable.

The royal family honor code is superior in that it sees people as they are; it gives us a completely workable policy, the exact drill to follow in any situation. God knows us and deals with us from His integrity; He demands that we know Bible doctrine and deal with Him, ourselves, and others from our honor-code integrity.

The relationship between the royal family honor code and Christian motivation clearly shows that the code is realistic and does not make any false assumptions about the human race. In the XYZ equation we discover that our motivation in life is called "hope"—hope$_1$, hope$_2$, hope$_3$. And for what do we hope? What do we eagerly anticipate? Certainly selfless altruism does not move us and inspire our spiritual momentum. Our honor code does not require that we set aside our own interests. Let me illustrate.

Often in history, soldiers have come from the lower classes; Napoleon's army in the Italian Campaign was the dregs of society, but it was nonetheless victorious. These soldiers were not motivated by the lofty sense of duty and patriotism that we sometimes assume beats in the breast of every man in uniform. A battalion commander, exhorting such troops before an engagement, would never have said, "Men, storm that fortified position and give your lives for the reputation of the Directory!" Such an appeal would have been beyond their level of thinking. No one would have obeyed! Instead, the commander would point out the objective, perhaps a fortress city on a hilltop, and say, "Soldiers, in that city is great wealth! If you capture it you will all be rich! Your *pay* is in that city!" And up the hill they'd go.

Now, the ultimate in life—and the purpose of life—is to glorify the Lord Jesus Christ; that is "the good." But when we enter the Christian life, we, like soldiers without love for country, do not know God, love Him, or even truly respect Him. But because He is glorified when He can bless us, our desire for blessings becomes a legitimate Christian motive.

The royal family honor code does not require that we affect a false humility and say, "Well, I really don't want anything for myself. I just want to honor Jesus." Eventually, we *will* be occupied with the Person of our Lord and will want only to glorify Him. But that comes *after* learning a great deal of the Mind of Christ. In the meantime, if a person cannot be honest before the Lord about his desire for blessing, with whom can he be honest? Imagine the legalistic frustration, hypocritical lip-service, and *dis*honor that would grow out of a code that refused to acknowledge normal human motivation!

Even as immature believers we are still spiritual royalty. Aristocrats are not expected to live on pretense; we are expected to think reality. God wants us to be phenomenally blessed; we are expected to comply with His desires. When we adjust to His justice, He is free to bless us without compromise to His essence. That is how tactical victories in the angelic conflict are won through human volition. It is a wonderful relief to learn that the lines of the old hymn, "not for reward, . . . but for the Lord," are contradictory. "Reward" and "the Lord" go together. The "humble" deprecation of self that refuses reward is the arrogant focus on self that refuses the Lord.

The XYZ equation belongs to all believers of all dispensations. Adam lived under it after he fell; Noah, Abraham, Moses, and David; you and I; millennial believers—we all live under it. It is God's plan for fallen mankind.

No factor in the equation is unique to the royal family. But concurrent with our entrance into the Y radical we find the unique factor that sets up our royal code. In the moment we are given God's righteousness we are also placed into union with Christ by the baptism of the Holy Spirit. *That* makes us royalty. Everything Jesus Christ has and is becomes ours. Our double portion of divine righteousness, both *from* the Father and *in* the Lord Jesus Christ, is the basis for the honor code. If imputed righteousness sets up a potential for blessings in time (P_2), our superior position in union with the King of Kings gives us a *double potential* for blessings! This is the privilege into which we are spiritually born.

Our royal function is traditionally called "the Christian way of life," but that term means different things to different people. It might conjure up ideas of observing taboos, of keeping the Ten Commandments, of being moral, of having no fun, of working in a church program, of being effusively nice, of dedicating oneself to Christian service, of practicing some psychological function, of getting involved in social action. Each of these is thought by some group or another to be the Christian life. But none is. The believer's code of honor is as much greater than any of these misconceptions as orientation to reality is greater than wishful thinking!

The code devised for us is superior even to the *true* systems under which believers lived in past dispensations. Nothing in the Mosaic Law, in ritual and sacrifice, in divine establishment morality, can compare to the way of life outlined for us. Our honor code is founded on the reality of what, in past dispensations, was merely a shadow of future things. The Cross, the strategic victory over Satan, and the battlefield royalty of Christ are now historical facts. The Age of the Church has temporarily interrupted the Age of Israel—God is forming a royal family for our victorious Lord—and the absolute superiority of our being in union with the God-Man defies description. The code of honor for such a royal family requires not merely morality but integrity—integrity oriented to reality.

Two factors determine whether we are living under the integrity of the code or are simply adhering to a standard of morality. First, for right thinking there must be Bible doctrine resident in the soul. The issue is, What do you think of doctrine? And second, for the application of resident doctrine there must be the filling of the Holy Spirit. The issue is, How rapid and consistent is your use of rebound? Since the honor code is executed through doctrine in the power of the Holy Spirit, a believer who is ignorant of doctrine or who fails to be filled with the Spirit is not living by the code. These two factors should look familiar. They are the believer's two adjustments to the justice of God in Y and Z radicals.

THE HONOR CODE AND DIVINE ESTABLISHMENT

The difference between integrity and morality is seen in the relationship between the royal family honor code and the laws of divine establishment. The honor code begins with human freedom, picking up where divine establishment leaves off.

Freedom is the basic concept of establishment, and establishment protects freedom by guaranteeing each of its integral parts: volition, privacy, property, and authority. No freedom is possible if even one of its parts is missing.

The honor code, too, protects our freedom, demanding that we respect the function of freedom's four integral parts in the spiritual realm as well. First of all, regarding volition, God is resolving the angelic conflict by allowing man, like the angels, to exercise free will. In His self-knowledge God has always known Himself to be able to win the angelic conflict, no matter what any of His creatures might decide to do. Before creating anything or anyone, He knew He would be glorified. He demonstrates His glory in that His plan *will* prevail. He therefore never coerces our free will; He never needs to! If sovereign God respects the decisions of people, we must do the same. There is no place for bullying in the Christian life. [50]

Second, our privacy is guaranteed by the royal priesthood.[51] We each represent ourselves before the Lord; as faces in a crowd we learn doctrine in the privacy of a congregation; we rebound for ourselves; we are blessed as individuals. God has custom-designed special blessings for each of us personally. The privacy of the priesthood is a basic provision of the code. That is why we must respect the privacy of other believers and why such intrusions as gossip, judging, and maligning are among the worst sins (James 3:5; Prov. 6:16–19).

Next, respect for property also carries over from establishment into the royal family honor code. No church, religious organization, or individual is ever authorized to violate your property. All spiritual giving, whether of your time, your money, or your service, is a matter of free will. It is never a matter of coersion, regardless of how subtle, nor of levy, whether called "tithing" or not.

The honor code principle which governs here is that no Christian production of any kind is ever the source of divine blessing. Even though proper-

---

50. Do not confuse the exercise of authority with bullying, whether you wield authority or are under it. Parents, for example, are responsible to God for controlling and training their children. Laying down the law for your children is anything *but* bullying.

51. See above, page 95.

ly motivated giving *is* commanded of believers, our giving is not why we receive gifts from God. We can do God no favors. Grace is not for sale. When we are specially blessed it is because we have the capacity from doctrine to enjoy that special blessing!

The honor code says we can do nothing to earn or deserve blessings from God. Divine blessings come down the grace pipeline, which *God* constructed and which He insulates and protects against all human intrusion. The way of life prescribed by the code is not one of striving to earn God's approbation but one of adjusting to His justice; His *justice* blesses us. The code says, "Advance to maturity! You will be blessed in no other way!" Ignorance of our own code of honor leads us to faithfully practice things which do not produce maturity.

The fourth factor in human freedom—authority—is defined in many areas of life by the laws of establishment. The honor code, too, demands that we orient to establishment authority in each of these areas. In addition, there is divinely delegated spiritual authority: the written canon of Scripture and the pastor-teacher in the local congregation. We must submit with academic self-discipline to the communication and policy-making authority of the pastor-teacher in the local church (Heb. 13:7, 17). He is the one responsible for teaching accurate doctrine and for enforcing policies in his congregation which insure the right of everyone to learn.

Upon the foundation of establishment, therefore, God builds for us a code that far exceeds establishment. Establishment calls for morality; the honor code demands integrity. There is a tremendous difference. Establishment merely protects freedom; the code tells us how to use the freedom we have. Establishment furnishes an environment; the code points out the objective within that environment: "the good," that final imputation in eternity at the end of a road of remarkable imputations in time. Establishment morality is avoidance of practices and activities which would destroy freedom, privacy, property, and authority. Honor code integrity is persistence in and faithfulness to a principle, a focus on the objective which God designed for us in eternity past.

> Is not your awe of God your confidence, and is not your
> hope the integrity of your ways? (Job 4:6)

In Job 4:6 we see that integrity is related to focusing on the goal; we also see where the believer's integrity fits into the XYZ equation. Hope is confident anticipation of future blessings, and included as part of the believer's hopes are the means of attaining those future prospects. Doctrine is the means of advance in the Christian life. Therefore doctrine is the essential; doctrine is the bulwark of our royal integrity. The royal family honor code does not reject morality; it surpasses morality. Any unbeliever can cultivate human morality; only through doctrine and the filling of the Holy Spirit can the royal family develop spiritual integrity.

ESSENTIALS AND NONESSENTIALS

Enroute to the goal of blessings in time, blessings in eternity, and the glorification of Christ, we are required by the code to avoid some things and practice others. With reference to ourselves we must avoid arrogance, which appears under pressure in the form of self-pity and under prosperity in the form of self-righteousness. With reference to others there is a series of principles we must follow.

First, we must know the difference between essentials and nonessentials. We are to be absolutely inflexible on the essentials of life. But when some nonessential is at stake, we should be as flexible as necessary. Thus we avoid pettiness, self-righteousness, and judging—and going off half-cocked—while permitting other believers the freedom to live their own lives before the Lord.

We are not called upon to change or reform others; Bible doctrine does that—from the inside out! Our prodding from the outside creates a false situation in the "victim's" soul. It coerces his volition and usually drives him away from the only true source of growth, *the* essential, the Word of God.

Under the code, therefore, we must often defer to immature believers who have ideas, traits, or habits that are obnoxious to us personally. The new believer who is positive toward doctrine tends to be over-zealous; he is inclined to judge and malign those who do not quite fit his idea of what a Christian ought to be (Rom. 14:3*b*). Unknown to him, many of those he might criticize are much more mature than he is; they have outgrown their background prejudices, pseudo-taboos, and hang-ups. For the immature believer, therefore, the honor code spotlights the privacy of the priesthood and says, "Do not malign."

The mature believer under attack by an immature believer faces a different problem. His tendency is not to malign but to be intolerant (Rom. 14:3*a*). He is tempted to swoop down and straighten out the little whippersnapper! The code stops him short, saying, "Tolerate the weaker brother. Be flexible in the nonessentials." The strong believer is required to be thoughtful and considerate. He is not to shake the weak believer's still-fragile confidence nor dampen his enthusiasm. Certainly he is not to use his own freedom to shock the new believer. If one of the strong believer's normal and legitimate functions in life offends the weak believer, the code says, "Do not practice it in his presence. Be discreet. Do not flaunt your freedom in front of those who are shockable and do not yet know how to use their freedom in Christ." This is the law of love (1 Cor. 8:13); it is incumbent upon mature believers. In contrast, the law of liberty (1 Cor. 8:9) applies especially to new believers who, through doctrine, are just beginning to shake off the chains of legalism. The law of love gives a greater responsibility to those who are more mature. Thus the principle: the honor code demands more of the strong than of the weak.

> Now we the strong [mature believers] are obligated [under the honor code] to keep bearing the weaknesses of the weak and not to accommodate ourselves. (Rom. 15:1)

The mature believer can be flexible because he knows that in due time the continued intake of doctrine will bring the immature believer into line with the truth. All the mature believer must do when faced with an over-zealous, under-taught, new believer is to recall how many people had to tolerate his own half-formed ideas while he was growing up!

Bible doctrine is the answer, but no one learns everything at once. Flexibility in the nonessentials means toleration; toleration means live and let live. Toleration under the honor code means live and let live as unto the Lord.

TWO KINDS OF LOVE

The next tenet of the code follows naturally from the principle of toleration. The code demands not only that we love all other believers—"love one another"—but also that we love all people—"love thy neighbor" and "love thine enemy." But how can we have high standards if we must love everyone? How can a believer have personal integrity and at the same time try to show the same love to a totally despicable stranger that he has for an admirable friend? Another honor-code distinction is imperative. We must understand the difference between personal and impersonal love. Personal love emphasizes the object of love; impersonal love, the subject.

> . . . Thou shalt love thy neighbor as thyself. (Rom. 13:9*b*, AV)

The phrase "as thyself" is often taken to mean "as *you love* yourself," but there is no basis in the Greek text for that interpretation. In fact, such a command could never come from God. Our attitude toward ourselves is the epitome of instability; the absolute righteousness of God would never set up so vascillating and inconsistent a standard for our conduct. One moment you might be arrogant and full of unrealistic, inflated self-love. Are you then to live in a dream world regarding other people, too? That would be a wonderful way to get swindled out of everything you own, but that is not the Christian way of life. Or, the next moment, you might regret some stupid thing you have done and hate yourself for being such a thoroughgoing dunce. Are you to despise your neighbor? Should you, out of neighborliness, apply your boot to the man next door everytime you feel like kicking yourself? Of course not. That is not the intent of the passage.

Romans 13:9 means exactly what it says. "As yourself" points to the source of the love: your own soul, the real you, the place where your own norms and standards reside. This love emphasizes the subject, the one who does the loving, instead of the object, the one who is loved. Indeed, the one who loves does not need to even know the object in any personal sort of way. This is impersonal love. You are commanded by the honor code to love *all* others on the basis of who *you* are, from your standards, from your integrity, not as a reaction or response to what they are.

"Love thy neighbor as thyself" does not set up self-love as a standard; it requires that you love others from the high standards of doctrine you have in your soul. It is therefore stable and consistent. Impersonal love demands an attitude *in you,* the absence of mental attitude sins, the relaxed mental attitude provided under the filling of the Holy Spirit. If someone maligns you, you do not lower yourself to dog-eat-dog (Rom. 12:17*a*). With your honor-code integrity you refuse to get involved in nonessential squabbles. You remain above the mob like the aristocrat you are. Your objective in life, the object of your hope and confidence, the source of your motivation and spiritual momentum, shines so brightly ahead that the divine commands to turn the other cheek, to feed your enemy, to bless those who persecute you, become a completely understandable part of the honor code.

Why must we have impersonal love for all believers? Because every believer possesses the righteousness of God. God respects the principle of His own integrity resident in each believer regardless of that individual's personal traits, habits, or ideas. In fact, justification is defined as God's recognition of imputed righteousness in every believer. We too are to respect the righteousness of God wherever it is found.

> . . . For God hath received him. Who are thou that judgest another man's servant? . . . (Rom. 14:3*b,* 4*a,* AV)

That is not to say that the Lord never disciplines those who possess imputed righteousness. He does. And He alone.

> . . . To his own master he standeth or falleth. (Rom.
> 14:4*b*, AV)

God takes out of our hands the responsibility of chastising believers who are out of line. When we judge others, we arrogate to ourselves equality with the justice of God! Judging is God's business, and we come into line for discipline ourselves when we try to preempt the supreme court of heaven (Rom. 2:3; cf. 14:10).

The honor code demands discernment, however, and we must distinguish between positive immature believers and negative reversionists. We are to follow a different policy toward each. While we tolerate the growing believer "for the purpose of *the good* [so he can attain the final objective of the plan of God]" (Rom. 15:1, 2), we must separate ouselves from those who "cause divisions and offenses contrary to doctrine" and who "serve not our Lord Jesus Christ, but their own emotions, and by good words and fair speeches deceive the hearts of the simple" (Rom. 16:17, 18). Total separation from those who are enslaved to their emotions through allegedly speaking in tongues is perfectly consistent with impersonal love, and is also an instance of inflexibilty in the essentials of doctrine.

Impersonal love also becomes the basis for personal love. Personal love is a very exclusive love. It emphasizes not the subject—you—but the object —the person you love. The special people who are objects of personal love include the Lord Jesus Christ, right man or right woman, family, and friends. Personal love requires the same integrity as impersonal love, but something more is added. You are attracted to someone; you know and deeply appreciate that special person. You are occupied with him; you have an emotional attachment to him. None of these are characteristics of impersonal love.

The believer who is never taught to distinguish between personal and impersonal love, who is told instead to love all people with the same love, overloads his soul. He ends up with either a hardened cynicism, a deep-rooted hypocrisy, or a nervous breakdown. For the rest of his life he is soured on Christianity by something that is not even Christianity! Our true way of life is based on the fact that God's integrity takes precedence over His love. When even human love is allowed to supersede human integrity, love becomes destructive.

RECIPROCITY AND AN ATTITUDE TOWARD DYING

Closely related to the honor code's provisions for love is the principle of reciprocity. The first century believers in Macedonia "decided with pleasure" to give a large sum of money to the Jews who lived in distant

Jerusalem, who spoke a different language, and who had a totally different culture—people they would never meet (Rom. 15:27). Furthermore, the Jewish believers in Jerusalem were reversionists and legalists; they would soon convince even Paul to forget grace (Acts 21:18-26). Certainly they did not deserve generosity. The Macedonian believers, however, were fulfilling the royal family honor code. The Jews were the original custodians of the Word of God. God had selected Jewish prophets to receive and write the Scriptures. The greatest communicators of doctrine were Jews. Christ Himself was a Jew. The Macedonians acknowledged their great debt to this unique people. The Gentiles had benefited from the Jews through doctrine, in spite of the evil then rampant in Judea. Now, from doctrine in their souls, these Macedonian Greeks were motivated to reciprocate by sharing their money with destitute Jewish believers. In this we see the basic premise of the honor code: right thinking results in right motivation, and right motivation results in right action.

The honor code closes with a confident look at death. The impetus of $X + Y + Z$ gives us a perspective on the purpose for our lives on earth. As we advance, we come to appreciate the reality of promised eternal blessings laid up for us in heaven. Hope$_3$ means that we are not afraid to die. If the circumstances demand it, we have no qualms about risking our lives for other members of the royal family of God. This maximum expression of impersonal love and reciprocity is a provision of the honor code (Rom. 16:4).

The royal family honor code is the only legitimate system that includes dying as a part of living. Death is not the exception to life; it is an integral part of life on earth. Thus, the believer who lives by the code faces death, when it comes, with the same integrity he has in facing everything else in life. For the mature believer, dying grace is a wonderful imputation from the justice of God so that death is not something to dread. When we understand that God thought about us in eternity past and long ago planned the exact time, place, and manner of death for each of us, we know we are in perfect hands. Unafraid of death, we are able to live in the devil's world with supreme confidence.

THE EQUATION AND EVIL

We have been familiarizing ourselves with how the XYZ equation works. We used it to clarify our spiritual responsibilities under the plan of God, seeing why and how we must adjust to His justice. We used it to categorize the various ways in which God sustains us in the devil's kingdom—establishment, logistical blessings, supergrace blessings, and the royal family honor code. We might continue, showing many categories of Bible doctrine in their logical relationship to the plan of God. For example, believers must understand the Biblical doctrine of evil. The principle of the equation is well known to Satan. Since he is a counterfeiter, and since the equation outlines the plan of God, we can better understand Satan's strategy of evil if we note how he attacks or attempts to counterfeit each factor in the equation.

In the X radical, the imputation of human life is opposed by the highly speculative hypothesis of evolution and by the philosophy of materialism. The imputation of Adam's original sin is attacked by the mistaken notion of the dignity of man and its corollary doctrine of noble human equality. The first potential is obscured by various psychological systems, including the idea that improved environment is the solution to life's problems. Of course, the Gospel is a favorite target for satanic attacks (2 Cor. 4:3, 4); he has a false gospel of his own (2 Cor. 11:3, 4). In all three radicals pertinent doctrine is opposed directly through negative volition, or indirectly through myriad distractions or rejection of the communicator's authority. Hope is debilitated into uncertainty. The first "plus" (salvation adjustment to the justice of God) is attacked by any system of salvation by works.

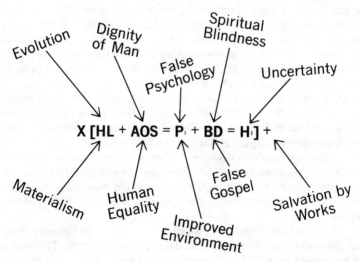

In the Y radical, the judicial imputation of all our sins to Christ is buried under denials of Christ's virgin birth (or under Mary worship) or is twisted into an incredible mysticism around the literal blood of Christ. [52] The judicial imputation of God's righteousness is rejected in favor of self-righteousness by sincere believers who butt their heads against the grace pipeline.

---

52. See Thieme, *The Blood of Christ.*

We could go on, noting the satanic opposition to each factor in the equation, but I think you begin to see the possibilities. You should be able to finish this analysis of evil yourself. I would like to conclude our study of the equation on a different note.

THE EQUATION AND FAITH-REST

Romans 8:28 reduces complex doctrine to utmost simplicity for a reason. The mature believer, suddenly hit with undeserved suffering, needs to latch onto something simple. He may be spiritually advanced, but he is not perfect. Mature believers are still human. When disaster or tragedy hits —especially when it comes without warning—mature believers are as susceptible to fear and panic as anyone else (1 Kings 19:1, 2). And what does fear do? It cuts off rational thought. Common sense flies out the window. Mental stability melts into panic. Emotion and imagination take over the soul. When he is suddenly caught off-guard, the mature believer can miss his opportunity to be the man of the hour; instead of glorifying the Lord in a sticky situation, the believer is in danger of bringing reproach on His name.

God wants us to use the doctrine resident in our souls; Satan and the forces of evil want to prevent us from using it. One of Satan's favorite ploys for making resident doctrine inaccessible is to create fear, especially fear of death. A believer who succumbs to fear cannot think clearly. In order to think, he must bring his fear under control.

A personal or national disaster, with the anxiety it engenders, is a complex situation. If an unsettled and frightened believer is to regain his mental stability and poise, he must reduce his life to its utmost simplicity. Then, reoriented and thinking clearly once again, he can turn around and handle the complex situation with doctrine. For just such contingencies, God provides a step-by-step technique for overcoming fear and for rapidly recovering mental stability. By following this procedure, the mature believer can apply the doctrine he knows before the opportunity has passed, before he fails the test.

"Faith-rest" is the technique which the believer uses in a pressure situation. He reaches out with his faith and claims a Biblical promise. The result is the moment-by-moment "rest" described in Hebrews 4.

> Let us therefore fear lest a promise being left to us of
> entering into His rest, any of you should seem to come
> short of it. (Heb. 4:1, AV)

The only thing we have to fear is failure to claim the promises of God, which put to rest our fears! The mature believer's faith first takes hold of a promise, then begins to think in terms of principle, and ultimately comes to doctrinal conclusions.

This technique for overcoming Satan's fear-panic ploy is presented in Romans 8:28–32. These verses supply the divine resources that the mature believer needs when sudden disaster—whether personal or collective —throws him temporarily off-balance. Let us pick up the context from Romans 8:25, excluding the parenthesis inserted in verses 26 and 27.

> Now if we hope [and we do, hope₃] for what we do not
> see, through fortitude [despite intense suffering] we stand
> in eager anticipation. . . . In fact, we know [hope₃] that
> to those who love the God [mature believers], He works
> all things together for the purpose of the good, for those
> who are elected to privilege according to a predetermined
> plan [X + Y + Z = the good]. (Rom. 8:25–28)

Romans 8:28 presupposes a long and persistent intake of doctrine. The believers in view have learned all the pertinent doctrines connected with hope₃; they know divine essence and Christ's uniqueness so well that they love Him; they are familiar with all the things that God is working together for the good; they understand the doctrine of election, the special privileges of the royal family, and the details of God's predetermined plan. But all this wealth of doctrine in their souls is entirely useless in the crisis if the fear-panic ploy blocks out its application. Just as concentration is necessary to learn doctrine, so also that same concentration is necessary to draw upon the doctrine in the soul. A person must be able to concentrate if he is to apply doctrine to experience. I call this "reverse concentration": instead of coming *in,* doctrine is moved *out* to meet the demands of the moment. But reverse concentration is possible only when the mind is stabilized.

For example, imagine yourself in an airplane cruising at 35,000 feet. You are all strapped in and comfortable, reading a fascinating book or enjoying the cloud formations below, when an explosion suddenly rocks the plane. An engine has blown. There is fire outside the windows. Now *that* is a sudden disaster! No matter how mature a believer you are, your first reaction is going to be fear. Why? Because you're human! As the plane goes into a stall, your stomach is in your throat. You feel cramped and confined. Everyone is in shock. People begin to whimper. Someone screams. Fear becomes contagious. The specter of death and total helplessness ignite uncontrolled panic. All the Bible doctrine in your soul—including all this doctrine we have been studying—is useless to you because rational thinking has been wiped out. Amid the hysteria, your reverse concentration is simply not working.

When the chips are down, what is the difference between cowardice and courage? The brave man *thinks* under pressure whereas the coward does not. One of the greatest virtues in life is the ability to think clearly in a crisis. That is the stuff of aristocracy! Being afraid is normal, but succumbing to fear and failing to control fear is absolutely unnecessary. Here is where Romans 8:28 and the XYZ equation come in.

Romans 8:28 is not only a principle to understand; it is a promise to claim. If you are a mature believer, the *fact* is that God works all things together for the good—for you! Hence, this terrifying plane ride is something that He is doing for your benefit and for His own glorification. That is the promise you need in order to stabilize your mind. And if the fear-panic ploy keeps seizing your soul, just keep claiming Romans 8:28. Claim it until it sticks and you begin to regain your mental poise by seeing this sudden disaster from the divine viewpoint. And don't just repeat the words like a magical chant. When I say, "claim a promise," I mean *think* of what the promise *means*.

Do you now see the difference between the King James version of Romans 8:28 and the corrected translation? All things do *not* work together for good; that is wishful thinking and self-deception! The true doctrine is that *God* works all things together for the good. That makes all the difference in a pressure situation. Everything depends on the One who is working. In a crisis, in the grip of fear, you must quickly refocus on the ability and integrity of God.

And what does God's integrity do? How does He make all things work together for good? Through imputations. Each imputation in the XYZ equation contributes to your stability under pressure. How do you "keep claiming Romans 8:28 until it sticks"? By using the equation. In the X radical, God imputed human life to your soul because He had a plan for your life. That plan goes on. Just because an airplane is hurtling to the ground does not mean that God has changed His game plan. The imputation of Adam's sin *proves* that God has a plan for you. God went to the trouble of imputing someones else's sin to you, so you could qualify for grace, while saving up your sins for the Cross. The only explanation for such a thing is that He has a purpose for your life! The rest of X radical—potential$_1$ (the possibility of salvation), the Gospel, and hope$_1$ (the expectation of salvation)—begins to define that purpose.

In Y radical, the first judicial imputation tells you immediately that if God meted out justice against His own Son, God will certainly mete out justice to you. And since you have His righteousness and are a mature believer, justice means blessings. Perfect God is bound by His own perfection to give you logistical and special blessings! It begins to dawn on you as the airplane plummets to the ground, that *God* is responsible for keeping you alive and that *God* is the One who decides when it is your time to depart from this life. The entire situation is in His hands; He always has everything completely under control.

By this time you begin to recover your poise; reverse concentration has started to pull out the doctrine stored under "XYZ" in your right lobe. There you sit in that burning, spinning airplane, a mature believer, having a ball. You are *thinking* even with people screaming and falling apart all around you. If the Lord is going to take you home—fine.

The factors in the Z radical tell you that you have eternal life irremovably imputed to your human spirit, and that special blessings from God's justice glorify Him in time. Indeed, dying grace is the final category of blessings in time. Again you realize the truth: the plane crash glorifies the Lord! You are using the assets of doctrine in your soul to make this roller coaster ride the most fantastic experience of your entire life. Potential$_3$ calls to mind the second *a fortiori:* "If God can bless me with such amazing stimulation and clarity of mind in a plane crash, certainly He has indescribably wonderful things for me in the perfect circumstances of heaven!" The doctrine pertinent to heaven stimulates the third hope; you confidently, dogmatically, immovably *know* that in a few seconds you will meet the Lord Jesus Christ face to face.

But if this airplane is *not* the Lord's means of bringing you home, you will survive. And that's fine, too. The plane will recover a glide, safely crash-land, and deposit you on terra firma. You will find youself looking up into the sky you just fell through, and you will know again that God has a plan for you. This will have been one more of life's wonderful experiences. Whenever you face danger, you will either go to heaven or continue your life as a mature believer. But whichever way it goes—so what? What difference does it make? The Lord has the option; all you do is grab Romans 8:28 and keep your thinking clear. God works all things together for good.

In a plane crash, even from high altitude, you might not have time to get past reestablishing your mental stability. Perhaps you run through half of the XYZ equation before the plane ploughs in. But in a crisis that gives you more time—you have terminal cancer, a special loved one has died, you have lost your life's savings, you are prisoner of war of the Communists—further divine assets are provided.

Romans 8:29, 30 is a step-by-step logical procedure to stimulate reverse concentration. In other words, after claiming Romans 8:28 and removing the fear-panic ploy, what next? You start a system of logic: point one, point two, point three, point four, point five; followed by two doctrinal conclusions in Romans 8:31, 32. This becomes a standard procedure, a checklist to use whenever any kind of disaster or pressure, whether great or small, creates fear and cuts off objective thought.

THE FAITH-REST TECHNIQUE
Romans 8:28-32

1. Claim a promise that stabilizes your mind.

God works all things together for the good.

2. Use reverse concentration in a logical rationale.

A. *Foreknowledge:* God thought about me in eternity past.
B. *Predestination:* God has a plan for me since eternity past.
C. *Election:* God chose me for the privileged part of His plan.
D. *Justification:* God can bless me now (first *a fortiori*).
E. *Glorification:* God will bless me in heaven (second *a fortiori*).

3. Reach doctrinal conclusions.

If God is for us who can be against us?
[If God] delivered up [His own unique Son] in behalf
of us all, how shall He not with Him give us
in grace the all things?

You need to know this system and be prepared to use it on a moment's notice. Imagine the worst situation, the one that seems most awful to you—rape, Communist torture, someone's death, whatever—and apply this technique to it. Even in your imagination there is no need to dangle on the fear-panic ploy. If God can handle the worst, He can handle anything less.

For [we know that] whom He foreknew . . . (Rom. 8:29*a*)

Verse 28 supplies the verb excluded in the elliptical style of verse 29. "We know" is the thinking that begins to draw upon the reservoir of doctrine in the soul. After stabilizing our minds by latching onto the utterly simple promise of Romans 8:28, we take the first step of clear thinking. We recall that God knew about this crisis billions and billions of years ago (Ps. 139:1-6; Matt. 6:8; Acts 15:8, 18; Heb. 4:13). That is a basis for comfort. If He knew about it, He did something about it.

. . . whom He foreknew He also predestined. . . . (Rom. 8:29*b*)

You can see that this is a recovery system, not a chronological delineation of the divine decrees. Other passages show the sequence of omniscience-decree-foreknowledge that is so important theologically (Acts 2:22).[53] Romans 8:29, however, jumps immediately to the printouts of the divine computer: foreknowledge, predestination, election.

By remembering predestination (also termed "foreordination" or "predetermination"), you take the logical step: if God thought about you in eternity past, He has a plan for you. Any catastrophe that strikes suddenly and throws you into a panic comes as no surprise to God. He included it in His plan for you. It is one of the "all things" that He is working together for good.

God's plan is designed to glorify God. It calls for Him to work in your behalf. He takes all the imputations, potentials, doctrines, and hopes, combines them with the changing circumstances of your life, taking cognizance of all your thoughts, decisions, and actions, and achieves a perfect, complete result. He designed this plan in eternity past. Your life, therefore, will be a combination of many things—prosperity and adversity, wonderful experiences and sudden disasters—but the combinations and changes do not alter God's plan one bit. They *are* God's plan! No matter what happens, God has built a wall of fire around you. His plan is all-inclusive and always remains the same. You are free yet totally secure. Only God could accomplish that.

The predetermined plan of God calls for us to gain our motivation and spiritual momentum from Bible doctrine. This motivation and momentum is designed to function under all conditions, disaster included. As the mature believer remembers this, his reverse concentration begins to pick up speed.

> Remember the former things long past,
> For I am God and there is no other.
> For I am God and there is none like Me,
> Declaring the end from the beginning
> And from ancient times things that have not been done,
> Saying, "My decrees will be established,
> And I will accomplish My good pleasure." (Isa. 46:9,10)

Despite negative volition or opposition from men or angels, despite all the disasters of life in the devil's domain, God is so wise, just, and powerful that He makes everything work together to accomplish His good pleasure. Romans 8:29 continues with the long-range view of what God's good pleasure is.

---

53. See Appendix B.

> For [we know that] whom He foreknew, He also predest-
> ined to be conformed to the image of His Son that He
> might be the Firstborn among many brethren. (Rom.
> 8:29)

"Conformed to the image of His Son" refers to the resurrection body; but conformity begins in time. At salvation, we were placed into union with Christ and thus became members of His royal family. This is positional sanctification. To positional sanctification is added experiential sanctification as Bible doctrine renews our minds: our thinking is conformed to the thinking of Christ through learning the Mind of Christ. The process is completed when ultimate sanctification occurs for the royal family at the Rapture; then we will all be "conformed to the image of His Son" by receiving bodies like His.

It is the Father's plan, not our human effort, that makes us like Jesus Christ. From the moment God knew that we would believe in Christ, that is, from eternity past, it has always been God's predetermined plan that we should have resurrection bodies. This fact, inserted here in the recovery checklist, begins to piece together the big picture. The objective for eternity future was established in eternity past as an absolute certainty. Whether a believer advances to maturity or becomes an evil reversionist, he will still receive a resurrection body. This illustrates the impartial justice of God upon which we totally depend. In spite of tragedies that may beset us, despite even our own failures, "underneath are the everlasting arms" (Deut. 33:27).

But there is a much greater purpose behind God's predetermined objective than simply to give every believer a new, beautiful, indestructible, and perfect body. From what we have studied regarding imputations, you should already sense what is building up. Do you recall where the resurrection body appears in the XYZ equation? God decreed a resurrection body for you in order to establish an affinity, a system of antecedence. His greatest desire is to perform a real imputation, the seventh imputation—"the good"!

Your resurrection body is marvelous in itself, but God wants to use it as a target for imputing to you eternal blessings, which are even finer yet! Predestination, therefore, as the second item on the crisis-recovery checklist, reminds us of an awesome potential God has given us (P_3) and sets the stage for perfect confidence in time. And what is that confidence? What is that stabilized mental attitude that the mature believer recovers after he controls the fear-panic ploy? That's right, hope$_3$. Even in a shocking disaster, the mature believer can have absolute confidence that, at the Judgment Seat of Christ, the justice of God will impute eternal blessings and rewards to his resurrection body. The final end is secure.

But how does this apply under the pressure of the moment? When the mature believer has stabilized his mentality by claiming Romans 8:28, he runs through the checklist, beginning in Romans 8:29, and quickly calls to mind God's guaranteed long-range solution. From that solution, he works back: if God will provide the resurrection body and ultimate sanctification regardless of personal failures or successes, obviously there is a solution to the short-range problem at hand.

The next item on the checklist carries on from the phrase "that He [Christ] might be the Firstborn among many brethren": God's plan calls for the battlefield royalty of our Lord to be fulfilled in the royal family.

> And whom He predestined, these same ones He also
> elected to privilege. . . . (Rom. 8:30*a*)

The verb *kaleo*, "to call, summon, invite, elect" (from the same root as *kletos*, "the elect," used in Romans 8:28), connotes the Church Age believer's royalty. Used technically here, *kaleo* means "elected to privilege." Note the logical sequence so far in this recovery procedure: we were in the *mind* of God in eternity past (foreknown); we were in the *plan* of God in eternity past (predestined); we were in the *privileged* part of God's plan in eternity past (elected)! Our royalty—the "holy station in life" to which we are elected (2 Tim. 1:9)—demands that we keep up our spiritual momentum, even when victimized by the fear-panic ploy. We should conduct ourselves like the aristocrats we are. And because our royal privilege is a grace privilege, we should follow the honor code principle that we never earn or deserve blessings from God.

In other words, when we have been victimized by the fear-panic ploy, we are not called upon to have a guilt complex about it or feel sorry for ourselves or try to make up for our failure. Fear is a sin; rebound says, Simply name the sin to God and move on. *Doctrine,* not sinless perfection, is our spiritual momentum. The pressure situation calls for *thinking.* We must waste no time breast-beating. Our thinking must be objective, not subjective. Instead of remorse, the content of our thoughts must be that God has a special purpose for us on earth, that this purpose is related to winning the angelic conflict, that we are alive to be blessed, and that God alone provides the blessings in the midst of any disaster that might come our way. Reverse concentration means right thinking, right motivation, right decisions, right action—even under the worst possible conditions.

> . . . And whom He elected to privilege, these same ones
> He also declared righteous. . . . (Rom. 8:30*b*)

This is familiar ground, and familiar ground is exactly what we need in a pressure situation. The verb *dikaiöo* is usually translated "to be justified," and we have seen that justification is God's stamp of approval. God imputed His righteousness to us then turned around and declared us righteous. Thus, justification completes the second judicial imputation (J_2) in the Y radical. We possess the central attribute of the essence of God, the principle of His integrity; and He recognizes that we possess something that belongs to Him.

That is what justification *is,* but the *purpose* of justification is that we might be blessed. This is the first *a fortiori:* if God could accomplish the most difficult thing in declaring sinful men righteous, it follows with greater reason that He can accomplish the less difficult task of imputing blessings to His own righteousness in us. In a crisis, what should immediately strike the mature believer is that this particular pressure situation is actually the blessing of undeserved suffering being imputed to divine righteousness in him! Righteousness *demands* implementation by the justice of God; that implementation glorifies God.

> . . . And whom He justified [declared righteous], these
> same ones He also glorified. (Rom. 8:30c)

The manifestation of God's glory secures the highest glory for His creatures. When He can impute special blessings to us, we have reached the total fulfillment of spiritual progress, that is, spiritual maturity. After attaining this lofty goal, we, thankfully, never run out of potential; we continue to advance *in maturity* by continuing to take in doctrine. Blessings become greater as we advance, but maximum blessing in time is still only the beginning; as we have seen, the sixth imputation is parlayed into the seventh. The infinitely greater blessings of eternity glorify God forever. Tragically, this—the whole purpose of God's plan—is overlooked by modern Christianity. The conversion of earth's blessings and prosperity into heaven's rewards is how we glorify God and He us.

This He decreed in eternity past to be His plan. We are not alive primarily to work for God; we are alive to be blessed by God. Working is merely a *result* of having followed His plan. The extent to which most believers are out of step with the plan of God almost defies description; their lack of resources for a crisis is utterly tragic. The Bible tells us how to get in step and stay in step—and how to store up divine operating assets: believe in Christ, rebound as needed, and keep learning the Word of God.

The rhetorical procedure for cranking up reverse concentration is now complete. The five-step process began with a backward glance into eternity past; it ends in present time with anticipation of eternity future. If we were in God's thoughts billions of years ago, we were His plan. If in His plan, in the privileged royal family. If elected to privilege, the first *a fortiori* applies:

justification is the basis for blessings in time. If the blessings of time are imputed to the righteousness of God in us, the second *a fortiori* also applies: blessings in time guarantee blessings forever.

Here we are in a hopeless disaster; but then again, here we are in the middle of God's amazing plan! We know where we are, from whence we came, and where we are going. We know and love the One who is in complete control. With stability of mind restored, with doctrine flowing from our souls through reverse concentration, we can deal with the problem at hand with calm and confident objectivity. The doctrinal conclusions we reach allow us to be in complete control.

> To what conclusion are we forced, face to face with these
> things? . . . (Rom. 8:31*a*)

There is only one possible conclusion. It is stated elliptically, without verbs, simulating the staccato thoughts of a person stabilizing in a catastrophe.

> . . . If God for us, who against us? (Rom. 8:31*b*)

The plan of God is greater than any possible opposition. "God for us" sums up foreknowledge, predestination, election, justification, and glorification. God's essence guarantees His plan; God's justice carries it out. There is no authority higher than the justice of God. When we are moving with the momentum of God's plan by adjusting to His justice, God is for us, and He has no rivals.

> . . . Greater is He that is in you than he that is in the
> world. (1 John 4:4*b*)

If, in a pressure situation, you are still afraid after seeing the rationale behind this first conclusion, you are not yet a mature believer. But don't be dismayed! We all start out immature with scanty doctrinal resources in our souls. God still has a plan for your life; you simply need to understand that fact more thoroughly so you will be better equipped to meet the next crisis when it comes. Failing a test should be a sobering reminder of the need to keep on learning doctrine.

What is it that says God is *not* for us? Arrogance, self-pity, self-righteousness, shock, emotion, panic, disorientation to the truth. When you persist in being afraid in a pressure situation, you are saying in effect that God cannot handle the situation, and your fear becomes blasphemous. You are maligning God's character.

Billions of years ago—before Adam, before angels, before even the universe was created, when nothing existed but God alone—God knew Himself. He knew His own strength, His own wisdom, His own love, His own integrity. He has always known Himself to be unlimited, perfect, totally admirable, and immutable. In His Self-knowledge, He knew, should He create angels and men, that He would be able to control the entire situation no matter what they might think, decide, or do, no matter how far they might go astray, no matter what evil they might invent, no matter how cataclysmic the disasters of history or of anyone's personal life. What's more, He knew that in every circumstance He would demonstrate His character and be glorified through it all! Your unchecked fear expresses ignorance of God and His plan. The truth is that God is infinite, without peer; and that the solutions He provides are infinitely greater than the problems they solve.

This should be all anyone needs in order to stabilize in a difficult situation, but God provides yet a second doctrinal conclusion. Designed to gird up the mature believer's ability to think clearly under pressure, this final conclusion adds specific details to the general conclusion of verse 31.

> Who [God the Father] did not even spare His own unique
> Son, but delivered Him over in behalf of all of us, how
> shall He not with Him graciously give to us the all things?
> (Rom. 8:32)

Here is divine encouragement. Here also is Christian motivation! The two *a fortiori* arguments motivate the believer; there is hope despite our present ignorance, despite our old sin natures, despite living in the devil's world. There is good reason to strive for the goal! Romans 8:32 reiterates this clear line of *a fortiori* thinking, which we first met in Romans 5:12–17. Not only are fear and panic put aside, but the objective—supergrace prosperity—is made dramatically clear, encouraging us to face the pressure situation with doctrine and to keep moving in the plan of God.

But look at Romans 8:32 for a moment. Do you see what is there? Divine integrity! The integrity of God is written all over this verse.

The verb *paradidomi* means "to deliver over" as a judge delivers over a condemned criminal to the executioner. We have been studying the thinking of this Judge: *"dikaiosune theou"*—the integrity, righteousness, justice of God. When sudden disaster or unexpected pressure stings us into a status of nonthinking, the recovery technique jogs our memory, reminding us of another "crisis."

There was a moment in which God, in His absolute, eternal, infinite, and perfect essence, had to make a crucial decision. What He chose is, for us, the ultimate encouragement. The Father had to decide whether or not to judge His beloved Son. It was an awesome, far-reaching decision. But in eternity past, God made up His mind to "not even spare His own unique Son," and in A.D. 30 He carried out that decision. The Cross has always been a fact in the divine decrees, and for the past nearly 2000 years, it has also been a fact of history. Justice before love! The justice of God always takes precedence over the love of God—in eternity past, in past history, now, and forever.

God could never love us for ourselves. The only human being He could love was the only sinless Man who has ever lived. We deserved judgment, but God desired to demonstrate His own glory through *blessing* us, not through *judging* us. The genius of divine integrity went to work. The Father chose to impute every human sin to Jesus Christ for judgment "in behalf of all of us." And the Son chose to take our place, submitting to utter humiliation and indescribable torture.

We are left speechless by what has been accomplished for us. But judgment and humiliation are not the final goal! If God did the most difficult thing in judging His Son for sins that were not antecedently His own, then with greater reason, when that same relentless justice turns upon us, it will not stop short of blessing those who have accepted the completed work of the Cross. In the dramatically understated words of Romans 8:32, "how shall He not with Him graciously give to us the all things?"

The verb *charizomai* means "to give graciously, to give beneficially, to give in grace"; we might even translate it "to grace out." From the moment of salvation, God surrounds us in grace—and what is grace? Have we suddenly switched from justice to love? Has sentimentality taken over? Certainly not. Grace is the policy of divine justice in blessing us. Because of justice—specifically because justice "graced us out" by imputing God's righteousness to us—God can and does now love us with perfect love$_1$. But, still, justice remains our point of contact with God. And we would want it no other way. Justice handled our worst; justice can now hand us God's best without skipping a beat.

But what are "the all things" that God has promised us? We look back only as far as Romans 8:28 to find the answer. The justice of God carries out the plan of God, which moves on inexorably. It behooves us to move in the same direction! God works all things together for good for the one who *is* moving in the direction of God's plan, that is, for the mature believer.

"All things" are the factors in the XYZ equation. They all lead to the final imputation and the eternal glory of the Lord Jesus Christ. Because Romans 8:32 reiterates the first *a fortiori,* however, "the all things" focus on blessings imputed in time to divine righteousness in us.

In times of crisis, the mature believer stabilizes his mind with Romans 8:28. Then through the reverse concentration outlined in Romans 8:29, 30, he calls upon the resources of doctrine which have been stored in his soul. The general conclusion, Romans 8:31, is that the justice of God is for us; nothing and no one can be against us. And, more specifically, in Romans 8:32, if the justice of God is proven to be "for us" in the most difficult situation of the Cross, then that same justice is working in our behalf in the "minor" crisis of the moment. Indeed, God *leads* us into crisis situations, just as He deliberately led the Jews to the edge of the Red Sea, so that we can *use* the doctrine we have learned. God blesses us with opportunities to practice thinking under pressure.

The whole objective of life is to qualify for blessings in eternity by being blessed on earth. When we are headed for such absolutely wonderful rewards from the hand of our glorified Lord, any trouble that besets along the way is no reason to lose our mental poise or to cease living by the Word of God in our souls. The mature believer carries on with the objectivity and clear thinking of divine viewpoint.

4
Conclusion

WHOSE RIGHTEOUSNESS?

DIVINE-VIEWPOINT THINKING stands on a simple premise: God has integrity, and He imputed half of His integrity to every believer. But in our generation, as in past generations in other nations whose apostasy finally required divine judgment, this premise of grace is cast aside. It is too simple for the arrogant.

Arrogant people are more comfortable when life is complicated. There is more room for self-importance when things are nebulous and abstruse, especially when cleverly or beautifully abstruse. People can think they are smarter or more creative than they really are when the overall picture is out of focus. Therefore, they decry simplicity as superficiality even though simplicity is the utter genius of God's plan. "*Imputed* righteousness?" people say. "That's too easy!" Unwilling to see that they already have something far more valuable than anything they could develop on their own, believers push divine righteousness out of their thinking and devote themselves to establishing their own righteousness.

> For I testify that they [the Jews of Paul's generation] have a zeal for God but not as a result of knowledge [of doctrine]. For not knowing the righteousness of God and by seeking to establish their own righteousness, they have not been obedient to the righteousness of God [they have not adjusted to the justice of God for salvation]. (Rom. 10:2, 3)

Paul was describing his own countrymen in A.D. 58; they were already locked in the arrogance syndrome that would necessitate the holocaust of A.D. 67-73. Although Jewish unbelievers are in view, this passage applies as well to Christians in this country who are full of zeal but not full of doctrine. Their apostasy has pushed the United States to the brink of national judgment.

Wherever we look in Christianity today, we find people building their lives on the sands of human righteousness instead of on the solid ground of God's righteousness in them. One of the major reasons for doing this, we have seen, is that believers are trying to orient to God through His love instead of through His justice. With the arrogance natural to human beings, believers feel they must do something to deserve God's love. Now *that* is a complex premise, not a simple one. *That* is the premise of Christian superficiality which becomes the tragedy of Christian reversionism. One thing that imputed righteousness does is to eliminate any possibility that human righteousness could ever be acceptable before God.

Yet on every hand, believers are working and doing and performing and striving. In all this they seek to establish their own righteousness. They may have a pet area of holiness—which is their own business and their own problem before the Lord—but they do not keep it their business. They advertise it, talk about it, impose it on others, and thus seek to establish their own righteousness. They do this often in the name of setting a good example, but that is a rationalization. Believers set the example in spiritual matters not by imposing their prejudices, trends, and frailties on others, but by making clear the integrity of God.

Too many believers today have set up a selective standard of righteousness, and by keeping that standard, they are smugly satisfied with their own lives. But they live a lie; they live a blasphemy by being contented with their own righteousness while disregarding the absolute righteousness of God. They construct a beautiful edifice not realizing that they are building a jail. They lock themselves in a cell of comfortable falsehood.

Life is meaningful and full of definition and purpose except for people who shut themselves off in their own self-righteousness, isolated from the truth of God. Often these are wonderful, attractive people, but the difference between those who are building their lives on God's righteousness and those who build on human righteousness is not that one group is attractive and the other unattractive. Instead, the dividing line is between cognizance and ignorance of that second judicial imputation.

Do not confuse yourself by using the wrong set of standards. Whether or not believers are fine, upright, admirable people is not the criterion. Believers are not blessed of God because they are wonderful, loving, and kind. As appreciated as these traits are, unbelievers can possess them, whereas mature believers can have abrasive personalities and may be real stinkers. God evaluates believers, not for overt characteristics, but for the doctrine in their souls (1 Sam. 16:7).

The standard is such that we must leave the judging to God. There is no place for mutual admiration societies, in which we flatter those who share our strengths and malign those in authority or those whose weaknesses we do not share.

It is easy to compare ourselves favorably with the obvious failures of others, to be critical and impatient. But none of us is perfect. We all will sin as long as we live. Although sin is never excused, sin is not the issue. God cannot bless us simply because we stop sinning or because we are very righteous in some respect. We could all use a little more human righteousness, but our righteousness is not the issue either. The issue is God's righteousness.

Self-righteousness comes from arrogance, and arrogance resides in all of us to some extent. It is the most basic, most awful, and best disguised of all sins. We can spot its obvious manifestations in others, but we never seem to see it in ourselves. Furthermore, we fail to see the arrogance in those who flatter us or who display some special intelligence or charm. Yet attractive, wonderful people with hidden arrogance can distract us from the Word of God. Doctrine must have first priority.

The truth of doctrine is our only hope. We are hopeless and helpless without it; doctrine is our contact with ultimate reality. In this regard, high intelligence, even genius, is no help. The perceptive *ability* of the mind is not the important thing; what is essential is the *content* of the mind. If doctrine or establishment truth does not reside in the soul, falsehood will fill the vacuum. When it does, a high IQ becomes a liability, having the power to draw in much evil. This is the story of many liberals who have brilliant minds yet whose souls are blacked out to the truth in both temporal and spiritual matters. If orientation to reality is the criterion for sanity, such highly intelligent, personally engaging, widely respected liberals are insane. Truth is not in them. With an untrue frame of reference, they cannot comprehend basic principles of establishment; spiritual truths are out of the question. Such liberals who claim to put so much stock in reason cannot be reasoned with. They are dead to clear thinking.

Evil is always self-destructive, and the liberal's self-destructive path is the alternative to the way of imputed righteousness: he is following the path of human arrogance, establishing his own righteousness. Thanks to the Word of God, as long as we orient to the integrity of God we will not wander off into self-righteousness.

How can you recognize your own attempts to establish your self-righteousness? There is an unmistakable sign. You are critical of some real or imagined failure in someone else. You will nag him—often in subtle ways—to do certain things and refrain from others, implying that he cannot do that and glorify the Lord. You forget that you too have an old sin nature which you must handle in the privacy of your own priesthood through rebound and GAP. You certainly do not realize that your own zeal for righteousness comes from the trend toward human good of your sin nature!

You will not only nag others, if given the opportunity, but you also nag God. Ignorant of God's Person and plan, spiritually unstable, trying to follow the latest traveling teacher's key to Christian dynamics, you unknowingly become a spiritual Xantippe. You say, "Look what I'm doing, God. Look at what I've achieved for You. Look at these hours in prayer, these new converts of mine, this tithe and this sacrifice. Look at my work among the destitute; see how I've loved those who are unattractive to me. Now, God, bless me! Give me what I want!"

The immovable justice of God does not respond. Perfect integrity is not impressed. The ignorant believer's zeal for God obscures the integrity of God. Christianity is rampant with such well-meaning Pharisees.

How can we as believers be "obedient to the righteousness of God"? We must *learn* that we *have* His righteousness and that we have possessed it since the moment of our salvation. We must understand that we cannot improve it. Nagging God is resolved by inculcating into our souls the doctrine of imputations, the framework for an expanding, systematic understanding of His Word.

Nagging others goes by the wayside under the tenets of the royal family honor code. When the righteousness of God is in focus, the weak believer stops looking at the strong believer with a critical attitude, and the strong believer does not treat the weaker brother with contempt and intolerance. The inevitable conflicts of self-righteousness are solved by recognizing that God's righteousness resides in *every* believer, and that justice imputes to righteousness exactly what God deems right.

The only reason any of us is alive and sustained in this life is that we have His righteousness in us. God's integrity is responsible for us every day of our lives. He provides the day; the food, shelter, and clothing; the chance to grow spiritually through testing; everything. He supplies whatever we need, and all this moment-to-moment logistical support is imputed from the justice of God to what? To the righteousness we establish? To the trend toward human good in our old sin natures? To the human morality required of believers and unbelievers alike? Of course not. God in His justice can impute logistical blessings and special blessings only to His own righteousness. Everything we have is by courtesy of the integrity of God.

This is the true perspective of grace. "Grace" is not a line of teaching which merely excuses our failures. It is not sentimentality. It is not a demand for human works. Nor is it vague or inscrutable. Much beautiful lip service to grace only obscures the integrity of God. Grace is the total fairness of God's blessings. When grace is taught as being some inexplicable, wonderfully nebulous divine sentiment, the reputation of the one teaching is established, but the reputation of God is ignored.

The grace of God is clear cut. Our complicated opinions are of no account. We must adjust to God's opinion. And what is His opinion? It is as simple as it is awesome: there is a perfect and irresistible affinity between God's righteousness in us and the tremendous blessings of His justice. As we persist in learning the Word of God, we conform our thinking to His. Doctrine renews our minds. Life gradually takes on a remarkable perspective. We develop the capacity of soul to enjoy special blessings far greater than anything we could possibly deserve. We are relieved from the impossible effort and strain of earning the approbation of God because *His* integrity *gives* and *His* integrity *receives.* God's integrity blesses God's own integrity!

All glory belongs to God. There is no need for us to intrude with our self-important complications. We are brought along only as beneficiaries, *royal* beneficiaries. As we realize that our lives must be built upon the solid rock of divine righteousness, we are motivated to continually submit ourselves to Bible teaching. As we learn Bible doctrine, what comes to shine most brightly in our souls is the Sum of God's glory, our magnificent Savior and Lord, Jesus Christ. Without Him we would have nothing. With Him we have "all things."

APPENDIX A

The Doctrine of Divine Essence

GENERAL OUTLINE OF THE DOCTRINE

THE DOCTRINE OF DIVINE ESSENCE

I. Definition.

    A. Derived from the Greek adjective *ousia,* "being, substance," essence means inner or intrinsic nature, true substance, a person's qualities or attributes. These essential qualities are invisible in many cases, manifest in some.

    B. Essence implies being or existence. We are thus dealing with the fact that God exists and that certain qualities or attributes belong to His essence.

    C. At no point does the believer feel his limitations more than when confronted with the responsibility of understanding and giving due recognition to the essence of God. On the other hand, never could any subject be as vitally interesting. God in grace has revealed Himself, and what is revealed of God's essence is revealed to be understood. The believer can and must master the information God has provided regarding His attributes.

    D. Since God is a Spirit, His attributes are invisible to the human eye. His qualities cannot be perceived by empiricism or by rationalism; they can, however, be understood through the third system of perception: nonmeritorious thinking, called faith.

    E. The believer is totally dependent upon divine revelation from the canon of Scripture to understand the invisible, immaterial, infinite, unlimited essence of God. There is no frame of reference in our character or in the life of anyone we know—or in the entire human race—that can help us understand or even properly illustrate the perfect character of God. It is totally beyond us, and while there is a parallel between the soul of man and the essence of God, the parallel is limited. The essence of God is unseen; man's soul is unseen. God's essence is real; man's essence is real. Divine essence has many attributes (such as sovereignty, righteousness, justice, love, eternal life, omnipotence, omniscience, omnipresence, immutability, and veracity); man's soul has attributes (such as self-consciousness, mentality, volition, and emotion). God's Being is invisible and real, with attributes; beyond that there is no parallel between divine essence and the human soul.

    F. When confronted with the essence of God, supergrace Moses was commanded to remove his shoes because he stood on holy ground (Ex. 3:5).

    G. The doctrine of divine essence recognizes the existence of the Godhead in three Persons, each Person having identical essence or attributes in the same amount from eternity past: the Father (1

Cor. 8:6; Eph. 1:3); the Son (John 10:30; 14:9; Col. 2:9); the Holy
Spirit (Isa. 11:2; Ex. 31:3; Isa. 6:8, 9 cf. Acts 28:25, 26; Jer.
31:31–34 cf. Heb. 10:15–17).

H. Therefore, God is one in essence, three in Person.

I. The oneness of God, called His glory, *is* His essence or character
(John 10:30).

J. All the attributes of divine essence are present in God, but all are
not always manifest at the same time. This is illustrated by light.
All the colors of the visible spectrum are resident in a ray of white
light, but different colors are individually seen under different circumstances of reflection and refraction.

II. The Correlation Between Essence and the Trinity.

The fact that God exists in three Persons is documented in Scripture
(Isa. 48:16; John 10:30 cf. Ps. 110:1; 2 Cor. 13:14; 1 Pet. 1:2).[54] When
emphasizing essence, however, the Bible says that God is one, "one"
being a descriptive adjective meaning one in essence.

III. The Concept of Divine Personality.

A. Mankind has personality because he is made in the image of God;
that is, having real but invisible attributes (which, of course, are
not the same as God's attributes). In constructing man, God
wrapped a body around the real person, which is the sum total of
his invisible attributes, called simply the soul. The statement that
"God created man in His own image" (Gen. 1:27) is often
misunderstood and distorted. Man is not *born* in the image of God;
he was *created* in the image of God. There is a vast difference.
Adam was created with a soul and a human spirit, without an old
sin nature. Since the Fall of Adam, we are born without a human
spirit but with an old sin nature so that we are totally incompatible
with the essence of God. With each person possessing a sin nature
and thus being inherently hostile to reality (the integrity of God),
there is no "dignity of man," no "brotherhood of man." All are
included under the doctrine of the total depravity of man.

B. Man's personality is based on the essence of his soul. The soul with
its characteristics is internal; the personality is external. Personality is a manifestation of how the soul functions.

C. There are many people in the human race, but they all have the
same essence. We might say that mankind is one in essence but
multitudinous in personality. The Trinity is one in essence but only
three in personality.

D. While mankind is possessed of the essential elements of personality

---

54. See Thieme, *The Trinity* and *Divine Essence*.

and is capable of their normal exercise within a limited sphere, God is the Source and embodiment of these essential elements which He possesses in the sphere of infinity and to an unlimited degree.

E. Nearly every page of the Bible asserts the personality of God. We derive our understanding of the personality of God from the manifestation of various combinations of His attributes throughout the Word of God.

F. God designs, executes, and empowers; these are activities of His personality.

G. God speaks of Himself as "I"; therefore, He is self-conscious and eternally Himself.

H. God thinks, makes decisions, and feels; again, these are activities of the Person of God, the superstructure of His essence. In other words, God *has* attributes, but God *is* a personality.

IV. The Attributes of God.

A. Those qualities and perfections which belong to God are termed attributes. ". . . the invisible things of Him [His attributes] . . . are clearly seen, being perspicuous by the things He has made [the act of creation is a function of God as a Person] . . ." (Rom. 1:20). This phraseology portrays the personality of God and behind His personality its source in the attributes of His essence.

B. Essence is the Being which is attributed to Him since the characteristics of this divine essence are eternally and inherently in Him.

C. Since the grace of God and the work of God are manifestations of His essential qualities (His attributes), it is important to understand who and what God is (i.e., to understand His attributes). Moreover, since Jesus Christ is God—the manifest Person of the Godhead (John 1:18)—to understand Him we must understand divine essence. After salvation we *belong* to God; therefore, we are designed to understand the thoughts and functions of God.

D. The difficulty in the study of divine essence is that it brings the finite mind of man into constant contemplation of and concentration on the infinite.

E. There are two categories of divine attributes, absolute and relative. While God is infinite and absolute in every sense of the word, His "absolute" characteristics are those outside our frame of reference which belong to the nature of God apart from His connection with creation. His "relative" attributes can be understood, at least in part, because they are *related* to such items in our frame of reference as time, space, creation, and moral beings. God is absolute; we are relative. Certain aspects of His attributes are totally beyond human comprehension; nevertheless, there is revelation regarding them. In technical theological terms, God's absolute attributes are intransitive, primary, and incommunicable, while His relative attributes are transitive, secondary, and communicable.

V. The Absolute Attributes of God.

    A. Spirituality.

        1. The true theistic concept of the universe is that the universe, having its source from God Himself, is composed of material and immaterial.

        2. Matter is material, but God is immaterial. "God is a Spirit" (John 4:24); His essential Being is a spiritual entity. "Spirit" means breath, something invisible but real; it therefore means that God is invisible but real. The Creator is immaterial (a spirit); in contrast, His rational creatures are a combination of material and immaterial (body and soul, 2 Cor. 4:7, 16). This does not keep God from being even more real than are visible, material things. It is a fact that He is a spirit; the conclusion is that God is life.

        3. God is life (Jer. 10:10; John 1:4; 14:6; 1 Thess. 1:19); God lives. He does not possess life as we do, life that began at some point and has a terminus down the line. There never was a time when God did not live. He has always existed; His life is called eternal life. Eternal life has no beginning and no end, in contrast to the life of the believer, technically called "everlasting life," which has no end but began at the moment of faith in Christ. All life is from God, but all life is not of God (does not belong to Him) as pantheism claims.

        4. The eternal life of God is imparted to all who believe in Christ (John 3:16, 18, 36; 10:10; 14:6; 20:31; 1 John 5:11, 12). Jesus Christ is "the way, the truth, and the *life*" (John 14:6). He *is* life; never was there a time when He, in His deity, did not exist. Eternal life has always resided in Him: "This is the record, God has given unto us eternal life, and this life is in His Son. He who has the Son has life. He who has not the Son has not life . . ." (1 John 5:11, 12). Furthermore, as the Creator, the Lord Jesus Christ is the Source of all life (Heb. 1:2). God the Father is also the Source of life, not from the standpoint of creation, but as the One who breathes the "spark of life" into the fetus when it emerges from the womb at birth. Moreover, God the Holy Spirit is the Source of life as the Agent of regeneration and as the One who places each Church Age believer into union with Christ at the moment of faith in the Gospel. By the baptism of

the Holy Spirit at the moment of salvation, the eternal life of Jesus Christ becomes our eternal life. Thus the Members of the Trinity are related to life in specific, different ways that never clash and are totally compatible with the operation of the Godhead.

5. Under spirituality as an absolute attribute, God is also personality (Ex. 3:14). Anyone who has life has personality. Thus, all human beings have personality merely as the outward expression of the soul. No one has personality until he has life. In other words, you do not have personality as a blastocyst, an embryo, or a fetus because you do not have life—only reflex motility—until God gives you the spark of life at birth. That is when personality begins, but it does not appear immediately. It emerges with growth and maturity.

   God is personality because He lives and has certain attributes, but His personality never emerged or developed. It has always been perfect, and it is manifest in both blessing and cursing. We learn to adjust to the personality of God by applying Bible doctrine under all circumstances. It is important that we adjust to the fact that God is a Person, a personality.

   God's personality is always consistent. He does not change. God is not going to adjust in the least to our personalities. *We* adjust to Him. God is infinite personality; we are finite personality. The infinite never adjusts to the finite.

   God's personality connotes self-consciousness and self-determination.

6. God recognizes Himself to be a Person (He says "I even I" many times in Scripture), and as such He acts rationally.

7. Animals are conscious but not self-conscious; they have determination but not self-determination.

8. Man is a person possessing to a limited degree self-consciousness and self-determination. We are therefore capable of having a definite and permanent relationship with God (on the basis of grace after the Barrier is removed).[55]

9. In contrast to man, God is infinite personality. His absolute will and absolute perfection characterize His motivation and design as well as execution (Eph. 1:9, 11). It is inevitable, therefore, that even the wrath of mankind—as well as anything man does to adjust to God—will praise God (Ps. 76:10). In the statement "the wrath of man will praise thee," the word

---

55. See Thieme, *The Barrier.*

"thee" is a *singular* personal pronoun referring to the Lord
Jesus Christ. Since Christ is the manifest Person of the
Godhead, He is the One glorified by creatures; it is He who
became man.

10. God is to an absolute degree all that constitutes personality. He
is Himself, and He knows Himself to be beyond comparison
with any other being. He has absolute self-respect, which is
part of His divine love (love₁). He also has love for the other
Members of the Godhead. God the Father totally respects and
loves the Lord Jesus Christ and the Holy Spirit. Christ loves
the Father and the Spirit, and likewise the Holy Spirit loves,
honors, respects, and holds in awe the Father and the Son.
There is thus an interaction among the Three, but there is also
within each Person of the Trinity a complete self-confidence
and totally deserved love for self. This is not arrogance; it is
perfect personality far beyond our imperfect status. If we have
total love for self, it is arrogance, a sin; if God has total love for
Himself, it is perfection.

If God did not love Himself, there would be no reason for us
to love Him. When we share His thinking through doctrine, we
come to share His own high opinion of Himself.

B. Infinity.

1. God is without boundaries or limitations. He unites all those
perfections which belong to His character: since His perfect
personality comes from His essence, His perfect attributes
overflow from His essence into His personality undiminished.
In other words, even though all His perfections coalesce into
His personality, no divine characteristic is in any way limited
by being related to the other divine characteristics.

Furthermore, space is no boundary to Him; neither is time.
These are simply boundaries to which we are related as His
finite creatures and which we understand.

2. God is infinitely perfect. He cannot be tempted, nor can He
sin. Sin has boundaries, standards, and measures, but God is
beyond standards and measures and therefore cannot sin. God
cannot tempt anyone to sin, but He can recognize sin in us.

3. God cannot be complicated with ignorance or absurdities (any
more than with temptation, sin, or the approval of sin—all
these roads deadend into divine justice).

We have ignorance, and we are often complicated with absurdities. Through ignorance of doctrine, we become en-
meshed in evil; the absurd is emphasized in legalism. In addi-

tion, all kinds of sins eventually become absurdities as well as carnalities. Absurdities are fantasies, and God is never involved with fantasies. He is totally related to reality without having even the minutest area of ignorance. He has a great sense of humor, but it too is perfect and does not fall back on absurdities.

If you are ever going to understand the infinity of God and how far above us and beyond us He is, you must understand that He is free from ignorance and absurdity. In His infinity, there was no ignorance to overcome. He never had to learn anything because He has always known everything there is to know. That is impossible for us to fully comprehend because we have had to learn everything we know, whether the easy way (by paying attention to instruction) or the hard way (by suffering from our own mistakes). The ignorance we face daily is something God has never experienced and never will. This will come out in greater detail in one of God's relative attributes, omniscience.

4. God may be self-limited, as in the case of the Incarnate Person of Jesus Christ in Hypostatic Union. The Greek word *kenöo* used of Christ in Philippians 2:7 means "to be deprived of the function of deity." Under the doctrine of kenosis the God-Man submitted to the plan of the Father. By taking on true humanity, He limited Himself and became the unique Person of the universe. Now Christ is not only God, equal with the Father and the Holy Spirit, but He is also true humanity, different from the other Members of the Godhead.

God's infinity is intensive rather than extensive. That is, God is not to be thought of merely as extending infinitely beyond time and space but as possessing within Himself infinite resources. He is the perfect Person who passes beyond all phenomena and constitutes the basis for them, as possessing within Himself a boundless supply of the infinite energy of His spiritual life and personality.

Infinite energy and power belong to God (Ps. 8:3). He does not sleep; He never gets tired. After billions of years He is still not worn out, and He never will be. We need to adjust to that: God is compassionate, but He is not absurd—so do not expect Him to sympathize with your lame excuse that you are too tired to take in doctrine and fulfill your responsibilities in life. When you need energy for doing His will, He provides the energy. By applying what we know of the infinity of God, we can see that

God will always provide and that we must therefore carry on no matter how we feel. God never condones give-up-itis. When you start making excuses, you begin to develop maladjustments to God and to the grace of God.

God's promises and the faith-rest technique are all related to His infinity: He has no limitations, and we can rest in that fact.[56] When we recognize His infinity, we can understand that He works all things together for the good; we can reverse our concentration to draw out from our souls the principles of God's plan and logistical grace; we can reach doctrinal conclusions and take control of any situation we meet. When we recognize the infinity of His energy and resources, we never construe the actions we take or the human energy we exert, as a result of the faith-rest rationale, to be a means of gaining God's approbation.

5. Infinity characterizes not only what God is but also all that God does: His holiness, His love, His veracity, His Word of truth. Moreover, all His characteristics require energy, and His energy is infinite. For example, His justice is characterized by infinity so that there is no room for absurdity, for distortions based on sentimentality, or for imperfect motivation. This all adds up to the fact that all His judicial verdicts and sentences are always true and correct. In fact, reality is the function of God's justice. Reality is the divine discipline and the divine blessing in your life; it is the justice of God dealing with our nation; it is the divine destruction of certain client nations and the divine blessing of others.

6. The divine motive is for His own glory, not for self-praise. This is not arrogance; it is perfectly compatible with His infinite attributes. He recognizes His glory, and He claims all glory in the interest of absolute truth.

7. Therefore, all things exist for the glory of God (Ex. 33:18; Ps. 19:1; Isa. 6:3; Matt. 6:13; Acts 7:2; Rom. 1:23; 9:23; Heb. 1:3; 1 Pet. 4:14). Apart from this fact they would not exist; because of it they do.

This is not to say that sinful, evil, self-righteous creatures glorify God; we certainly cannot and do not. We can never impress God. The only thing that impresses God and glorifies God is what God Himself does. We gain from a relationship with Him; He cannot gain from us because His perfect

---

56. See Thieme, *The Faith-Rest Life.*

character is infinite with no room for improvement or gain. Because we are creatures with free will, when we are positive toward Bible doctrine to the point of spiritual maturity, God is free to do things for us that glorify Him in a fantastic way as we go along for the ride.

There is no contradiction in the fact that even the wrath of man (or of any creature) will praise God (Rom. 3:5-23; Ps. 76:10). We were born with old sin natures; we were spiritually dead the moment we became physically alive. Not merely dead to God, we were antagonistic to Him, in total violation of His integrity. But from His integrity God found a way to save us by judging our sins in Christ on the Cross. And in His integrity Christ presides as the Chief Justice of the supreme court of heaven (John 5:22, 27), the other two Justices being the Father and the Holy Spirit. Christ's infinity demands His glory in His decisions regarding human beings and human history. Judgments are continually being handed down from the supreme court of heaven, and whenever Christ renders a judgment, whether for blessing or cursing, whether to an individual, a group, or a nation, He Himself is glorified in providing that judgment.

God's glory was before all creation (John 17:5), and it will exist after history as it did before.

8. Infinity has three basic characteristics.

   a) Self-existence.

      (1) God exists eternally, unsustained by Himself or by any other source. God had no beginning, and His Old-Testament name, Jehovah, means "the Self-existent One." He is the Source of sustaining but does not need it Himself. In other words, He eternally exists as an infinite Person who does not need help from anyone. We, on the other hand, must have help from Him, and since He is the infinite Source with infinite capacity, He provides for our needs.

      (2) God's existence is unalterable. That is why we adjust to Him and He does not adjust to us. Moreover, He is the Cause of all existence outside Himself, but He has no cause for Himself. By application of this principle, if God caused us to receive His life, He can also afford to give us some of His energy: the source of the energy with which you are thinking right now is God's infinite ability to supply. This is an indirect, impersonal supply line to

the entire human race, since everyone requires energy to think. The direct line for believers is called grace.

We have a relationship with God, and there is no higher relationship in the universe. There is nothing beyond God—relationship with Him is the peak. When we made our first adjustment to His justice by believing in Christ, we entered into *the* perfect relationship. We are related to the One who has no cause. He *is* the Cause, but He *has* no cause. He is, in addition, totally familiar with every secondary cause outside of Himself, which means that He has every attribute necessary to make Him the perfect Supreme Court Judge.

b) Immutability.

(1) God is unchangeable. He cannot change; we do the changing (Ps. 33:11; Mal. 3:6; Heb. 13:8; James 1:17).

(2) God cannot be better or worse than His essence. He never had a day when He was better or worse, in contrast to us, for whom every day is better or worse. We have good days and bad days; we are up today, down tomorrow. But God never had a hard day and has never been unhappy. There is a vast difference between creature and Creator; you cannot give God a good day or a bad day, but He can certainly give you either!

(3) Even the anthropomorphic representations of the Lord Jesus Christ in Scripture merely represent His perfect attitude toward variations in man, in history, and in time. God Himself does not change. When man changes, God seems to change, but in reality God remains consistent with His own character. As a weathervane does not change its shape while turning with a shift in the wind, so God merely brings into view a different aspect of His unchanging Person and plan when we change.

God has the ability to handle any situation in life with whatever is necessary; therefore, the fact that He meets one set of circumstances with discipline and another set with deliverance does not mean that His immutability is compromised. It means instead that He is wise and just and that He knows when to do what. He does not deal with everything the same way—that would be stupidity, not immutability! God deals with everything according to the information He possesses, which is total.

We must do the changing if we are to be blessed by

Him. The only way to change in the right direction is to take in doctrine every day because the changes are made in the soul, the battleground of the angelic conflict. Maximum adjustment to God is spiritual growth and maturity, but if we do not change by adjusting to God, we will change by falling into reversionism. One way or the other, we *will* change. And if we go into reversionism, we will still get special attention from God—the pain of divine discipline.

Related specifically to the supreme court of heaven, the Chief Justice is perfect with no contradictions. He is immutable yet able to evaluate different situations in different ways. Since He is unchangeably perfect, His pronouncements are always perfect.

(4) Immutability is consistent with God's freedom and ceaseless activity. God simultaneously deals with millions and millions of people who come under His special attention. He dictates to us; we do not dictate to Him. For specified activities, He has delegated some of His authority to pastor-teachers (all sorts of male believers are given this spiritual gift at the moment of salvation), and we adjust to God's infinite, immutable, ceaselessly active authority by adjusting to the right pastor-teacher's authority.

God is free to act according to His essence. The fact that He is immutable means that He cannot change His own nature, not that He cannot act as His divine nature dictates. Therefore, God is always at His best. There is a false doctrine which states that because man failed in the Garden, salvation is God's second best. Supposedly His first best was to perpetuate that perfect environment. The ultimate conclusion of such a false teaching is that if we are nice and good enough, we might someday deserve God's first best, and He will establish another Eden. That is not only blasphemous and legalistic, it is satanic evil. God is always at peak performance. No characteristic of God can change; His justice, the watchdog over all His attributes, makes certain of that when He deals with man.

c) Unity.

Unity means that God is consistent, not that there is only one Person in the Godhead. There are three Members of the

Trinity, and unity means that each of those Persons is consistent with Himself and with the other Two. They are a perfect Team. Neither the Father, the Son, nor the Spirit ever violates or compromises any divine attribute, and together their activities are always perfectly coordinated. They think the same way; never has there been the slightest disagreement among them, and there never will be.

There is our security. We have a relationship with the Members of the Trinity, and it is consistent in every way. When we believed in Christ, all three Members of the Godhead agreed that we were saved. We will not arrive in heaven only to discover that the Father or the Holy Spirit has some additional requirements! They all agree that we possess their own righteousness and eternal life. There is no dissension about the fact that we are fully qualified to live with them forever. There is one perfect, absolute, infinite Spirit (Isa. 44:6), and divine unity means that three Persons possess it (John 5:44; 17:3; 1 Cor. 8:4). This fact refutes such false doctrines as polytheism and tritheism.

C. Perfection.
  1. The intellect, affections, and character of God are perfect; His perfection involves absolute truth, love, and holiness.
  2. Truth (Ps. 25:5; John 17:17; 1 John 5:6).
  Not merely true to other beings, God is true to Himself. The fact that God is veracity toward others is secondary (cf. veracity, below, as a relative attribute related to moral beings). The primary fact is that billions and billions of years before any creature existed, the Father, the Son, and the Spirit was each true to Himself and therefore had perfect integrity. They always possessed perfect integrity based on truth. Man says, "I am telling the truth"; God says, "I *am* the truth" (John 14:6). Man often finds it easy to adjust to others by lies and deceit, but God has never made such an adjustment. Jesus Christ is a totally true Person.

  God does not hold the truth as being something He acquired; He *is* the truth from eternity past. The truth has never been diminished or compromised in Him; God is the Source of truth. Therefore, God is the Source of Bible doctrine. From the truth that God is comes the truth we have in writing. Every form of knowledge, every truth, dwells in God in absoluteness, thus the dogmatism of Bible doctrine. The divine attribute of truth guarantees that divine revela-

tion in any form—spoken (pre-Canon) or written (Canon)
—is accurate, perfect, and absolute (Deut. 32:4; 1 John
5:20; John 6:32; Heb. 8:2).

There is a vast amount of truth that will not be revealed
until we get to heaven, but whatever God has revealed for us
in time is designed to be learned and understood. If we are
to adjust to the truth of God, we must acquire truth in our
souls through the daily function of the grace apparatus for
perception (GAP). We do not naturally possess the truth
within ourselves; we are born liars because the old sin nature
resides in us (Rom. 3:4). Therefore, whatever integrity we
have cannot be compared with the integrity of God.

Although people often adjust to each other by lying, we
cannot deceive God; we must adjust to His justice through
Truth: the Truth of the Gospel, the Truth of rebound, the
Truth of Bible doctrine.

3. Love (1 John 4:7, 16).

As with all the attributes of God (especially His absolute attributes), love belongs to the Being of God. We are speaking
of love$_1$, not of the anthropopathism, love$_2$. God's love cannot be disassociated from His eternal Being (1 John 4:8),
and never is His love diminished or improved. Thus, God is
love whether or not He has something or someone to love.
His nature is to bestow Himself, to give of Himself, and His
nature remains the same whether or not there is an object
for love, whether or not there is an occasion for love. In
other words, billions of years before the creation of the
universe, God's love was not less because there were no objects, and it is not increased after creation. The explanation
for this is that the only object that is ever worthy of God's
love is God's own eternal, unchangeable integrity. His love
for His integrity is revealed in His perfect righteousness: He
never compromises what He loves.

God's attribute of love is different from human love,
which God does not possess. Even if we understand human
love, that is no guarantee that we understand God's love.
Divine love in its totality is beyond our comprehension. His
love, for example, contains no emotion. Emotion is essential and wonderful in human love, but infinite God does not
feel and emote as do finite beings. His love needs no support; ours does. Another difference: in God's love there is
no deception—only the inviolable demand of perfect truth

and integrity—while our love is often blind. Furthermore, whereas God's love needs no object, our love is not love unless it has an object. God's love is part of His immutable Being in spite of objects or opportunities.

In the Scriptures, human love is often ascribed to God as an anthropopathism. Love₂ accounts for divine motivation in human terms that we can understand. We recognize that we are often motivated by human love; certain human activities can be understood only if we relate them to love. When God does similar things—like blessing or disciplining man—His motivation is much more complex than mere love. Actually, divine motivation is the sum total of His absolute, infinite, perfect Person; but to explain God's actions toward man, the Bible often resorts to language of accommodation that describes them in our frame of reference and makes them understandable to us. Related to man, God's motivation is put into operation, not through His love, but through His justice (cf. below, the relative attributes of righteousness and justice).

God does not love us because of what we are or are not. He loves us because of who and what He is. Specifically, He loves His own righteousness with an infinite love, and since we possess His righteousness as of the moment we believed in Christ, He loves us (Gen. 15:6; Rom. 5:3). God's love is always related to His integrity. Thus, He is very particular about whom He loves and admits into heaven. Jesus Christ is the only One worthy, and only through His merits are we acceptable. This is grace. There is absolutely nothing we can do to earn the love of God or the right to live with Him forever; we are qualified only by nonmeritorious faith in Christ.

4. Holiness (Lev. 11:44, 45; Deut. 32:4; 1 John 2:29).

   a) Holiness, or divine integrity, is made up of God's righteousness and justice. He has had absolute righteousness and perfect justice from all eternity past (Ex. 15:11; 19:10–16; Isa. 6:3).

   b) This holiness is required of men (2 Cor. 7:1; 1 Thess. 3:13; 4:7). God is unchanging in His holiness, and He cannot have a relationship with any creature where less than perfect holiness is involved; He must get the green light from His holiness before any relationship with man is possible.

      c) God's holiness is maintained by His will. That is, His holiness or integrity is His unchangeable Self; and His infinite perfection asserts itself as the highest possible motive, energy, and objective; and His will is the executive of His Being.

VI. The Relative Attributes.

  A. Related to Time and Space.

    1. Eternity (The Attribute Related to Time).

      a) Like all divine attributes, eternity applies to the Being of God. Eternal life belongs to the very essence of God. His eternity means that He has always existed and will always exist; there was never a time when He did not exist. He never had a beginning; no one preceded Him; nothing caused God to come into existence. Time is merely His invention for the convenience of His creatures.

      b) Because God is the Cause and Origin of time, He is not subject to time (Deut. 32:40; Ps. 90:2; 102:27; 1 Cor. 2:7; Eph. 1:4; 1 Tim. 1:17). He invented it for us, but He does not need it Himself. He had to invent time before His relative attributes became manifest. He has always possessed His relative attributes, but they were dormant in contrast to His absolute attributes which were and are always active. Time is the way God manifests His eternity to us, and we adjust to an eternal God by possessing eternal life. Still, we continue to think in terms of time, and, in fact, we cannot live without time.

      c) Both time and space, though without substance, are objects of His creation. If God was gracious and thoughtful enough to give us time, we must give time back to Him. In other words, basic giving in the Christian way of life is giving of time. Whenever we worship God in any way, we are giving time to Him. All Christian service, including the giving of money, is secondary. The primary means of giving time, and the most important phase of worship, is taking the time required to learn Bible doctrine. Our eternal life comes in two phases, life on earth in time and life in heaven in eternity. Here on earth, God gives us one day at a time, and we must recognize that a portion of that day belongs to Him for learning His Word.

      d) God is not in time, but time is in God.

      e) God transcends all creation, including time. To Him, "one day . . . is as a thousand years, and a thousand years as one day'' (2 Pet. 3:8*b*).

f) God is logical and therefore does not need to be chronological (Rom. 12:2), but He can be chronological if He so chooses. For example, time began with creation, and since the successions of history truly exist, God, who sees according to the truth, recognizes them. Furthermore, God always accomplishes in time what has to be done in time as part of His great plan. Thus, the variations of blessing and adversity that come in our day-at-a-time lives are merely part of an overall plan to bless us in eternity as well as to provide security for us and bless us in time.

g) Time, which is finite, has both succession and duration. Its duration is measured by its successions; for example, the duration of a day is measured by the succession of minutes or hours.

h) In contrast, eternity, which is infinite, has duration only. Duration without succession is still duration, but it is immeasurable. Therefore, God, who is infinite, is eternal and has duration only. In fact, eternity *is* infinity in its relation to time. Time is a line of procedure as far as man's concept is concerned. But eternity is a circle, reaching into infinity.

2. Immensity (The Attribute Related to Space).

   a) God is not subject to the laws of space. As He did with time, God invented and created space. Space is large, but not as large as God.

   b) God cannot be more or less than He is.

   c) God is the cause of space. He put order into space, which extends for billions and billions of light years. Space is one of two boundaries God has given to creatures, the other being time. Between our salvation and physical death, we as believers operate within both space and time exactly as the unbeliever does. When people fantasize, they lose track of where they are, but they are still in space. When people travel into outer space, they find themselves in a "timeless" situation, but they are still in time. We can never escape time or space, and it would be a disaster to do so—our entire orientation in life is tied to time and space. For example, when God commands us to "forsake not the assembling of yourselves together [to learn the Word of God]," He has to provide us with the means of complying with His order. He gave us time and space so that we could be at the right place at the right time.

d) In relation to space, God is immanent (in space) and transcendent (outside of space).

e) Omnipresence describes space in relation to God; immensity describes God in relation to space.

f) Since God is the Creator, the Cause of space, if space were defined as having boundaries, God would exceed those boundaries to infinity. Since God has the ability to construct time and space and is inside them as well as outside of them, He also has the ability to handle smaller problems such as our adversities and difficulties. Our personal and national problems are not nearly as hard for God to manage as it was for Him to invent the day or the cubic foot. Knowing this, we have no cause for worry.

B. Related to Creation.

1. Omnipresence (Deut. 4:39; Ps. 139:8; Prov. 15:3; Acts 17:27).

a) God is eternally present everywhere. The whole of God is in every place.

b) This is not pantheism, since pantheism denies the Person of God.

c) God is the total of His essence. Without diffusion, expansion, multiplication, or division, He penetrates and fills the entire universe and everything beyond the universe to infinity (Ps. 139:7; Jer. 23:23, 24; Acts 17:27).

d) God is free to be local. He was with Moses on the mountain (Ex. 19:20; 24; 18); He resided in the Holy of Holies in the Temple as the Shekinah Glory (Ex. 40:34; Lev. 16:2). He "became flesh and tabernacled among us" (John 1:14) while at the same time existing throughout all space and beyond all space.

He knows firsthand our weaknesses, our problems, our circumstances. He is personally interested in us every moment we are in time, and He is available to help us immediately. He is a perfect Counselor—He always has time for everyone simultaneously. Omnipresence means He is personally there, an eyewitness to every activity of our lives and of all human and angelic history.

2. Omniscience.

a) God is wise; He has perfect wisdom. He knows perfectly and eternally all that is knowable, whether actual or merely possible. Everything that has been known or ever will be known—for example, every discovery in the advance of science—has been known to God since eternity past. Never was there a time when He did not know everything that is knowable. In other words, God could pass any examination on any subject at any time (or on all subjects at the same time), and He could have done so in eternity past. Moreover, God never learns anything because He has always known everything; He knows the end from the beginning (Ps. 33:13–15; 139:1–4; 147:4, 5; Prov. 15:3; Isa. 36:9, 10; 44:28; Mal. 3:16; Matt. 6:8; 10:29, 30; Acts 15:8; Heb. 4:3, 13; 1 John 3:20).

b) Omniscience can be categorized three ways:

    (1) Eternal. Because God is eternal life and omniscient, He has always known everything (Acts 15:18).

    (2) Incomprehensible. Many things are incomprehensible to us, but because of His infinity, everything is clearly comprehensible to God. The Bible reveals only a small fraction of God's knowledge (Rom. 11:33).

    (3) Wise. Total wisdom as well as total knowledge belongs to God's omniscience (Eph. 3:10).

c) Every detail of all creation and history is in God's mind at all times and always has been from eternity past. This is God's mentality as connected with His infinity.

d) Therefore, the future is as perspicuous to God as the past.

e) God foreknows the future. Since all events take place according to His counsel (the divine decrees), He foreknows, but His foreknowledge is not predetermination. He knows every step you will take, but He never interferes with your volition (cf. Appendix B).

f) God foreknows the function of every free will; He knows what other beings will choose. He knows we have a free will—in fact He gave us our volition—and He knows which way we will jump in the function of our free volition in every situation in life.

g) Although He never interferes with free will, God is gracious and all-wise and therefore does not merely sit on the sidelines. He may determine which choice is made through His gracious influence, for example, through Bible doctrine resident in the soul of the believer or through His control of the variables of life that are beyond human control—often erroneously called "fate" or "luck."

h) God's knowledge is not subject to development, reasoning, regretting or foreboding. His knowledge is always total and perfect; therefore, it cannot develop beyond what it already is. God knows all the conclusions as well as all the premises; hence, even though He is totally reasonable and rational in all things, He never needs to reason things out. This also means that we can never second-guess God; there is no way we can improve on His system. We can simply go along with His perfectly wise policy, which has our best interest in mind. But what if we choose not to follow the divine course? His plan goes right along without us.

Satan is the best illustration of what happens to someone who tries to outsmart God. The devil's entire strategy boils down to an attempt to outsmart, second-guess, and out-maneuver God. Satan thinks he has a better plan than God's and wants to put it into effect and take God's place. The result of Satan's brilliant though arrogant efforts to improve on the divine plan is the confusion and evil we find in the world today. Eventually Satan's rival plan will result in his own destruction in the Lake of Fire forever. While believers will never see the Lake of Fire, their imperfect and unwise plans can create misery for themselves and others.

Since God's thinking is not subject to regrets, foreboding, or depression; all that He knows never makes Him unhappy. If we knew just some of the details God knows, if we could see the future, we would be upset immediately. Our country is headed downhill, and if we knew what was in store for us as a nation in the next few years, we would be shocked and terribly unhappy about it.

3. Omnipotence.

   a) God is all-powerful; His power is infinite. He is able to do all things which are the objects of His power within the range of His holy character; that is, He can do all things which are not self-contradictory or contradictory to His own nature. For Him to do contradictory things would not imply power but impotence!

   b) God will never make right wrong nor will He act foolishly. He never abuses His power; His power is perfect and beyond our comprehension (Isa. 44:24; 2 Cor. 4:6; Eph. 1:19, 20; 3:20; Heb. 1:3).

   c) If God is limited at any time, it is because of a self-imposed limitation consistent with His plan and essence.

   d) God can do all He wills to do, but He may not will to do all He can.

C. Related to Moral Beings.

1. Veracity and Faithfulness.

    a) God is infinite perfection in veracity and faithfulness, which are expressed to us in Bible doctrine. Thus, His *absolute* attribute of truth, under the category of His perfection, is related to man through the *relative* attributes of veracity and faithfulness.

    b) Veracity (Ps. 33:4; Heb. 6:18; Num. 23:19).

    God honors Bible doctrine resident in the soul of the believer. This is one of the great principles to be derived from the doctrine of divine attributes: God *is* Truth as an attribute; therefore He must honor Truth resident in our souls. God honors His Word wherever it is found; maximum doctrine in the soul constitutes maturity adjustment to the justice of God or total relationship with the integrity of God. From this it should be obvious why we cannot grow by our works or good deeds, not even by such normally legitimate works as witnessing, giving, prayer, etc. As a matter of God's veracity, spiritual growth can be achieved only by the consistent, persistent intake of Bible doctrine. Since God honors His Word, His Word in the souls of believers is the only thing that will save our country.

    c) Faithfulness (Deut. 7:9; 1 Cor. 1:9; 10:13; 2 Thess. 3:3; 1 John 1:9).

    Because He honors doctrine in our souls, God faithfully provides divine logistics to support us on earth during our period of spiritual growth. Thus we are able to continue in history and continue in GAP no matter what the historical climate happens to be. Even in a period of national decline and destruction, God faithfully takes care of us: death cannot touch the believer until God is ready to take him home. Not only is the believer protected in a time of disaster, but one of the blessings to the mature believer is historical impact. The believer whose soul is saturated with doctrine, who is fully adjusted to the justice of God, who possesses a total relationship with the integrity of God, is like an Atlas supporting the world. This is the case, whether known or unknown to those around him.

2. Mercy and Goodness (Ex. 22:27; 34:6; Ps. 116:5; 1 Pet. 2:3).

    a) Mercy is grace in action.

    b) Mercy is God's infinite love in action toward the objects of divine affection. Therefore, if Category One Love is our love toward God, God's mercy is Category One Love seen from the other side—His love toward us, creatures who possess His own perfect righteousness.

   c) God is absolute good, in contrast to the policy of Satan which is evil and contains relative good or human good.

3. Justice and Righteousness.

   a) Infinite integrity or holiness acting toward others is justice. The absolute attribute of holiness is broken down into the relative attributes of righteousness and justice. Thus when divine holiness is related to us, it takes the form of either righteousness (the principle of integrity) or justice (the function of integrity).

   b) God's righteousness is perfect, demanding perfect justice.

   c) God's judgments are perfect, demanding perfection.

   d) Justice administers the penalty which righteousness demands. That is why God can never become sentimental and eventually let everyone into heaven. On the other hand, justice administers the blessings of which righteousness approves.

   e) In righteousness is God's love for His integrity revealed.

   f) In justice is God's hatred for sin revealed.

   g) God is not arbitrary in any way. Integrity demands integrity; righteousness demands righteousness; justice demands justice. God's nature cannot change. Therefore, that which is contrary to His righteousness must be punished, and that which is adjusted to His justice must be blessed.

   h) God must continue to be integrity; that is, He must demand and execute punishment for both sin and evil as long as He is what He is.

   i) His penalties are not vindictive but vindicative. With unchangeable sin and evil there is unchangeable condemnation and judgment; thus, God is proven to be consistent.

   j) In salvation, God provides in grace all that He demands of the unbeliever; and through rebound, God deals with the sins of the believer.

   k) In Himself, God's spirituality or personality is supreme, but in relationship to man, integrity (righteousness and justice) is supreme.

VII. Other Divine Characteristics.

   A. The Freedom of God.

     1. Freedom is not truly an attribute; God's sovereignty is.

     2. God must be consistent with Himself; He cannot compromise His essence.

3. The Incarnation and spiritual death of Christ was the only way the free will of God (His sovereignty) could provide salvation for man. In other words, God is free to bless man only when man is adjusted to His justice, first of all at salvation, then at rebound, and finally at spiritual maturity.

B. The Affections of God.

1. His affections are the feeling aspect of His consciousness as distinguished from the cognitive aspect.

2. Anthropopathisms ascribe to God human characteristics which He does not possess, but they explain divine policy to us in terms of human attitudes.

3. For example, repentance (but God does not really change His mind) (Gen. 6:6).

4. Hatred (an expression of divine justice) (Rom. 9:13).

5. Anger (but God's judgments are never capricious or based on passion) (Rom. 1:18).

6. Scorn (Ps. 2:4).

7. Benevolence (Rom. 8:32).

8. Compassion (Lam. 3:22-32).

9. Longsuffering (Num. 14:18).

10. Happiness (God is infinitely happy in Himself with absolute freedom from fear, anxiety, regret, foreboding, or annoyance).

C. The Authority of God.

1. God's authority is derived from all His attributes.

2. God has absolute authority over possible things and actual things.

3. Over possible things, God is sovereign in that He leaves them as merely possible and not actual or destines them to become actual at a specific point in the future.

4. In this realm, God renders account to no one. He acts in conformity with His own perfect character and consults no one for advice or encouragement. He is perfect and cannot be less than perfect in any decision He makes.

5. In relation to existing things, God is the final and absolute authority (Ps. 145:14; Matt. 20:15; 1 Tim. 6:15). God delegates and establishes systems of authority in the human race; we call these systems of delegated authority "the laws of divine establishment." Designed for believers and unbelievers alike, these authorities are necessary for the perpetuation of the human race. For example, each individual holds the authority over himself in the function of self-discipline; this is the

mechanics of using his God-given free volition. Likewise, in marriage, the man is in authority over the woman; in the family, parents are in authority over their children. Law and law enforcement, as well as the military, are systems of authority under the principle of national government. Governments, however, have no authority to invade the privacy of law-abiding citizens or to regulate their personal lives or legitimate businesses.

Government wields authority as a servant of the people with the specific limited duties of internal and external protection, along with a basic amount of administration. Legitimate government is simply the administrator of certain rights which belong to the citizens of the nation but which have been entrusted to the government for objective, just, and dispassionate execution. Furthermore, the laws of divine establishment limit government to the national level and below. Internationalism gives rulers more power than they can properly handle, and freedom cannot be protected.

6. The authority of God rests in three facts:

   a) God is the Creator. God gave existence to every creature and to all things; therefore, His authority extends over them. He has the right to save or judge, reward or discipline. This right, however, is restricted by His own perfect essence. He is therefore compelled to discipline the reversionist under the influence of evil. He is also compelled to bless and reward the mature believer under the influence of doctrine. This exercise of authority is always consistent with His own essence and plan.

   The Creator's absolute and sovereign ownership of all things is contrasted with the secondary rights which men recognize in the ownership of private property under the laws of divine establishment. All the wealth of the world belongs to God (Ps. 50:10). Consistent with His will and perfect character, He can give blessings or remove them according to His personal handling of each individual as that person is adjusted or maladjusted to divine justice (Job 1:21).

   b) God has redeemed us. He purchased us out of the slave market of sin. He freed us at the Cross, giving us the right to choose for or against His plan of salvation and, subsequently, to choose for or against Bible doctrine. He bought us with a price; therefore, He has authority over us.

      c) God has provided Bible doctrine. The authority of God is expressed in doctrine, and our obedience to His authority is related to the amount of doctrine resident in our souls. If we go with God's authority, there is tremendous blessing; if against, tremendous cursing.

VIII. Categories of Anti-theistic Theories.

    A. Satan has many approaches by which he tries to destroy our understanding of the character of God.

    B. Polytheism is the belief in a plurality of gods, as in the Phoenician, Greek, and Roman pantheons.

    C. Pantheism is the philosophy that God and the universe are one, that the universe conceived of as a whole *is* God. It denies the transcendency of God, the fact that God exists outside the universe. This puts boundaries on God. Pantheism also denies the personality of God, claiming instead that He exists only as the sum total of all the forces and laws of the existing universe. Pantheism falsely asserts that since God does not go beyond the universe, He did not create the universe.

    D. Materialism is that form of atheism that denies the existence of God and claims instead that material substance is the basis of and explanation for all things. It contends that instead of being imputed by God to our immaterial souls, life is a product of what is material. This is the philosophy of Communism.

    E. Deism asserts that God is personal, infinite, holy, and the Creator of the universe, but claims that He personally abandoned His creation when completed. Thus, He intended the universe to be self-sustaining and self-promoting by the forces resident in it. Deism rejects the Word of God and any suggestion that He intervenes in human affairs. As a rationalistic movement of the 17th and 18th centuries, Deism's adherents included Thomas Paine, David Hume, Thomas Jefferson, Edward Gibbon, and Voltaire.

    F. Idealism is a system of thought which contends that the mind is the only entity and that the material universe is no more than an impression or illusion of the mind. Some idealists believe in God but deny His creation of material things. Their philosophy spawns asceticism.

    G. Evolution states that the cosmos has developed from a crude, homogenous material into its present heterogenous and advanced state by means of its own resident forces.

      1. Theistic evolution claims that although God is the Creator of the original materials, evolution is the method by which all development has been accomplished, from a supposed primor-

dial state into one of completeness.

2. Atheistic evolution rejects the existence of God and claims that matter is eternal and self-developing.

H. Positivism is a system of thought which accepts as true only what can be verified by literally pointing to it. This school of philosophy claims that reasoning is mere redundancy, and it attempts to squeeze all thinking into a system like mathematics. It disregards both God and the human soul.

I. Monism takes the view that there is only one kind of substance or reality instead of two (e.g., mind and matter—dualism) or more (e.g., a plurality of independent substances—pluralism).

J. Biblical theism is where we stand: the doctrine of the essence of God.

APPENDIX B

The Doctrine of Divine Decrees

GENERAL OUTLINE OF THE DOCTRINE

THE DOCTRINE OF DIVINE DECREES

I. Definition and Description.
- A. The decree of God is His eternal, holy, wise, and sovereign purpose, *comprehending* at once all things that ever were or will be—in their causes, courses, conditions, successions, and relations—and *determining* their certain futurition.

    This is meant to be a concise, technical definition; each phrase carries a wealth of information. This definition relates various attributes of God's essence to His "purpose" for angelic and human history. It identifies the source of the divine decrees as being the omniscience of God "comprehending" all things in eternity past. It also portrays divine volition "determining" or choosing, before anything existed, which things would actually become historical events. The doctrine of divine decrees develops the various aspects of this definition.

- B. The several contents of this one eternal purpose are, because of the limitations of our mentality and faculties, necessarily perceived by us in partial aspects in both logical and revealed relations. For this reason we often use the plural, "decrees" to express the many facets of God's plan. Actually it is all one decree, given billions of years ago in less than a second and covering everything in all of what to us is past, present, and future history (Ps. 2:7; 148:6; Dan. 9:24). At the time of the decrees, all history was yet future.

- C. The decree of God is His eternal and immutable will regarding the future existence of events which will happen in time and regarding the precise order and manner of their occurrence.

    Here, and throughout the doctrine of divine decrees, we use the term "will of God" in a technical sense. In common usage, the "will of God" refers to what God desires of an individual or group in a particular situation,[57] but that is not the "will" in view here. We mean the decision He made in eternity past, from His attribute of sovereignty, which established that certain things would actually come into being while other things would not. We mean His sovereign choice as to what will take place in time. (We are so dependent on God that nothing can even exist apart from His decision to make it exist!)

    Many things that occur are results of angelic or human free will acting contrary to God's desires. He nevertheless decided or willed that these things would take place. Thus He makes our voli-

---

57. See Thieme, *Divine Guidance.*

tion truly free. How He could do this without compromising His perfect essence is the story of the justice of God.

An example of something that God willed to exist is *you!* You are a responsible, rational, freewill individual who lives in the twentieth century. You and your freedom, etc. were decreed billions of years ago. You exist today because you are part of a very old plan.

D. The divine decrees are the eternal plan by which God has rendered certain all the events of the universe, including both angelic and human history—past, present, and future. God's decree rendered all things as certain to occur; He decided that they *would* exist. In doing so, He did not interfere with angelic or human free will. In fact, He decreed that we would have free will! In giving us volition, He also decreed that our decisions, whatever they might be, would certainly take place—even those that are contrary to His desires. Being omniscient, He had the good sense to know ahead of time what we would decide, and He not only decreed that those decisions would exist but He also decreed the exact manner, consistent with His integrity, in which He would handle our decisions.

E. The decree of God is the chosen and adopted plan of all God's works.

F. The decree of God is His eternal purpose, according to the counsels of His own will, whereby for His own glory He has foreordained whatever comes to pass.

G. The decree of God is the sovereign choice of the divine will (His attribute of sovereignty) and mentality (His omniscience) by which all things are brought into being and controlled, made subject to His pleasure, and producing His glorification (Isa. 46:10; Eph. 1:9). The Father, the Son, and the Holy Spirit pre-existed everything. No one was above them; no one originated them. (God has no origin.) Anything the Members of the Trinity decide to originate is decided with two concepts in mind.

1. It is for their *pleasure.* We do a variety of things for our pleasure or entertainment, but God's pleasure is, we might say, somewhat broader in scope. His perfect happiness is part of His infinite character, so His pleasure is not impulsive or frivolous. Nevertheless He snapped His fingers and billions upon billions of light years of space instantly came into being. Then He created creatures with free will—beautiful, powerful creatures called angels. Their history is largely undisclosed to us, but eventually, from their own free decisions, some of these creatures got out of line—the Fall of Satan and the revolt that

began the angelic conflict.

God always knew that some of the angels would revolt. Therefore, in the same instant that He decreed to create the universe and the angels, He also decreed that at a certain point in time He would create another type of creature. Like the angels, this new person would have free will and would be designed to share God's happiness. But he (and his progeny) would also become the demonstration of the fullness of God's essence to those angels who had impugned God's character. So, for God's pleasure, He created Adam. Now, long after the Fall of Adam, God's pleasure is our adjustment to the justice of God. Salvation, spirituality, and spiritual maturity free God to bless us.

2. What the Trinity decides is also for their *glory*. God has always existed in perfect glory; anything He does reflects His glory and results in His glorification. God does not depend on us for His pleasure or His glory; He enjoyed these things in eternity past when no one else existed. He is expressing them in us and toward us: we are here as part of God's pleasure and glory.

3. It is the pleasure of God to permit creatures to exercise free volition. We should have no illusions about ourselves. We are here, not to glorify ourselves, not to impress God, but to line up with His pleasure and glory.

H. Picture the decree of God as a giant computer. In eternity past God fed facts from His omniscience into the computer. These "facts" are differentiated from mere potentialities, the "alternatives," which He also knows in His omniscience but did not decree. The facts include every thought you would ever have, every decision you would ever make, every action you would ever take. When He decreed (or fed into the computer) the fact that you would exist as a free agent, He also decreed —simultaneously—that your every thought, decision, and action would take place. He fed into the computer the decisions He knew you would make about sin, about rebound, about human good and evil, about believing in Christ, about walking down the street, about the laws of establishment, about doctrine, about spiritual production, about everything. He also fed other facts into the computer. Based on knowing how you would use your free will, He fed in logistical grace and, for those who would advance to maturity, special blessings in time. He knew every situation you would face—every problem, every heartache, every personal or historical disaster, every failure or success—and

He provided the solution to each problem. Moreover, He supplied everything you would need to face them in complete security with perfect orientation and inner happiness. Capacity for happiness comes from understanding these things, from having doctrine in your soul. One obvious conclusion: there is never an excuse for complaining.

I. The computer of divine decrees prints out facts about believers under the categories of election, foreknowledge, and predestination. It also prints out facts about unbelievers under the categories of condemnation, reprobation, and retribution. No unbeliever is ever "predestined" to go to hell.

J. The decrees of God are the sum total of God's plan, designed in eternity past, relating to all events of all classifications, collected into one single all-comprehensive whole through God's omniscience.

K. The omniscience of God is the key to understanding the decrees. God has three kinds of knowledge.

  1. Self-knowledge. God knows Himself; He has never had to learn anything about Himself; His self-knowledge has always been total, perfect, complete. He is aware of His own essence and the unlimited capabilities of each Member of the Trinity. Unlimited and subjective in self-knowledge, the Members of the Trinity know each other.

  2. Omniscience. God knows all things outside of Himself. God knows all things about believers and unbelievers both the *actual*—which He Himself foreordained, decreed, programmed into the computer—and the *possible*— which could have happened but did not because He did not decree it, did not make that particular decision, did not enter it into the computer. His omniscience is unlimited and objective.

  3. Foreknowledge. This subcategory of God's cognizance acknowledges only what is in the decrees, in the plan. It is a computer printout of the actual facts (not mere possibilities) regarding the function of the believer. The term "foreknown" is used in Scripture of believers only (and of Christ). His foreknowledge is limited and objective.

II. The Mechanical Function of the Computer.

A. Stage One, the Omniscience of God.

  1. In His omniscience, God knows perfectly, eternally, and simultaneously all that is knowable, both the actual and the possible.

  2. Such perception and sagacity is totally compatible with His

essence. God would not be God unless He always knew all about everything.

3. God is eternal; His knowledge is eternal. He is sovereign; His knowledge is superior. The link between His superior knowledge and our inferior knowledge is Bible doctrine.

4. The Creator's knowledge is infinitely superior to the creature's knowledge or intellect.

5. Every minute detail of both angelic and human creation is completely and perfectly in His mind at all times.

6. The omniscience of God perceives the free as free, the necessary as necessary, together with all their causes, conditions, and relations, as one indivisible system of things, every link of which is essential to the integrity of the whole. Every cause and effect is related to another cause and effect and to another and another. In this one, all-comprehensive, interdependent system of cause and effect, man's volition is the uncaused cause of human function so that the course of history is just as man thinks it, wills it, does it. When you understand this, you realize that you have no reason for complaining, for falling apart in a crisis, or for feeling left out and sorry for youself. God never tampers with your volition; "predestination" does not mean that He forces you into a course of action.

7. Time does not limit God's knowledge. To Him, the future is as perspicuous as the past.

8. The omniscience of God knows the alternatives to history—the possible as well as the actual.

9. God knows what would have been involved in every case where a man's decision might have been different from what it was. Imagine that you are confronted by twenty possible courses of action and must choose one. Even though God knew which way you would choose to go and decreed only that one to become reality, He knows all the repercussions of each alternative.

10. Omniscience is one of the three categories of divine knowledge.

11. Omniscience knows every thought, decision, and act in human history, how they all relate to each other, and how they relate to all the possible alternatives.

12. The foreknowledge of God makes nothing certain but merely acknowledges what *is* certain. It knows what is already in the decrees regarding believers only.

13. For believers, there are at least three categories of printouts from the computer: foreknowledge, election, and predestina-

tion (sometimes called foreordination).

14. Foreknowledge means that nothing can be certain until it is first decreed; only then can what *will* happen be foreknown. God knows all actual events as certainly future because He has decreed them to be certainly future.

15. God's decrees relate equally to all future events of every kind— to the free actions of moral agents as well as to the actions of necessary agents; to the sinful, human-good, and evil as well as to the morally correct, divine-good, and honorable.

16. The decrees alone establish certainty. For the believer, "foreordination" and "predestination" are synonymous with the decrees.

17. Foreordination is an act of the infinitely intelligent and wise God in determining the certain futurition of events in the life of the believer.

B. Stage Two, the Decree Itself.

1. The omniscience of God fed into the computer only the facts.

2. This was accomplished in eternity past—simultaneously, not in stages.

3. The decrees have become the complete and consummated right of the sovereignty of God determining the certain futurition of all things in human history.

   a) Whether you realize it or not, God has rights. No decree can become complete without the sovereignty of God. Because He knows the end from the beginning, God wills certain things to happen.

   b) Since, in eternity past, God exercised this right to make things certain, when we say "certain futurition of events," we mean events which are future from eternity past. Thus, we mean all events throughout all time. Many areas of the decrees have been fulfilled historically, up to and including this present moment; but all were future when decreed, including those still future today.

   c) Because of how infinitely complex this decree happens to be, we must conclude with a doctrine: God is smarter than we are!

4. No event is directly effected or caused by the decree. The decree merely establishes what will be caused, but the decree itself is not the cause. The fact that a thought or action on your part is in the decree does not mean that the decree caused you to think or do it. The cause is your own free will. Your thoughts are in the decree because, billions and billions of years ago,

God had the wisdom to know *what* you would think and to not omit from His planning the fact that you *would* think it!

5. But the decree itself provides in every case that the events shall be affected by causes acting in a manner consistent with the nature of the event in question. As an example of this principle, the cause of some events is the free will of man.

6. In the case of every freewill act of a moral agent, the decree itself provides at the same time the following:

   a) *The agent shall be a free agent.* Far from coercing anyone's volition, the decree establishes volition.

   b) *His antecedents and all antecedents of the act in question shall be what they are.* Once something happens, that's it. It is part of the system of cause and effect; it becomes part of the basis for other things happening down the line. Wishful thinking cannot change what has already occurred.

   c) *All present conditions of the act shall be what they are.* God is not going to make reality suddenly vanish or become different or reverse itself. God enables us to orient to reality and to face the facts. If our arrogance or simple ignorance leads us to make decisions which overlook certain facts, those facts nevertheless are what they are. For example, if we do not adjust to the justice of God, the justice of God is still a reality, and it will adjust to us through discipline.

   d) *The act shall be perfectly spontaneous and free on the part of the agent.*

   e) *The act shall be certainly future.* That is, it will definitely take place, at a certain time, after the decree is given.

   Perhaps you do not recognize the significance of these five points, but they knock hyper-Calvinism right out of the box! Hyper-Calvinism is a distortion of the sovereignty of God to the point of excluding the free will of man. It is a ghastly fatalism, in contrast to the wonderful teachings of the Word of God regarding divine sovereignty and human free will. Let me illustrate.

   God knew in His omniscience that the woman and the man would commit sins in the Garden. He knew all the repercussions of those two acts throughout history, but He still decreed that Adam and his wife would have free will, decreeing also to furnish timely and wonderful provisions for them and their progeny. But never in any way did He coerce their volition. God did not suddenly shout, "Look out! Satan is about to tempt the woman! I'm going to keep him from doing so! I'll kill the serpent! There will be no serpent! There will be no human history!'' That is the kind of nonsense implied by the hyper-Calvinist's distortion of God's sovereignty. Another implication, perhaps more famous but equally ridiculous, is the false notion that since unbelievers go to hell, God *predestined* them to go! Unbelievers go to hell of their own volition: they freely decide to reject the Lord Jesus Christ as Savior.

Actually, John Calvin (1509–1564) was an excellent exegete of the Scriptures, generally speaking. But like the followers of any good Bible teacher, some of those who came after him misrepresented him and have applied his name to doctrines that would have made his hackles rise.

Hyper-Calvinism is not correct, but neither is the Arminian view. (An Arm*e*nian comes from Armenia, a country in the Caucasus Mountains; but an Arm*i*nian is a person who accepts a system of erroneous theology named after Arminius [1560–1609].) Arminius and his followers distort the sovereignty of God in the opposite direction. They claim that man's volition is beyond God's control, that man can cause things that are not in the divine decrees. This is totally false; nothing can be certain until God decrees it to be certain.

Perhaps you have never been exposed to it before, but what we have been presenting is orthodox theology, that is, *Biblical* theology. Orthodoxy is something few people recognize today; hardly anyone is still a student in this field. Most men who are truly students of theology are trying to reconcile theology and philosophy. The inevitable result is that they reject the authority of the Word of God. From their attempts come such false doctrines as neo-orthodoxy, existentialism, etc. Great strides are being made—great erroneous strides!

If many scholars are wrong, there is also error on the other extreme, far removed from the realm of disciplined study. Holy rollers claim to base their teachings and practices on the Bible. But they are so far from being orthodox that they center all their beliefs on a distortion of the gift of tongues. The true gift fulfilled its purpose and was removed more than nineteen centuries ago. As do many ''theologians,'' the holy rollers live in the middle of heresy not orthodoxy.

Fundamentalist Christianity is now so plagued with emotionalism and with pastors who promote clever ideas rather than teach accurate theology, that it has nearly ceased to be true theological fundamentalism. Orthodoxy is being neglected, yet orthodoxy is the study of Bible doctrine.

Orthodox theology is a complete system in which one area of Scripture sheds light on other areas. Because the Bible does not contradict itself, everything in the Bible must agree with everything else as part of the system. By persistently studying the Bible from its original languages, by immersing himself in its historical context, and by diligently comparing Scripture with Scripture, the pastor, under the filling of the Spirit, continually refines, expands, fills in, revises, and improves his systematic communication of doctrine. This is how the pastor develops a thorough understanding of doctrine and how breakthroughs come to light. Without such a regimen of study and teaching, the pastor cannot present systematic theology to his congregation. The doctrine of divine decrees is a basic category of orthodox theology; we are not surprised, therefore, that in spite of its importance it is a subject of which the vast majority of people are ignorant.

7. The decree vested solely with the will of God what His creation should be. For example, God alone decided in eternity past what human beings would be like: we would be rational creatures with free will. Our souls would have self-consciousness, mentality, volition, and emotion; Adam would be body, soul, and spirit as he came from the Creator's hand. By way of a ludicrous illustration, God did not decide to give us two heads, five legs, a thirty-foot tail, and the brains of a horse. Nor did He design us with an old sin nature; that came from Adam's negative volition.

8. Because God cannot contradict His own nature, the essence and attributes of God necessitated His willing the highest and best for mankind. When God created man, He created the highest and best compatible with His plan. Adam was not greater than the angels, but his body, soul, and spirit and his environment were all absolutely perfect. Of course, some of the highest and best that man received at creation has been lost through the Fall. The same perfect God who created mankind now condemns us. But He still wills the highest and best in that He now offers perfect salvation and magnificent blessings in

time and eternity. Because we have free will, we may miss all of
this, but it is still available.

C. Stage Three, the Printouts.

1. The printout from the computer of divine decrees, which
   relates to believers, includes election, foreknowledge, and
   predestination.

2. "Predestination," "foreordination," and "predetermination" are synonyms and refer to the decree. These terms
   describe the act of the infinite, eternal omniscience of God
   which determined the certain futurition of events related to the
   believer.

3. Foreknowledge is not the same as omniscience but is more
   limited in scope. Omniscience knows both the actual and the
   possible; foreknowledge includes the actual only.

4. Being omniscient, God knows all that would have been involved had He adopted any one of an infinite number of plans of
   action. He also knows all the consequences had *man* chosen a
   different course of action within the realm of his own volition.

5. Foreknowledge refers only to those things which God *did*
   decree or adopt as the plan of God—those things related to the
   believer only.

6. Only the decree establishes certainty or reality; only reality can
   be foreknown; nothing can be foreknown until first decreed.
   We can see where Arminianism departs from orthodoxy: it
   holds falsely that events can occur without being decreed by
   God to occur.

7. God's decrees never originate from His foreknowledge.
   Although all three exist simultaneously in the mind of God,
   omniscience, the decree, and foreknowledge must be separated
   into a logical sequence for us to understand them. First comes
   omniscience, then the decree, then foreknowledge. The decree
   is based on omniscience; foreknowledge is based on the decree.

8. Election is the plan of God for believers only. All the elect are
   believers, but not all believers are elect. Election means
   "chosen, selected, set apart for privilege." There are three
   elections to privilege: the unique election of Christ, the election
   of Israel, and the election of the Church. All Church Age
   believers are elect members of the royal family of God. (In this
   outline we are not attempting to delineate the entire doctrine of
   election; we want to clarify how God elects those who are
   elect.)

   Technically, election is God's complete agreement with

His own foreknowledge; "elect according to the foreknowledge of God" means that He simply agrees with Himself (foreknowledge) and puts a stamp of approval (election) upon what He decreed (1 Pet. 1:2). God elected or chose believers in the sense, first, that He *knew* ahead of time that, if given free will, they would freely choose to believe in Christ; second, that He *decreed* that such an act of faith would actually occur; third, that He *agreed* not only that their positive volition to the Gospel would occur at a certain point in time but also that all the blessings of salvation plus certain unique blessings would be their eternal possessions (Eph. 1:4; 2 Thess. 2:13).

Election is *declared* through God's foreknowledge; election is a *function* of predestination. Predestination permanently relates the Church Age believer to the plan of grace (2 Tim. 1:9). Furthermore, predestination means that, in union with Christ through retroactive and current positional truth, the Church Age believer shares the destiny of Christ (Eph. 1:5). We also share the election of Christ which occurred in eternity past (Isa. 41:2; 1 Pet. 2:4, 6).

9. God's gracious and unconditional covenants to Israel can be fulfilled only to the elect—to those physical Jews who are also spiritual Jews through faith in Christ, the Messiah. The true Jew is not merely the physical seed of Abraham but the spiritual seed as well. Unless the racial Jew follows the pattern of Abraham in salvation, he is not elected (Gen. 15:6; Rom. 4:3). Romans 9:6 explains how God can have an elect nation: "all (racial) Israel is not (spiritual) Israel."

10. The unconditional covenants to Israel are promises for the elect Jews only; that is, for those who have believed in Christ and thus possess God's imputed righteousness and eternal life. God has chosen one nation to be the basis for the spiritual blessing of the entire human race. But that election cannot violate the very principle of human history—free will. To become a citizen of this elect nation, the individual Jew must become one of the elect; he must believe in Christ. The covenants to Israel are eternal; their recipients and beneficiaries must have eternal life. To be a physical Jew but not a spiritual Jew is a great tragedy.

III. The Characteristics of the Divine Decrees.

A. The decrees include all the facts of history. These are the facts which were fed into the computer by the omniscience of God.

B. There is one all-inclusive will and purpose of God concerning all that ever was or will be. Think of it as a computer tape. Your entire life is on tape. Your tape begins with your first breath, and everything in your life from then on is recorded on the tape. You do not know what the future holds for you, but God does. He recorded it billions of years ago.

C. This divine will and purpose originated entirely within Himself. The tape is in the mind of God; He alone designed it entirely for His satisfaction, compatible with His essence, and related to His eternal glory and pleasure. It pleases God to run your tape to the end. He knows what is on it, and He is running it for you.

D. Space and time are the battlefield, the overall setting in which we live. These broad concepts are in the decrees, but so are the details which reach down to the minutia of life. Even the minor detail of the fall of a sparrow is known to God; every hair that drops from your head is included in the decrees.

E. The doctrine of procession describes how the Members of the Trinity function under the decrees: the Father sends the Son (John 3:17), the Father and the Son send the Holy Spirit (John 14:16, 26; 15:26; 16:7). Among themselves, the Members of the Godhead function in a way which is immanent (complete and changeless), intrinsic (within the Godhead), and subjective (subjectivity is perfect when God is dealing with Himself).

F. How the Godhead maintains and supports the believer is transient (the tape keeps playing), extrinsic (these actions occur outside of the Godhead), and objective (our point of reference is the perfectly fair justice of God).

G. The decrees are efficacious. "Efficacious" refers to the direct work of God: His work always succeeds in having its intended effect; the decrees actually determined all that ever was or will be.

H. The decrees guarantee certainty. The foreknowledge of God makes nothing certain; it merely perceives what *is* certain.

I. The omniscience of God feeds the facts into the computer while foreknowledge reads what the computer prints out.

J. The decrees of God are all-comprehensive. Not the slightest confusion could exist as to one of even the smallest events without confusion to all events. All events are interwoven and interdependent. You might assume that the decrees eliminate the need for prayer, but that is not true. God looked down the corridors of time to see what believers would ask in prayer. Effective prayer makes requests which God can answer in the affirmative; these answers —the things we ask in time—are incorporated into the decrees in eternity past (Isa. 65:24)! Prayer is a powerful weapon in the angelic conflict when wielded by the mature believer who knows what he is doing (Phil. 4:6; Col. 4:2).[58]

K. The decrees are also eternal, which means that God never gains in knowledge.

L. What God has known at any time He has always known.

M. This means that the decrees were all decreed simultaneously—in eternity past. God is never surprised by anything we do or fail to do. He knew everything simultaneously, built divine provisions around the free choices we would make, and included the whole thing in the decrees billions of years ago. The decrees existed before man, before angels, before the existence of the universe; the decrees pre-existed every creature and every thing.

N. The decrees of God are perfect. God is perfect; God's plan is perfect. The only thing imperfect in God's plan is man.

O. God's perfect plan includes all imperfect persons, but He maintains His perfection and integrity through His policy of grace. God never loses His perfection, and His plan never fails even though man is imperfect and often fails. Because we are imperfect creatures in a perfect plan, the plan must be based on God's justice. That is why we must believe in Christ, why we must rebound, why we must advance to maturity. We must adjust to His perfect justice.

P. The decrees of God are unchangeable and certain. Nothing will ever arise to necessitate a change in the decrees. Everything was known and decreed (made certain) in eternity past. God's decree is unchangeable because it deals only with reality. It is certain because omniscience always knew that these things would occur under the circumstances of their particular moment in history. The changelessness of the decree is one of the great blessings of logistical grace. There are no erasures, corrections, or deletions; no last minute changes; no chance of becoming lost in the shuffle. All the provisions for all our needs are absolutely secure.

If you do not accept that statement, your rejection of it was known to God and was decreed to actually exist at this time as your own expression of your free choice. But God also knew that the statement was nonetheless true.

Q. The decree is the free choice of divine sovereignty. God is not bound to follow a necessary pattern or course, but once having decreed it in eternity past, once having said "This is it," God is bound by His infinite faithfulness, truth, and incorruptibility to

---

58. See Thieme, *Prayer.*

complete what He has begun. God will play out your tape to the end. Once He decreed you to exist, that became the plan; the future events in your life *will* occur—tomorrow, the next day, and the next. You will never suddenly cease to exist. God is bound by His eternal, infinite, perfect essence to play your tape.

R. God has decreed ends as well as means, causes as well as effects, conditions and instrumentalities as well as the events which depend upon them.

Let's take an example from ancient history. The rise and fall of empires and the movements of entire populations are sweeping in scope and impressive from our human point of view. But they are just as much in the decree as are the daily occurrences in our individual lives.

Long before He created the universe, God's omniscience knew all about the historical role to be played by the Assyrians. Not only did He decree that they would be a great power, but—in the same instant—He also decreed that all the historical trends which led to their ascendancy would also occur. This included a complex chain of events. The western Aryans (or Indo-Aryans) would come out of the mountains of Asia to dominate the Hurrians who lived in Mesopotamia, while the eastern Aryans moved south into India to conquer the Dravidians. In Mesopotamia, these Indo-Aryans and Hurrians (together forming the vast Kingdom of Mitanni) would become degenerate. From farther to the west (now called Turkey) would descend the attacking Hittites who, after conquering Mitanni, would mysteriously turn around for home, leaving a power vacuum. Into this vacuum would rise the Kassites from southern Mesopotamia, and these people would be absorbed by the Assyrians.

There are no accidents in history. God knew all of these developments in the ancient world billions of years before they occured. He knew the causes, conditions, and successions of history. He knew how all these events were interrelated and what their eventual effects would be upon the Jews (who were by this time settling into the Land after the Exodus) and upon the rest of mankind throughout human history. Even though some of these events preceded others chronologically, even though the rise of Assyria depended on the fall of Mitanni, all were decreed by God in the same instant.

As an application from this glimpse of historical ebb and flow, we can have confidence in our Lord Jesus Christ, the God of history, who is so magnificent in His power as to make today's

awesome Soviet military buildup pale in comparison. If we are adjusted to the justice of God, who can be against us? (Rom. 8:31).

S. Some things God decreed to do Himself. We call these "immediate" things, in contrast to "mediate" things which He
decreed that some other agency, such as the free will of man, would
perform. For example, creation is "immediate." There had to be a
place for God's creatures to live, so He created space. Space is in-
comprehensibly vast; it is absolutely mind-boggling in size. For a
basic unit of measure we must use the distance light travels in a
year! And then we must think in terms of *billions* of light years with
still no end in sight! Our awesomely powerful God produced space
in a split second so that angels and man might have somewhere to
live. The angels inhabit all of space, whereas we live in a very small
part of it to resolve the angelic conflict. On this planet and on this
planet only is the angelic conflict being resolved.

God also decreed that He would "immediately" create time.
He set the earth on its rotation and orbit to give us our standard for
measuring time. Besides space and time, salvation too was decreed
to be provided by God Himself. Likewise, Jesus Christ's control of
history is "immediate"—He often takes a direct hand in a matter
rather than relegate everything to secondary causes.

T. God accomplishes some things, however, through the action of
secondary causes acting under the law of necessity. Thus the
decrees include both primary and secondary causes.

U. Other things God has decreed to promote or permit free agents to
do in the exercise of their own free will and self-determination. On
one hand, man's own volition is responsible for sin, human good,
and evil from the old sin nature. On the other hand, man is free to
believe in Christ through nonmeritorious postive volition and be
saved.

V. One category of events is rendered by the decree of God to be just
as certainly future as any other category. All events are equally certain to occur whether caused directly by the sovereignty of God or
caused by the free will of man. Primary, secondary, or tertiary,
every cause for every event is equally in the decree and *will* occur.

IV. The Will of God and the Divine Decrees.

A. There is one all-inclusive will or purpose of God concerning all that
ever was or will be from the beginning of human history until its
termination on the last day of the Millennium. God has known
every thought, decision, and action that has ever occured or will
occur; all these things come into being through one computer.
Many things are printed out by the computer of the divine decrees,

but first they were all *in* the computer.

Remember that we are not referring to "God's will" in the sense of divine guidance for the believer's life. By "will of God" we mean His sovereign decision as to what would come into existence; in other words, the divine decrees.

B. This will and purpose of God originated within Himself long before any creature of any kind existed. His will is always consistent with His perfect essence.

C. The will and purpose of God—that is, the divine decree—was objectively designed for His own glory, pleasure, and satisfaction.

D. All creatures have been placed in space and time; all events related to space and time were instantaneously and simultaneously decreed. The fact that all events were decreed results in divine action. Of course, the divine action which is most interesting to us is His work of grace—the policy of His justice in blessing believers. But there are many other categories of divine action; they fall under two classifications.

   1. Divine actions within the Godhead are immanent, intrinsic, and subjective.

   2. Divine actions related to creation are transient, extrinsic, and objective.

E. God did not decree Himself to be. God existed prior to and outside of the decrees, so that the divine decrees do not act upon God; He acts upon the decrees.

F. God's decrees are efficacious—having the power to produce the intended effect: they actually determine all that ever was or will be. They include God's directive will, permissive will, and overruling will. These three categories of divine will describe the manner in which God's sovereignty controls history; they are subcategories of divine action as related to His creation. In particular, these three categories show how divine sovereignty actually deals with human volition. The will of God (as to what would exist, i.e. the divine decree) calls for God's will (His attribute of sovereignty) to function toward us in certain ways (*directly* stating what He desires of us or *permissively* allowing us to go our own way or *overruling* our decisions—not letting them have their intended results—in order to protect us and the rest of mankind from our own negative volition and to preserve and perpetuate His own marvelous plan).

G. All things depend on God's will (the decree), and nothing is certain apart from God's will.

H. God's decrees originate from His own omniscience, and in eternity past the decrees separated fact from fiction.

I. We must make clear the distinction between God's omniscience and His foreknowledge.

J. God's decrees do not originate from His foreknowledge.

K. God's foreknowledge makes nothing certain; it merely perceives what the decrees have made certain. Prophecy never determines history.

L. Nothing can be foreknown until it is first decreed.

M. Foreknowledge is God's cognizance of what He has decreed regarding believers. In logical order: omniscience programs the computer of divine decrees, and the computer prints out various categories of information for foreknowledge to read.

N. We must also distinguish between the decrees of God and the desires of God. The decrees merely establish the facts of history; many things are included which God does not desire. They are in the decrees because the omniscience of God knew that, given free will, His creatures would reject the divine design. All sins are acts of volition, and although God never approves of sin, He put them in the decrees because He knew we would commit them. The decrees deal with reality, with certainty, with what actually happens. Just because God decrees a particular event to take place does not mean He approves of it.

O. Sin, human good, and evil are not the desire of God, but they are in the decrees because people do these things from their own volition.

P. God desires His perfect will, but angels and men use their God-given freedom to violate the desires of God. The very fact that sin and evil are in the decree is proof that our volition is truly free. The decrees are the all-inclusive will of God; they contain all the facts of history—both the decisions which please God and those which displease Him.

Q. God does not desire to cast His creatures into the Lake of Fire, but it is decreed as certain for all men who reject Christ as Savior (2 Pet. 3:9). His desire is for all unbelievers to come to a change of mind toward Christ. For those with negative volition at God-consciousness or Gospel-hearing, the Lake of Fire is decreed and becomes a computer printout called retribution.

R. God does not desire to discipline believers, but it is decreed as certain for all believers in reversionism or carnality. Remember this principle before you start to misapply doctrine and say that because God is love He would never cause you misery and pain. God desires to express His perfect justice toward you; if you do not permit His justice to bless you, His justice will not hesitate to discipline you. We were created as free agents responsible for our own decisions. Either we adjust to the justice of God or the justice of God will adjust to us.

S. We must distinguish the decrees of God in eternity past from the actions of God in time. The action of God in time is the execution of the decree.

T. The execution is not the decree but logically follows the decree.

U. Distinction must also be made between God's decrees and God's laws.

V. The laws of divine establishment regulate human conduct; they are set up for human volition to obey. By protecting and perpetuating the human race, these laws give each of us a chance to be evangelized and, after believing in Christ, we have the opportunity to grow spiritually without interference or coersion. The laws of establishment can be broken by our volition, but the decrees cannot.

W. We cannot violate the decrees because any decision we make was known in eternity past and was included in the decrees.

X. The decrees are the all-comprehensive will of God and are only partially revealed in Scripture; the laws of God regulate man's conduct in time and space and are completely revealed.

V. The Blessing of Man and the Divine Decrees.

A. The omniscience of God in taking cognizance of the Fall of man graciously provided a plan for blessing man based on imputations from divine justice.

B. This plan involves the omniscience of God feeding into the computer of the divine decrees seven imputations which provide maximum blessing for mankind in time and eternity.

C. The decrees of God contain the historical reality regarding every human being's level of attainment in this grace plan. Freedom means that some attain all these imputations while others do not. Freedom insures *inequality*. (The road to equality is the road to slavery.)

D. Nonmeritorious human volition can fall short of any potential in God's plan.

E. The extent to which each individual advances in this plan was known to God in eternity past. This was fed into the computer. God knew that some would remain unbelievers, that others would believe but remain spiritually immature, that a few would advance to maturity. Those who reach maturity receive blessings in time and even greater blessings in eternity; they glorify God and bring Him pleasure.

F. In too many cases, the potential exceeds the reality. The potential is totally known to God's omniscience, only the reality is in the decrees.

G. Our attainment of divine blessings through imputation is the means God has chosen to glorify Himself and to give Himself pleasure.

H. The glory of God is related to the believer's advance to maturity and the resultant imputation of divine blessings.

VI. The Glory of God and the Divine Decrees.

A. The decrees unite in one all-inclusive and final objective the glory of God (Prov. 16:4; Rom. 11:36; Heb. 2:10; Rev. 4:11).

B. Since the Members of the Godhead were alone before all creation, the decrees of God concerned no one but them. The decrees were designed to glorify those who were there when they were made, not to glorify us who were not there. The Father, Son, and Holy Spirit had infinite glory in eternity past and will have it in eternity future. Whatever they do in the interim—from the creation of the universe to the conclusion of history—must bring them infinite glory. (Generally the decrees relate to the glory of the Lord Jesus Christ because He is the manifest Person of the Trinity.) When history terminates, God's glory will be as perfect as it was before time began. Our failures do not stain the glory of God. His glory does not depend on us; we depend on His glory.

Grace is born of the glory of God. Grace means that God does all the work which adds up to our blessing. Whether in time or eternity, divine blessing is all grace. The only things related to us that can glorify God are what God Himself accomplishes (such as imputing His righteousness or providing doctrine). That is why He despises our self-righteousness and hypocrisy. He has no use for our legalism and human good, and He severely disciplines the legalist. When we begin to glorify ourselves, our accomplishments, our knowledge, or our experiences, we are kidding ourselves and setting ourselves up for divine discipline.

Any time we are blessed of God, we can count on one thing: we did not earn or deserve it. It is God's doing, exhibiting *His* glory, and we do not have to keep looking over our shoulder expecting to lose it! Once we understand His glory, we will certainly not want to intrude on it; we will want to go along with it. And there lies the blessing.

C. Being infinite, God the Father, God the Son, and God the Holy Spirit are worthy of all glory.

D. God's glory is what He is. (Here we have the entire doctrine of divine essence!) Receiving glory is nothing new to the Trinity. All three Persons have always had it and always will. In eternity past, they did not need to add anything to what they already had; God has never suffered any kind of deficiency. They found infinite pleasure in each other; they were perfectly satisfied and perfectly happy. As part of that pleasure they simply decided to create a universe and put free creatures in it—first angels, then men. The Members of the Trinity knew what such creatures would do, and based on that, they made many further decisions.

E. Since He is the Origin and Subject (not the object) of the decrees, God will inevitably be glorified by every thought, every decision, every action in human history. The good and the bad are included; sin, evil, *everything* will all add up to the glorification of God. In other words, the plan of God began with glory and will end with glory; it is never held up; it never stops; it moves on with you or without you, no matter what you do. If you remain an unbeliever, you will go to hell; and God's glory will remain uncompromised and untarnished. If you believe in Christ, you will go to heaven, again consistent with the glory of God. Both in time and in eternity God's character is vindicated in everything that occurs. Even "the wrath of man shall praise Him" (Ps. 76:10).

F. God is glorified not only in what He is but also in what He has decreed.

G. Since the manifestations of His declarative glory secure the highest glory for His creatures and their greatest good, it is inevitable that blessing or glorifying any creature brings glory to God who, through grace, is the Source of everything. Imputing blessings to mature believers glorifies God, emphasizes His grace, and excludes human works.

H. To the finite mind, the decrees are many, but to God, they are all one plan embracing both cause and effect, means and end.

I. The decrees include every detail in the experience of every creature, including such minute aspects as the number of hairs on your head. Even in a national disaster, when many mature believers will be isolated and alone, they can still do their jobs and live their lives as unto the Lord, knowing that God has not forgotten them.

J. The decrees of God are those sovereign purposes of God which are efficaciously accomplished by God alone, apart from all creature ability, mentality, talent, counsel, or cooperation. He did not ask our opinion but Himself decreed what He wanted to decree. He is the Origin; His is the glory.

K. God is glorified and pleased in the momentum and advance of believers within His plan.

L. The omniscience of God knew in eternity past what thoughts, motivations, decisions, and actions would carry one believer to maturity and another into reversionism. God has prepared the most magnificent things for the mature believer—imputations from divine justice. He has prepared horrible discipline for the reversionist.

M. While omniscience knew the actual and potential, only the actual was fed into the computer of decrees. Anything decreed by God will inevitably glorify God; it could not work out any other way.

N. The divine decrees are executed through imputation from the justice of God.

O. The seven imputations—five real and two judicial—add up to the glory of God.

P. The decree of God allows maximum blessing for any believer but recognizes that human volition can fall short of any potential.

Q. Only response to doctrine can fulfill the maximum blessing desired by God for the believer.

R. The extent to which a believer advances is the extent to which the decrees of eternity past were declared for that individual.

S. God had the good sense to know beforehand how far each believer would advance, and that was decreed.

T. In too many cases the potential far exceeds the reality.

VII. Human Freedom and the Divine Decrees.

A. The plan of God and the decrees of God are totally consistent with human freedom. God does not limit, coerce, or violate man's self-determination.

B. We must distinguish between what God causes directly, such as Christ's spiritual death on the Cross, and what He permits indirectly, such as sin, human good, and evil.

C. God created man with a free will—volition in his soul. God therefore permits that free will to function in human self-determination. Otherwise man would never have fallen. God permitted the Fall; it was not His directive will. But His permissive will is as much a part of the decrees as is His directive will. Remember, the decrees are human history in the mind of God in eternity past.

D. God is not the author of sin, human good, or evil. Free will is the source of these things.

E. Both sin and the Cross were fed into the computer of the divine decrees. Sin is the permissive will of God; the Cross, the directive will. Sin is neutralized by the Cross; this is an example of how God permits man's free will to oppose Him yet maintains His own integrity and wins in the end.

God the Father, God the Son, and God the Holy Spirit knew that the two greatest systems of human law—Jewish and

Roman—would meet at the Cross and that both would break down and fail. (The law did not fail; those administering it failed.) The Members of the Trinity knew that hearsay would be accepted as evidence, that the facts would be omitted, and that the whole succession of Christ's seven trials would be a railroading of the law. Nevertheless, the precise manner in which Christ was convicted and crucified was decreed in eternity past because God knew the freewill decisions of every individual involved. He knew the mob mentality and the decisions of every member of the crowd that shouted, "Crucify Him!" He knew the conspiracy of the religious Pharisees. He knew the nature of religion because He knows Satan's every thought, and religion is from Satan.

Christ's execution was the sum total of human evil and reversionism. It was the quintessence of sinfulness—sinfulness related to religion. The religious crowd crucified the Lord, yet God's purpose was carried out by the *free* choice of man—even by the free negative volition of the evil, reversionistic men in the Sanhedrin.

It was religion that put Christ on the Cross, but it was the justice of God the Father who used the crucifixion for His own purpose. Now *there* is a neat little twist! God used religion, the devil's ace trump, to provide our salvation! Religion reached its evil peak only to inadvertantly provide the grace way of salvation as the justice of God imputed the personal sins of mankind to Christ and judged them on the Cross.

This once again shows that no matter how great the creature may be—and Satan is the smartest of all creatures—God is always greater. Satan finally came up with this "smart" way to get rid of Jesus—Roman crucifixion. But through this supreme masterpiece of satanic conspiracy came our salvation. God not only uses the wrath of man to praise Him (Ps. 76:10), but He uses the wrath of angels as well! It was a combined satanic-human operation that put the Lord on the cross. Satan thought he had accomplished his objective, and in no way had his volition been coerced. But all he had done was to contribute to our Lord's objective. There is the beauty of the divine decrees!

F. No decree itself actually opposes human freedom.

G. Man is free to glorify and serve God, but the manner of glorification and service is prescribed by God and is not left to man's freedom or imagination. In other words, God did not ordain the tongues crowd to glorify Himself; He ordained the intake of Bible doctrine. Nor did He ordain witnessing, prayer, or any other

Christian production to be the means of spiritual growth.[59] We must understand what is His plan and what is not. The daily function of GAP is His plan for our growth.

H. If the result is to be spritual growth and divine blessing, our freedom is limited to positive volition toward Bible doctrine.

I. Man's use of his freedom to reject doctrine results in divine discipline. Either we adjust to the justice of God or the justice of God will adjust to us.

J. The believer's objective is to use Bible doctrine resident in his soul to determine the will and pleasure of God regarding his life and modus operandi.

K. In this way, human freedom becomes merged into God's will. God is pleased, and man is blessed beyond description.

VIII. The Practical Application of the Divine Decrees.

A. Since the decree is the sum total of God's plan and purpose in eternity past, it centers around the Person of the Lord Jesus Christ (Eph. 1:4–6; 1 John 3:23).

B. Therefore, the free will of man must face the issue of Christ and His work on the Cross. Faith in Christ is man's entrance into the plan of grace. At the Cross, the sovereignty of God and the free volition of man meet for the glory of God and the advantage of mankind. The basis for this meeting is the justice of God.

C. Under the divine policy of grace, the work of salvation is accomplished by God while man gains the benefits apart from human merit or ability. The definite antagonism between divine justice and human works means that human works are set aside in every phase of the plan of grace.

D. God's plan in eternity past was designed to include all events and actions, related to their causes and conditions, as part of one indivisible system, every link being a part of the integrity of the whole. Each link is as important as the whole. The whole is the integrity of God making all the links properly relate through grace. This is how He makes all things work together for good.

E. Without violating human volition, God has designed a plan so perfect that it includes directive, provision, preservation, function, cause and effect for all believers.

F. Under this plan, God has decreed to do some things directly (such as creation or salvation), some through secondary agencies (as through Israel or the Church), and some through individuals (as through the Apostle Paul—or through *us*).

---

59. See above, page 93.

G. Thus, there are primary, secondary, and tertiary functions within the plan of God. It does not matter into which of these categories any action falls; all constitute one great, all-comprehensive plan— perfect, eternal, unchangeable, with no loss of integrity. We are part of a magnificently perfect plan designed to give us everything that is wonderful in time and eternity. If our spiritual momentum carries us to supergrace, we *will* be blessed!

H. The plan of God is consistent with human freedom. God is not unfair; He does not limit or coerce our freedom. He graciously provides guidance as to how we should *use* our volition. The only revelation of the divine decrees is found in the Bible; therefore, the highest priority in the Christian life is the reception of Bible doctrine.

Some things God permits; other things He causes. Some things please Him; others do not. But God always recognizes reality. This is one of the most important aspects of our relationship with Him: everything which is decreed is reality and, like God, we too must face the facts.

Because God deals with reality, His plan must deal with things as they are. His solutions start with what is, not with what is not. There is no wishful thinking in God. He never rationalizes anything. He never blesses us out of sentimentality. He never blesses us because *we* think we're spiritual. He never blesses us because of our character, our plans, our ideas, our schemes, our self-righteousness. He blesses us always and only on the basis of *His* character.

Anyone who keeps trying to vindicate himself before God will never understand the righteousness of God, how it relates to divine justice, or how both characterize the decrees.

I. Again, God created man with free will.

J. And the fact that man can go contrary to the will of God proves the existence of truly free volition.

Index

SUBJECT INDEX

References to figures are printed in italic type.
Numbers in boldface refer to definitions.

SCRIPTURE INDEX

FIGURE INDEX